T0114061

PRAISE FOR *JAGUAR IN THE BODY, BUTTERFLY IN THE HEART*

'Jaguar in the Body, Butterfly in the Heart *is a magnificent adventure story that travels like an arrow right into the heart of what it means to be a conscious human being. Like all stories told with unflinching honesty and humility, this one has the potential to heal the reader, and help him or her remember who they really truly are.*'

DR CHRISTIANE NORTHRUP, *NEW YORK TIMES* BESTSELLING AUTHOR OF *GODDESSES NEVER AGE* AND *WOMEN'S BODIES, WOMEN'S WISDOM*

'Jaguar in the Body, Butterfly in the Heart *charts the journey of a young man treading the path of an ancient vocation in a modern world. In his wise, funny and tender book, Ya'Acov Darling Khan writes of his teachers and experiences with compelling generosity and practicality, and lessons abound. Shamanic teaching that is accessible and divine.*'

SOPHIE DAHL, AUTHOR

'*Ya'Acov Darling Khan has written an exquisite and important book that places the great and deep work of shamanism in its rightful context in this critical time in human history. For too long, shamanism has been seen as a left-field weekend pastime that is divorced from the challenges that we face as a species. Ya'Acov's story of his 30-year initiation into the shaman's world is an invitation for us to look deeply into what matters most to us and to find the courage to live from this place. Ya'Acov's book is vital for all of us who are ready to find the passion, dedication and courage to bring our visions to Earth and to leave a legacy for our descendants that we can be proud of.*'

LYNNE TWIST, CO-FOUNDER OF THE PACHAMAMA ALLIANCE AND AUTHOR OF *THE SOUL OF MONEY*

'*An important shamanic ritual involves "dismembering and remembering" – releasing dysfunctional patterns of thought and behaviour in order to embrace beneficial new ones. Through this beautiful book Ya'Acov offers that ritual for a world of humans who need to rebalance and remember themselves and their relationship with all else. He sings the shapeshifter's song; that song awakens a new dream, it manifests a new reality.*'

JOHN PERKINS, *NEW YORK TIMES* BESTSELLING AUTHOR

'As our world rocks with each new onslaught of unresolved human pain, there comes a bright light to remind us that we have resources far beyond our own: that we have help if we ask for it and that help is transformative. Written with integrity, authenticity and the flowing, addictive poetry of a born storyteller, Ya'Acov's book is a must-read for anyone who seeks to share in the bounty of the greater spirits of this world and beyond.

Ya'Acov's journey as a shaman began long before the current fashion for all things shamanic. When it comes to spirituality, many people talk the talk, but few actually embody the teachings in their day-to-day life.'

MANDA SCOTT, TEACHER OF SHAMANIC DREAMING AND AUTHOR OF THE *BOUDICA* SERIES AND *INTO THE FIRE*

'Ya'Acov Darling Khan's journey reveals the hard path that goes from a sincere but innocent day-dreaming about shamanism, to the struggles, doubts, failure and eventual victories to be found for those who travel far enough and persist for long enough to discover the secrets of shifting consciousness, and then bring them back to the world of our everyday affairs.

What I love about him and the journey he shares in this book is that his passion for the Spirit has always been so strong, and was not broken when ego-driven fantasies were shattered again and again by the bitter-sweet kiss of everyday reality.'

VICTOR SANCHEZ, RESEARCHER, AUTHOR, TEACHER AND FOUNDER OF EL ARTE DE VIVIR A PROPÓSITO (THE ART OF LIVING PURPOSEFULLY) AND TOLTECAS.ORG

'Ya'Acov is a medicine man of the highest integrity. His shamanic skill and embodiment transcend culture to reach the universal place of humanity and spirit. One doesn't declare oneself a shaman, the people do. When we are in the rainforest together, the indigenous people line up for healings with Ya'Acov, who works side by side with the elder tribal shaman.

In his book, Ya'Acov demystifies the original vocation, one often shrouded in misperceptions and aggrandizement in modern times. As our current systems and structures break down, more and more people are turning to the ancient shamanic worldview of interconnectivity and meaning. Jaguar in the Body, Butterfly in the Heart *provides a blueprint for how to authentically walk the path.'*

DAVID TUCKER, PACHAMAMA JOURNEYS DIRECTOR

'As the first generations of Westerners who were taught by traditional shamans and healers slowly matured through decades of practice, it was inevitable that gradually new forms of shamanism would appear. Ya'Acov Darling Khan is an experienced shamanic teacher who represents a shamanic practice that is thoroughly body-based yet spiritual, archaic yet contemporary. His words will inspire all those who follow the path of spirit.'

DAAN VAN KAMPENHOUT, FOUNDER OF THE PRACTICE FOR SYSTEMIC RITUAL, AUTHOR OF *IMAGES OF THE SOUL* AND *TEARS OF THE ANCESTORS*

'With self-depreciating humour, honesty and openness, Ya'Acov carries us with him as he weaves the story of his journey from youth to adult to elder. Writing with grace and love, he invites the reader to travel through the landscapes of his shamanic path. A compelling mixture of mysticism and down-to-earth living.'

CHRIS ODLE, MEDICINE MAN

'Ya'Acov is a masterful storyteller who takes you deep into his real-life story of magic, shamanism and a lifelong commitment to waking up! I have run joint workshops with Ya'Acov and can say without doubt that in both the dream and waking worlds he is the real deal!'

CHARLIE MORLEY, LUCID DREAMING TEACHER AND AUTHOR OF *DREAMS OF AWAKENING* AND *DREAMING THROUGH DARKNESS*

'I am totally convinced that in order to live something you have to dream it first. In Jaguar in the Body, Butterfly in the Heart, I discovered the most beautiful examples of how you can find your teachers and precious knowledge in your dreams and then in your life. Bravo to Ya'Acov Darling Khan for showing us that it is possible in such a beautiful and poetic way and encouraging every reader to look forward to experiencing this mystical path.'

SERGIO MAGAÑA OCELOCOYOTL, AUTHOR OF *THE TOLTEC SECRET* AND *CAVES OF POWER*

'If, like me, you think too many are jumping on the shamanic bandwagon, this book is about the real thing. It takes precise introspection, total humility and great courage to take the shaman's initiatory journey. An entertaining description of a tough, exacting apprenticeship, this well-written personal odyssey takes the sham out of shamanism. An inspiring read.'

DR EVA CHAPMAN, PSYCHOTHERAPIST AND AUTHOR

'It is amazing how long it took this man to recognise that he was a shaman. If you have ever wondered what it takes to be a genuine shaman and what the shaman's world is like, then this is the book for you. Brilliant and engrossing, it is a great read and a fabulous account of an inspiring journey.'

PROF. JAKE CHAPMAN, AUTHOR, SYSTEMS TEACHER, DEMOS ASSOCIATE AND ENLIGHTENMENT MASTER

'Ya'Acov's intelligent voice is clear and simple as he tells his astonishing tale of life, love and learning. I have been lucky enough to hear many of these chapters as they have unfolded in his life and have often been struck by his honest struggle to accept his real nature: he has now grown fully into that reality, and it is a joy to witness.'

MATTHEW BARLEY, PROFESSIONAL MUSICIAN

'Ya'Acov Darling Khan is one of the leading lights in a remarkable reawakening of authentic shamanic practice in the West today. He is a rare emissary between worlds.

A true story of mystery, mysticism and magic, his account of a life lived in shamanism is essential reading for anybody who wants to understand how this perennial form of spirituality can help us heal our deepest wounds and live richer, more authentic lives. Fusing remarkable encounters with shamans from the Arctic to the Amazon with a white-knuckle account of his lifelong spiritual quest, it shows the urgent relevance of shamanism in addressing our modern-day dilemmas.'

MATTHEW GREEN, AUTHOR OF *AFTERSHOCK: THE UNTOLD STORY OF SURVIVING PEACE*

'This book is an antidote to the Western culture of "weekend shamanism" which often misunderstands shamanism as separate from daily life and commitment to action, using it to fortify a sense of self rather than to do the humble, hard, fierce work of confronting who one really is.

Ya'Acov stands up now in this role, not to polish his own ego, but in service of life, to remind us of the true nature of shamanic practice in this critical time for our species.

He is also a wonderful storyteller. I have watched Ya'Acov crafting this book with the same attention to detail that he brings to all his offerings and I am sure it will bring you courage and encouragement for your own path with heart.'

SUSANNAH DARLING KHAN, CO-CREATOR OF MOVEMENT MEDICINE, AUTHOR AND CREATOR OF NUMEROUS CDS

JAGUAR
IN THE BODY
BUTTERFLY
IN THE HEART

JAGUAR
IN THE BODY
BUTTERFLY
IN THE HEART

The Real-Life Initiation of an Everyday Shaman

YA'ACOV DARLING KHAN

HAY HOUSE

Carlsbad, California • New York City
London • Sydney • New Delhi

Published in the United States by: Hay House, Inc.: www.hayhouse.com®
Published in Australia by: Hay House Australia Pty. Ltd.: www.hayhouse.com.au
Published in the United Kingdom by: Hay House UK, Ltd.: www.hayhouse.co.uk
Published in India by: Hay House Publishers India: www.hayhouse.co.in

A catalogue record for this book is available from the British Library.

Interior images: 1, 57, 113, 177 © Ashely Foreman

Tradepaper ISBN: 978-1-4019-6338-5

Printed in the United States of America

This book is dedicated to seven extraordinary people. My wife Susannah, our son Reuben, my mother Angella and my father Brian, Bikko Máhte Penta, and Jake and Eva Chapman.

Susannah, the finest woman I know and my beloved for more than three decades, a Medicine Woman in your own right, a beautiful songstress and creator of many albums, and a very fine and inspiring teacher. More than anyone, you have witnessed, challenged and supported me on this journey. We have always danced on the edge, and even though we have fallen many times, still you are here, and still we are together. My gratitude to you for the way you have loved me into being is way beyond words. You are and always have been the one for me and so it will be forevermore.

Reuben, son shine, like your mama, you know the best and the worst of me. Watching you grow into the fine young man you are, is and has been the most wonderful journey. You taught me how to be your father, and I could not be prouder of who you are becoming. To have you walking the road you are on gives me hope for all our futures.

My mother, Angella Carne, your constant love and support, even in difficult times, and the faith you gave me in life, have been at my back always. Your kindness and quiet wisdom were the ground on which I learned to walk.

My father, Joseph Brian Carne. You were the rock that sharpened my blade, the force against which I could measure my own. And though we *never saw eye to eye whilst you lived, without you I would never have discovered the adventure my life has become. I miss you.*

Bikko Máhte Penta, for so long, my hidden guide. The shaman who taught me that strength without humility has no value, that power distils itself through the patient silence of the land, and that being a shaman is something that I was born into. I miss you too.

Finally, Professor Jake Chapman and Dr Eva Chapman, elders and friends who have been like no others. You have supported me to be who I am, nothing held back, full power, whilst at the same time, making sure that I keep my feet on the ground and keep questioning myself. And you have shown me this through example, the best kind of teaching there is.

CONTENTS

FOREWORD

Ya'Acov Darling Khan has written an exquisite and important book that places the great and deep work of shamanism in its rightful context in this crucial time for the human species. It is both a personal and archetypal story. He honestly shares his struggles about the challenges of being a shaman in the modern world and he does so refreshingly without self-importance. Many times, I found myself moved by the story of a life devoted to finding a modern expression of shamanism that is appropriate to the times we are living in.

We live in critical times for our species and our relationship with the Earth that is our home. We are now being faced every day by the limitations of the cultural story that we have been telling since the industrial revolution began, namely that 'more is best'. As our colleagues in the Amazon and indigenous peoples everywhere are telling us, we need to remember that the Earth is a living being, and like all living beings, she has her limits. We need to find a new story that is appropriate for the realities of our time in which we remember that in fact every single of one of us that lives depends on the intricate balance of life that is our biosphere. This has always been true, but our modern way of life has created an imperative for us to find a new way if we are to carry out the sacred task of passing life on to the generations that will follow in a better state than we received it.

Throughout our human story, shamans have had the job of reminding us that we are part of the web of life and that we need to honour and learn to live in balance with the forces that shape our lives. For too long, shamanism has been seen in popular culture as a left-field weekend pastime that is divorced from the challenges that we face as a species. But in reality, shamanism has never been solely about trancing out or getting high on the latest medicine or technique to come into fashion – it's about living in a way that honours that which gives us life, feeds us, waters us, and gives us warmth and shelter. It is about the quest to find our place in our community and the wider community of life on which our own lives depend. It is about bringing our visions to Earth, and in so doing, finding what is ours to contribute. It invites us to live in a balanced way, asking for what we need in order to give everything we've got in gratitude for the gift of this life.

Shamanism is about passing on the torch of life, received intact from those who came before us, tending it and helping it to evolve in the short time that we hold that torch. It's about being in touch with the spirits of a place, not through belief, but through a committed relationship with the land we live on and care for. It's about recognizing the passing of the seasons and taking time to honour the different stages of life through appropriate initiation. It's a tradition that is as old as the first drumbeat and, despite the fact that its practitioners have been cast as charlatans and quacks, it has survived brutal oppression across the world over the centuries.

Interestingly, as it retreated into the silent and untouched places that remain on this Earth, those same places became more and more threatened by the mistaken story that the world is ours to do with whatever we see fit. In the last three decades, shamanism has risen like the phoenix and traditional shamans from these hidden worlds have been feeling the call from nature itself to share their knowledge once again in the hope that we will remember our responsibilities before it is too late.

From a young age, Ya'Acov was drawn to the spirit world of shamanism. He pursued this yearning throughout his adult life, studying and practising shamanism with many gifted teachers around the world. In this magical memoir, he tells the story of his 30-year initiation into the shaman's world. The way he describes his often extraordinary experiences, far from making us feel like lesser mortals, invites and challenges us to look deeply into what matters most to us and to find the courage to live from this place.

His story describes a modern-day shamanic initiation in a world where our connections to the old ways have been cut but not destroyed. His searching and commitment are clearly the results of his love for life. His stories of meeting traditional shamans from the very north of Europe to the dense jungles of the Amazon made me both laugh and cry in recognition of the ways in which we all need to wake up from our walking blind in the dark.

He and his wife, Susannah, have dedicated their lives to protecting 'the wild' inside us and in nature and to rediscovering a modern-day shamanism that is relevant to the challenges of our times. Their Movement Medicine work is a contemporary shamanic practice that invites all of us to discover the ongoing and evolving mystery of who we are and to put that knowledge in the driving seat of our lives.

I believe that the most important work of our times is to dedicate our brilliant creativity as a species towards finding sustainable, socially just and spiritually fulfilling solutions to the challenges we now face. In this task, shamanism has an important gift to offer. Ya'Acov has deeply integrated what he has learned from his indigenous teachers and the work that he and his wife offer is a wonderful thread in the tapestry of brilliant responses I see growing on my travels around the world.

I feel it important to mention that Ya'Acov is highly respected amongst our indigenous partners in the Amazon, where he is accepted as a practising shaman. His book is vital for all of us who are ready to find the passion, dedication and courage to bring our visions to Earth and to leave a legacy for our descendants that we can be proud of.

Lynne Twist, co-founder of the Pachamama Alliance
and author of *The Soul of Money*

INTRODUCTION

I'm sitting in front of a small lake with a lively stream behind me. I'm surrounded by the old oaks who have lived here an awful lot longer than I have. They stand majestic in the landscape, singing and dancing with the wind. The sun is up and I've been here all night praying for help in sharing my story with you in a good way.

I am a shaman. Not because I tell you I am, but because my teachers have told me so. I wanted to be a shaman, God knows why. Most of the indigenous people I've met think it's bizarre in the extreme that some people in the industrialized world want to be shamans. However, it's taken me more than 30 years to make peace with and find the use of being a shaman in the modern world.

Shamanism embraces a whole host of practices in its core intention to remind us of our place in the web of life and our need to live in balance with the seen and unseen forces that shape our universe. Since time immemorial we humans have been banging drums and going into trance in order to connect with and learn from these elemental forces, whether they are expressed as lightning, the power of the waters or the wind, or the force that keeps the seasons turning. Shamanism doesn't rely on faith, but invites us to learn from direct experience. When I discovered it, I found both a language for my own experience and the methods to deepen it.

The first time I was publicly called a shaman, I was in a small hall on the edge of Dartmoor. It was the early 1990s and I'd been invited to a workshop by an Indonesian movement meditation master called Suprapto Suryodarmo. He introduced me to the group as a shaman.

I was shocked and my face reddened. There were both students and friends in the room and the public display of my embarrassment only embarrassed me further. I felt branded, even ashamed. Finally, a man who knew shamans, for whom shamanism was a part of his culture, was publicly acknowledging me. Wasn't that what I'd dreamed of? It was, but the shame I felt was deeply shocking. It showed me my journey had hardly begun.

I went to my teacher at the time, an extraordinarily creative woman called Gabrielle Roth. She was known as 'the urban shaman' for her work with ecstatic dance and ritual theatre. She told me that the only reason it was difficult for me to accept being a shaman was because I thought that being a shaman made me special. Once I'd realized that being a shaman was simply a vocation, I'd be over it.

This incident made me think back over my journey so far. I'd been brought up in a culturally traditional Jewish family that still celebrated and honoured the major festivals of Judaism and lit the candles every Friday night. At seven I wanted to be a rabbi. At 13, I was bar mitzvahed. I was a regular attendee at the synagogue. I loved it. I was really into God. Matters of spirit concerned me every bit as much as going to see my football team play at the weekend. We went to pray. Then we went to the match.

At the same time, I was having a bunch of experiences that nobody could explain to me. I spoke to the dead. I travelled out of my body each and every night, and the world of my dreams was far more real to me than the waking world. I struggled to integrate the two. Maybe if I'd been living in the forest, my family would have taken me to the shaman and I would have begun my apprenticeship. Instead, because of my blackouts and 'strange symptoms', I was taken to a specialist, who thought I might have epilepsy. I didn't tell him that I was choosing to leave my body. What was natural for me became problematic.

When something is left in the dark and not given attention, it goes through all kinds of contortions to seek the light. And that's what I did.

When I discovered shamanism, at 19, I recognized that finally here was something that made sense of my experience. So why, all these years later, was I feeling ashamed of it?

My shame, it turns out, wasn't just personal. It was wrapped in the experiences of shamans who had been mercilessly and viciously attacked for generations. In Europe, the Church was quite successful at destroying the spiritual traditions that preceded its own creed. Later, the scientific establishment took over as purveyor of *the* truth.

But the spirit of shamanism is as old as the land itself and has endured. Though there are as many forms of shamanism as there are landscapes within nature, each invites us to access the intelligence of life itself and learn how to live in balance and harmony with the environment.

In the past 30 years, there has been a massive rise of interest in shamanism and it has swept back into the industrialized world from the places where it survived. Like many others, I felt a hunger to reconnect to something that I could experience directly rather than just believe in. Since then I've been through heaven and hell many times over in order to find something that is down to earth and real, honours the old ways and yet is appropriate for the challenges and realities of our times. My initiation into the shaman's world has taken me to the wide-open spaces and etheric light of the Arctic tundra and the timeless magnificence of the Amazon rainforest, before planting me alongside the granite guardians of Dartmoor. Along the way, I've had many struggles, victories and defeats. At times, I've been battered and bruised and confused. At others, I've experienced the magnificent mystery of life and laughed like a lunatic when the cosmic joke of it all has come into central view and I've recognized who I actually am and what I'm here for.

I've seen again and again how my unconscious reactions to my own history have obscured the simplicity of the matter and had me seeking out more and more fantastical experiences in order to prove that spirit is for real. The shamanic path is full of pitfalls. There are so many ways to get confused, distracted and fall into illusion. It's taken me a long time to learn to trust myself.

In these times of deep loneliness of spirit and what I have recently heard described as 'nature deficit disorder', there are many lost souls desperate for some wise shaman to tell them how to live and what to do. The shaman has become a romanticized and exotic figure. But shamans are human beings who have a particular predilection for matters of the spirit. They are far from infallible. Indeed, most indigenous shamans I've met, remarkable as they are, have had little or no training in personal awareness or the kind of power dynamics that exist when vulnerable people seek healing from those more in touch with their power. The road I travel on is littered with people who have suffered the consequences of imagining that the wisdom that an indigenous shaman possesses in one field will be automatically transferred to all other areas of the psyche and of life.

I didn't want to write a book that would have people chasing dragons in shamanic fantasies. Or to get into a war of paradigms and try to convince others that what is true for shamans and shamanic practitioners is true for everyone. That isn't helpful. Nor is the practice, all too common in the shamanic revolution, of viewing the rational mind as the devil incarnate. Quite simply, I hope that my own journey, and the many mistakes I have made along the way, may serve as guidance for the many people from all walks of life who are now exploring shamanic rituals and practices.

The bottom line is that I've had hundreds of experiences that I don't understand. It's quite possible I never will. However, I've found again and again that if I'm able to build a bridge between my experience and the way I live and act, then the part of me that needs concrete answers to ineffable questions tends to quieten down. Ultimately, no matter the intensity of our shamanic training, it's life itself that teaches us how to use the power we access in a responsible way.

Shamans walk with a foot in both worlds. There is no point in being in touch with spirits and visions if we're not able to bring them to Earth.

In my travels, I've found that shamans tend to be at once the most down to earth of people and able to recognize that waking up each morning and finding themselves in a body on a planet travelling through space at 67,000 miles an hour is an everyday miracle.

We live in extraordinary times. I witness our great capacity to harm. And I witness our great capacity to act with unprovoked kindness. I witness an ongoing battle that is taking place in humankind. Maybe it's always been like this, but now that we are so many, the consequences for the rest of life have become much more severe. This battle can happen externally, between two opponents, but for me, as I suspect for us all, the truth is that it is going on inside me. I recognize it as the fight between the part of me that wants to stand up for 'the wild' inside me and in nature and the part of me that wants comfort. Only by resolving it will I find peace.

It is essential that we all resolve it, for our current way of life is seriously endangering our own species. We are messing with the future as if it belonged to us, and it doesn't. Creation does not belong to us – we belong to it. So, we have brought ourselves to a crossroads. We have created an imperative to wake up to the consequences of our choices. We have generated the need to design a new guiding story that breaks through the trance we've fallen into.

This morning I heard the prime minister of Bhutan, a tiny country in the Himalayas, talking passionately about his country's commitment to remaining carbon negative for all time. More than that, he is calling for us all to follow his country's new denomination of success. It's called Gross National Happiness (GNH).

Things are changing. There is every chance we may use the crisis we have created as a way of waking up and recognizing the sanctity of life. Shamanism can help us in this. It can help us to remember that we are all part of the web of life. It can remind us that our perception isn't fixed and neither is the story that we are born into nor the one we choose to tell.

There's an old prophecy that you may have heard about. It concerns the eagle and the condor. The condor represents the peoples of the heart who live close to nature and who wish to preserve her delicate balance. The eagle represents the cultures of the mind who use this form of intelligence to invent, create and recreate. It was said that the culture of the condor would protect and live in balance with the Earth and all of creation for a while. This would be followed by a time in which the culture of the eagle would wrap its long wings around the Earth and nearly squeeze the life out of her. It was foretold that the outcome of these long cycles would be that the eagle and the condor would learn to fly together in the same sky – the peoples of the heart and the cultures of the mind would learn from the best of each other's knowledge and create a new dream here on Earth. The time the old ones were talking about is now.

I hear the old shaman's drum calling us to journey. It's time to share my story with you just as it is, just as it happened, and leave you to do with it what you will.

Part I

COMING DOWN
TO EARTH

DISCOVERING THE PATH

'You know you're in love [with life] when
you can't fall asleep because reality is
finally better than your dreams.'

Dr Seuss

The shaman's song stills the night air and the whole forest listens. A jaguar is hunting. An impossibly blue butterfly floats by. The gentle humming of the jew's-harp is a rhythm in the silence. I follow it as far as I can. I hear a song being sung. The voice is impossibly high and its sweetness is pure medicine for the heart. It reaches out in all directions at once. Through the song, the shaman hears the hearts of everyone in the story. Their stories are invited out into the light to be acknowledged, purified and healed. Each story has its own note and the shaman sings until the cacophony becomes a harmony, like the song of the forest. Only then does the shaman stop singing.

I've been yearning to hear this song for so long and tears are falling from my eyes. When I open them, I'm in a room with a wooden floor. The 44 dancers are coming to rest. The stillness in the room is like the stillness in my heart.

And then I realize that the song is mine.

It has come through me.

I have become the hollow bone.

Susannah, my beloved wife and long-time partner on this adventure, and David, a friend of many years, are looking at me. They feel it too.

As I look out into the room, I see that the dancers are deeply engaged with their own journeys. They haven't noticed at all. And then I know it is the real thing.

The shaman's song that I've travelled the world in search of has arrived.

It's early spring in 2003. We've been in the Arctic now for three days. Anka told me that we needed to let the clean Arctic air blow the noise of the city from us. She's a big, powerful Sami woman and I don't really know her very well. I don't know if I trust her. Last night, we had a sauna in our little chalet and she tried to seduce me. I said no very clearly, but even then I had to say it twice. Afterwards, I wondered if any of what she'd told me was true.

I'd met her a few months before at a workshop I was teaching in Oslo, in Norway. She was one of 44 dancers on a five-day shamanic dance workshop. Life truly has a sense of humour and the fact that I'd ended up teaching movement was proof of that. I hadn't been the dancing type. Not unless I'd had too much to drink, and even then I'd only dance to 'Welcome to the Monkey House' by an obscure band called Animal Magnet. But the dance had called me and had become my teacher and my guide.

Ever since I was a child, I'd been looking for a way to understand and make use of the experience of life I was having. Aren't we all?

My experiences had seemed quite ordinary early on. Talking to my dead great-grandmother as she sat on her old chair at the top of the stairs was no big deal until I realized that talking to the dead was weird for most of the people I knew.

Since then, my journey had taken me to many places. And on it, I'd met and worked with some extraordinary teachers. They'd shone like stars in the darkness, the light of their souls aflame with the knowledge they'd come here to share. And yet, above all of them, for the past 12 years there had been a presence, quiet but always there, like ancient stone, running deep like the roots of an old silver birch. His voice had been calm and shimmered like the ripples on a fjord. I called him the Old Man of the North. I assumed he was a dream figure, an inner archetypal wise man, but I was wrong. He was a real human being and I'd come here to meet him.

This story, like all stories of this kind, started a long time ago. As we drove along the wide highway, the Arctic tundra rushing by on both sides, my mind stretched back over the years. If the man we were going to meet wasn't the man I'd been dreaming of, the very foundations I'd built my life on would shatter.

I was awash in an ocean of feelings and doubts, but underneath it all the quiet hum of a shaman's song calmed me. Despite the doubts that nagged at me, pulling me this way and that, I knew that this man was the man who'd given me such good guidance for all those years.

Unbidden, he'd come into my dreams the week before Susannah and I had been going to teach our first shamanic dance workshop. I'd been terrified of teaching. I'd had no idea if I would be capable of guiding people through the dance. I was barely out of nursery school myself as a practitioner of ecstatic dance. And, as I said, the very fact that I was starting out on the road to teaching through dance was a joke. But as I lay there one night, after another day of intense preparation for our first 'Life Dance' event as the newly formed 5 to Midnight Gaia Dance Project, there he was – a calm presence, drumming, reindeer in his eyes, singing in a language that spoke directly to my heart, 'Be calm. All is well. I am with you.'

I didn't dare ask him who he was. I didn't want to break the spell of the dream. I simply sat with him and listened to his drum and his song. And he remained with me all week, coming into my adrenalized sleep every night to sing me into a place of trust. Even when Susannah and I began to teach, he was still there when I closed my eyes, offering me guidance and support.

I came to rely on him. Whenever I walked into a room to lead a shamanic journey, there he was, as constant as a heartbeat. As time went on, he became more and more helpful. He'd often give me a sense of what was going on for the people we were working with, advise me to look out for dangers along the way or give me specific advice about how to work with the group. For the first 10 years of our relationship it never occurred to me that he was a real person. But now I was about to meet him.

⟡

We'd arrived at Alta airport in the north of Norway three days before. Anka had told me which flight to get and that she would meet me when the plane stopped in Trondheim to pick up passengers.

It had been six months since we'd met at the workshop. She'd danced deeply and powerfully and many times I'd watched her going into trance and contacting her spirits. She was a shaman too, trained in many Western techniques but rooted in the traditions of her people, the Sami.

At the end of the workshop, she'd come to me to say thank you. Then she'd asked me a question that on the surface had been straightforward: 'Don't you have a story to tell me?'

I'd hesitated. Two years before, after receiving guidance from a teacher I had at the time, I'd started my search for the Old Man of the North. For some reason I began to tell her about it.

She asked me to describe him. I didn't just describe him but also his house and the landscape it was situated in, which I'd seen many times in dreams and visions.

She nodded as I spoke and then answered matter-of-factly, 'Yes, I know him. I'll take you to meet him.'

My heart jumped into my mouth. I was both shocked and elated. Could this be real?

She hadn't finished. 'I warn you, though, he will test you. Even if we travel all that way up north, he may refuse to meet you. He'll look for your buttons and push them mercilessly. He'll want to know what you're made of.'

The slightest possibility that she actually knew who this man was and where he lived was more than enough encouragement for me to face a few tests. The thing was, I didn't want anything from him. I simply wanted to meet him and thank him face to face for all the support he'd given me over the past decade. I also knew that if it *was* him, it would obliterate the doubts that my rational mind had about this shamanism business being more in the realm of science fiction than everyday life.

So now Anka and I were leaving the little 'sauna incident' town of Kautokeino and driving towards the Finnish border. We'd spent the first two nights in the tiny hamlet of Láhpoluoppal, staying with a friend of Anka's who was a children's storybook writer. She was writing stories in her native tongue to keep the Sami language alive. Her daughter was training to be a lawyer and wanted to work in the local government in Karasjok. From them, I'd learned a little more about the Sami story, which, sadly, was as horrific as the stories of other indigenous people coming into contact with the 'civilized' world.

The first night I was there, I'd dreamed that I was hunting with the Old Man. We were hunting reindeer in a strange environment. There was a building there that had a curving, sloped roof that reminded me of a ski jump. And as we hunted, we came across a huge ski jump right in the middle of the town. It seemed completely out of place.

My shaman guide was teaching me how to hunt, and soon enough we trapped a reindeer and killed it. We took out its heart and ate it. I had been a vegan for many years, so eating reindeer heart was a surprising departure from my normal diet! But the Old Man had talked to me at length about the relationship between the reindeer and the Sami people. He'd explained that it was similar to the relationship between the Plains Indians of North America and the buffalo. The reindeer was sacred to the Sami people and to hunt it and eat of its flesh was a very strong welcome to this land.

The next day, Anka had decided it was time to call the Old Man and ask his permission to visit him. He didn't speak any English, but I could hear from the tone of his voice on the phone that he wasn't happy.

'What's he saying?' I asked.

'He wants to know how old you are.'

'Tell him I'm 39.'

She did. There was a pause and then Anka held the phone away from her ear as he responded with a gruff bark of a sentence.

'What now?'

'He says, "Tell him to go home." He's sick of young men coming to see him and asking him stupid questions. He says he won't see you.'

I couldn't help laughing. I don't know why. It wasn't funny. We'd travelled thousands of miles to see this man and he was sending me away before he'd even met me. But I felt steady inside myself. As far as I was concerned, we'd been hunting together the night before and I asked Anka to tell him that.

'And please tell him we'll be there tomorrow after lunch to see him,' I added.

I heard a laugh and Anka nodded. 'He says it's okay. He'll see us tomorrow.'

First test passed, I thought, glad that Anka had warned me.

As we left the town, Anka started singing a traditional *yoik*, the Sami name for the spirit songs through which humans can communicate with the spirit of anything, be it a person, a rock, a place or the many spirits that populate the vast and wild landscape in which the Sami live. She told me it was the Old Man's *yoik* and that he would know through her singing it that we were on our way.

I listened and sank into the melody. Something deep inside me recognized the song, and my heart started to beat a little faster.

⁂

As we drove south, away from the chalet, I was astonished to see the strange building from my dream and the ski slope right there in the middle of town. Everything about the journey had a familiar feel to it. The boundary between dreaming and waking life was blurred so that at times I really wasn't sure if I was awake or asleep.

It wasn't long before we drove around a corner and into the scenery that I knew so intimately from the past 10 years.

'This is it!' I almost shouted with joy. 'My God, is this real?'

I pinched myself and looked at the palms of my hands, a reality-check practice that I'd learned from lucid dreaming. My hands were perfectly normal, so I was awake, wide awake, no doubt about it. And yet I was inside the world of my dreams. And there was the small wooden house with a deck overlooking the river.

We pulled off the road and parked. My heart was racing and I tried to breathe deeply to calm myself, to no avail.

We got out of the car and walked towards the house. I saw the small *lavo*, a structure almost exactly the same as a Native American tipi, and the pile of reindeer antlers that was as familiar to me as my own home. Even the small round stone altar was there.

A small man was standing on the deck, looking out over the river. He didn't turn around immediately. He looked up into the sky and I watched as a beautiful eagle flew into sight and called out. Then he nodded and turned round.

It was him. It really was. I couldn't believe my eyes.

As we approached him, Anka introduced us: 'Bikko Máhte Penta, this is Ya'Acov Darling Khan. Ya'Acov, this is Bikko Máhte.'

We shook hands and I looked into the eyes of the man who had been such a source of guidance and inspiration to me for so many years. I knew him so well. And yet apparently I'd never met him. My mind did a few somersaults and landed firmly on its back and upside down.

At that moment, where the world of dreams and the world of so-called reality fused into one seamless union, my life changed forever. This was an undeniable happening that crushed any semblance of control my rational mind had worked so hard to hold on to.

We all sat down on Bikko Máhte's wooden bench. I had prepared so many things to say to him, but now that I was there, there really was nothing to say. And so we sat under the cool Arctic sun and the vast sky as the river danced by and the wind sang through the trees.

After a while, Anka asked Bikko if he wanted her to translate.

'We have been communicating very well already for many years,' he responded.

For now, there was nothing more to say. My mind became like the sky and we sat quietly, not saying a word, for several hours.

I sensed some tension between Bikko and Anka. She hadn't mentioned her attempt at seduction and I certainly wasn't going to bring it up. But although something uneasy still rumbled in the space between us, I had to acknowledge that she'd done precisely what she'd said she would six months ago in Oslo. She'd brought me here to meet the Old Man of the North.

*

That first visit went by in a flash. I walked on the Old Man's land and sat by the river, and every now and again, with Anka translating, we said a few words to each other. I stayed in his house. He watched the TV news. He cooked reindeer stew for us. I ate it – I knew better than to turn down a gift like that.

That first night, I dreamed that we were under attack. As I looked out, I could see the steeples of the local churches. They seemed to be bristling with malevolence as they pierced the night sky. I felt a mixture of fear and outrage. I asked for guidance and was shown a ceremony.

In the morning, I asked Bikko Máhte and Anka about my dream. Anka explained that there were several churches in the area, all competing for the hearts and minds of the local population. They were at each other's throats all the time, but they all agreed that shamanism was the devil's work. And, since Bikko Máhte was a practising shaman, he was doing the devil's work.

I told them about the advice I'd received in my dream and Bikko Máhte asked me to do the ritual I'd been shown. So Anka and I drove into town and found the local store and I bought the four small round pocket mirrors I would need. We returned to the house and I prepared myself for the ritual.

Later in the afternoon, as the sun was going down, I took my drum and the mirrors and went out onto the land. I drummed and sang to the spirits for more than an hour. The more I drummed, the quieter my mind became and the stronger I felt. It was as if the power of the land itself was coursing through me. The ferocity I felt inside me was now as sharp as the edge of a sword. But I wasn't angry. I had no intention to do harm, only to do my best to offer some protection to a man who was holding the sacred tradition of his people safe.

Bikko Máhte had been drumming on that land for more than 30 years. I cannot overestimate the courage it had taken for him to do that. Since Christianity had arrived in the Sami lands, the Church had instilled the cold fear of hell into the bodies, hearts and minds of these gentle people. A tradition that had kept them living in healthy balance with the land for many thousands of years had been brutally repressed by those who thought they had the sole word of truth written in their holy book and the right to impose it wherever they went. In an attempt to break the backbone of the Sami culture, they had decided to punish anyone found playing, making or owning a drum. The death penalty wasn't uncommon for this 'offence'. All drums found were burned. The drum, the very heartbeat of the people, was transformed into a symbol of evil.

Bikko Máhte had grown up in this atmosphere of fear-driven religion. And yet his spirit was the spirit of a shaman, just as his father's and grandfather's had been before him. Shamanic dreams started coming to him in his twenties, and in those dreams, he was given a drum to play. And he was told to make a drum.

He was confused and afraid. His confusion stretched him like a skin across a great divide. On the one side, there was all the knowledge of his ancestors and the spirits. They had lived in balance with their environment and, for the most part, in peace. On the other side, there was the new religion, the religion that had brought a mixture of the great light of Christ and a whole bunch of strange and twisted ideas about the devil. He didn't know where to turn.

But then it came to him. He knew there was an old drum on display in the museum in a nearby town called Karasjok. He would go and stand in front of it and ask for guidance. He planned to stand as close to it as possible and ask everything he believed to be good and true if the drum was evil or a force for good. He felt in his heart that his ancestors had known the power of the drum and had used it for healing and balance. And yet he wasn't unaffected by the fear that had been so deeply instilled in his people.

So off he went to Karasjok. The drum was so old that the skin had blackened with age. He stood in front of its display case, praying for guidance. After some time in deep concentration, he saw three bright stars appearing on the drum.

The way he understood this message says much about the struggles the Sami people have been through. On the one hand, the three stars represented the holy trinity from the relatively new kid on the block, Christianity. On the other hand, they represented three of the old Sami divinities showing up to remind the young shaman-to-be that the drumming tradition of his ancestors had shone its light in the darkness for many thousands of years and that he needn't be afraid. The often uneasy relationship between Christianity and shamanism is as present in the land of the Sami as it is in so many places around the world where imported religions have blended into the ancient traditions that preceded them.

So, more than 40 years ago, Bikko Máhte crafted himself a drum in the way his people had done for many generations. At the time he was training in the traditional crafts of his people. He developed into a highly respected craftsman and when I met him he was teaching at the Sami Institute in Kautokeino. He told me that although his teacher at the time didn't approve of him making a drum, he nevertheless gave him the keys to the workshop so that he could work on his drum project over the weekends. And thank the spirits that he did. I know that his clandestine support of his student has brought immeasurable riches to my life and to the lives of many others. Bikko Máhte's life as a shaman had begun.

As I drummed, all of these stories presented themselves as images in my mind. I felt the pain of what we as humans have done to indigenous cultures and to the ancient practice of shamanism throughout the world. I felt that pain in my heart and I sang to the four directions, north, south, east and west. As I had been shown in my dream, I planted one of the small round mirrors facing outwards in each of the four directions and I called to the spirits of the elements that I had learned to associate with each direction. Then I spoke to the trees and the rocks and the spirits of the land and asked them to create a circle of protection around the perimeter of Bikko Máhte's land. The mirrors were planted to do what mirrors do: to reflect back whatever came their way.

When I had completed the ritual and went back into the house, I was astonished to find that three hours had passed. I was tired from my work, but content. We ate and then it was time for me to pack my bags and return to the UK.

Before I left, I made sure that Bikko Máhte knew how grateful I was for all the years of support I'd received from him. I felt sure that we would see each other again. I had the sense that my journey with him had just turned a new corner. A whole new landscape lay ahead.

Chapter 1

ON THE ROAD TO A FIRST SHATTERING

'It can take years to mould a dream. It takes only
a fraction of a second for it to be shattered.'
MARY E. PEARSON, *THE KISS OF DECEPTION*

I'd met the first person who had the ability to come into my dreams
and remind me that I was dreaming years before, in 1987. At that
time I'd recently begun a serious course of study in shamanism. I'd
been lucky enough to meet some great teachers and had started what
turned out to be an eight-year apprenticeship with the Deer Tribe Metis
Medicine Society.

I was apprenticed to a curly-headed Austrian medicine man called
Batty Thunder Bear Gold. He had a great name and an even better
sense of humour. He taught from a sofa and smoked Indonesian clove
cigarettes all day long. In the smoke-filled rooms of his workshops,
I'd been learning about the medicine wheel, the four directions, a
cosmology called the '20 count' and the pathway of study and ceremony
that the Deer Tribe offered. I'd also been learning not to take myself too
seriously; the sound of deep belly laughter was never far away when
Batty was around.

The leader of the tribe was called Harley Swiftdeer. He was quite a
character and was loved and admired by some and pilloried as a total

charlatan by others. Whatever the truth of the matter, he had a brilliant mind and the teachings he brought together provided me with a starting-point.

At that time, having studied filmmaking and photography at college, I was offering something called ritual photography, the purpose of which was for the client to end up with a photograph of their true self. In order to get there, we used costume and theatre and previously taken images to engage in a creative dialogue about what happened when I pointed the camera at the client in the studio. Did they hide? Did they show off or perform? Were they nonchalant? And what would it take for them simply to allow the camera to see them as they were? I'd woken up with the idea one day and just got on with it. It was minimally successful, but the people I did work with really got a lot out of the experience. And looking through the camera lens taught me more about seeing what was in front of me. I learned to see the language of the body and started to see that it often revealed a deeper truth than the spoken word.

My photography work gave me just about enough income to survive. I was living in a community in Mornington Grove in London's East End. We were 14 people living in two houses next door to one another. I had to cook once a week and keep the stairs clean. My rent was minimal, I was surrounded by good people and it was an excellent place for me to fall apart in. And so I did. I was in therapy and going to as many workshops with the Deer Tribe as possible.

In that same period, I met the wonderfully enigmatic Arwyn DreamWalker, the first person who was able to come into my dreams. She was a wiry-haired medicine woman who was half Cherokee and half Irish. She was very connected to the Navajo people and had teachers in Peru as well. She was a consummate dreamer.

I met her for the first time in the early summer of 1987. She was teaching a workshop at a place called the Centre for Alternative Education and Research (CAER) on the southwestern tip of Cornwall in England. It was situated amongst some beautiful and ancient woods and had a *fougou* in the garden, an Iron Age underground ritual chamber. There was also a beautiful gypsy caravan in the grounds that Arwyn would regularly invite us to meet at for our night-time dream work. She liked it because a caravan is for travelling and she liked to go places in her dreams! The mornings of the workshop were always taken up with discussing where we'd been and what we'd done in our dreams.

Arwyn never missed an opportunity to give us a teaching, and the Irishwoman in her had a sharp sense of humour. One lunchtime, she came into the kitchen and asked the 20 or so students who were eating lunch, 'How many of you have spirit animals who are carnivores?'

At least 15 of us put up our hands.

'And how many of you are vegetarians?' she asked.

At least 12 of the 15 raised their hands, including me.

'Mmmm,' she said, 'if I were a meat-eating animal, I wouldn't hang out round a bunch of vegetarians for long! You have to feed the spirits you work with, look after them and honour them and their way of life.'

I wasn't sure if she was joking or not, but one look at her face made me realize she was perfectly serious. I would have to rethink the idea of having a rattlesnake for a power animal!

Arwyn was a wonderful teacher for me. She was full of crazy wisdom and the joy of her craft. Looking back now, I remain amazed at her commitment to sharing her knowledge and at ours to do whatever it took to take it in.

Lucid dreaming had been part of my life since I could remember and I was delighted to discover that it was an important aspect of our study with Arwyn. At one point I had a long lucid dream that profoundly changed the direction my life was going in.

That particular dream began with being with my therapist, a diminutive and very sweet man from Malta named Manas Marmara. He told me to lie down and guided me to deepen and soften my breathing.

As I did so, a remarkable thing happened: I felt myself growing way beyond the edges of my physical body. I felt hemmed in by the wooden walls of the room we were in, but, with a little effort, seemed to pop through them. And still I was expanding.

As I felt my hands touching the stars, something about the sensation felt very familiar, and then I remembered. Every night for years and years when I was a child, I used to have this experience. I would fall asleep with it. I don't know where I got it from, but I did it every night from the age of seven to my early teens. I loved it. It put me in touch with a reality that was more real for me than the world I was learning to live in. I would just lie in bed and let go. And the more I let go, the more I would expand. And I would keep going until my thumbs could tickle the stars and I was as expanded as I could be. At that point I would ask the same question, night after night, year after year. That question brought joy into my life. I loved the feeling it gave me, which I can only describe as a seven-year-old's version of awe at the mystery of things.

The question was: 'If God created all of this, then what created God?'

I can't tell you where that question came from, but it was my absolute delight to ask it. I didn't expect an answer. The joy was in the question itself and the quietness of the night beckoning me into the magical world of my dreams.

I woke up from the lucid dream in the middle of the night, very moved to have remembered that experience. I wrote it all down and went straight back into dreaming.

In a second dream, I was in a ritual with Arwyn and some Hopi elders. Arwyn gave me an old mask and asked me to put it on. I did as I was asked, and the moment I placed the mask over my face, I stepped into another reality.

I found myself in a time and place many centuries before, in the desert of what is now New Mexico. I was dancing in front of a fire and chanting in a language that I didn't recognize. As I chanted, I heard the rumbling of distant thunder in the hills. I could see clouds moving in and I seemed to be singing to them. Within a few minutes, rain began to fall and I felt the desert landscape drinking it in. I could almost hear the sound of life coming back to the dry land. My song intensified and I recognized that I was singing to call the rain. My song was an intimate conversation with the weather spirits. I knew them well and I knew their songs. I had become a 'weather worker' and yet some part of me was vaguely aware that it was the mask that was lending me this power and that I was in a dream.

When I woke up, it was raining outside. I felt connected to the rain in a way that I'd never done before. I felt so grateful for the waters and for the first time saw them as the bringers of life. One dream had deepened my relationship with the weather in a way I hadn't even known was possible. And I knew that the mask was responsible and I knew, in the way that knowledge lands without thought in that gateway space between dreaming and waking, that I was to tell Arwyn about the dream and that this was a momentous point in my life.

I was right about that, but not at all in the way I thought.

Having written down my dreams, I took out a pipe that Manas had given me and sat down to do my morning prayers. The pipe was a magnificent Native American prayer pipe with a buffalo carved into the clay bowl and the stem beautifully decorated with leather and fine beadwork. I'd been overwhelmed by the generosity of the gift, and even though I knew that I would only look after the pipe for a short time, I'd set out to learn how to use it in a way that honoured its origins.

I was acutely aware that the pipe was from a tradition that, like all shamanic traditions, had been desecrated by those intent on replacing the 'superstitions' of the old ways with the 'enlightenment' of Christianity. The arrogance and cruelty of our European ancestors knew no bounds. I felt that I'd been given the pipe as a way of remembering how to pray directly from the heart and learning how to have an intimate and ongoing conversation with the Creator. I accepted it as a loan, knowing that once I'd remembered how to pray in this way, I'd return it to its homeland. I didn't want to play at being a Native American.

One of the first things that I learned about the pipe was that when the bowl and the stem were together, it was sacrilege not to tell the truth. Alongside that, speaking 'across the pipe' was a way of showing others that you were attempting to communicate something sacred and of great importance to you.

And so, having prayed, I went to look for Arwyn. I found her at the breakfast table. I asked her if I could speak to her 'across my pipe'. She looked at me with that magical squint that always made me feel quite naked and agreed to listen to what I had to say.

I told her my mask dream. As I related it, I could see that my words were having quite an impact. Arwyn's eyes were wide open and she was listening deeply. She asked me to describe the mask again. And then she called her colleague, Brigit, to come and listen to my dream.

It turned out that a few months before, Arwyn and Brigit had been given exactly the same mask that I'd seen in my dream. They'd been told that someone would show up who would be able to explain to them what it was for. Seemingly, that person was me.

I was somewhere between shocked and elated as Arwyn explained this to me. She told me there and then that I needed to go and visit her in the USA and study with her. She said she would take me to visit her Hopi teachers and that there was much to learn.

I was so excited. I'd read the books of Carlos Castaneda, as everyone interested in such things had at that time. He was a young student from the University of California, Los Angeles, who'd met an old Yaqui sorcerer called Don Juan who'd demolished his fixed perception of the world and introduced him to one far more magical and mysterious. Now I felt as if I was in the pages of one of his stories. I, too, had found my teacher. I was on my journey and there was no stopping me.

Except that a few weeks after this, Susannah and I went on holiday to Portugal and what happened there split my world asunder.

❧

Chapter 2

A PORTUGUESE DREAM

'All men dream, but not equally. Those who dream
by night, in the dusty recesses of their minds, wake in
the day to find that it was vanity: but the dreamers of
the day are dangerous men, for they may act on their
dreams with open eyes, to make them possible.'

T.E. LAWRENCE

Susannah and I were rough camping on the beach of a little-known
resort close to Faro. A few days in the sun seemed just the medicine
we needed to take a breath and do a little integrating. It was an intense
time. We were now both apprenticed to Batty Thunder Bear Gold of the
Deer Tribe, which meant that we had committed ourselves to a course
of study and a series of ceremonies, some of which were carried out in
groups, and some of which were designed to be done at home alone.
We were also working with two UK-based Deer Tribe teachers, Heather
Campbell and Sue Jamieson. On top of that, whenever Arwyn was in the
country, I made sure to be wherever she was teaching.

I had no idea what was waiting for me on that little beach, but I dare
say that the dream that visited me there would have found me wherever
I was. I was travelling towards that confrontation at a rate of knots.

I was, however, blissfully unaware of it. I was completely into what I
was discovering and Arwyn's invitation had given me what I mistakenly
thought of as the confidence I needed to continue. Now that a medicine

woman had recognized me, I believed that I was well on the way to becoming a shaman, and I was loving the adventure. I was 23 years old.

But our holiday was like the dance of the seven veils for me. Each night I was stripped of a little more confidence, until by the end of the week the raw layers of self-doubt and fear that my self-importance was doing a fine job of masking were all visible and exposed.

On that first night, I had a lucid dream. In the dream, I was flying and I was going somewhere very specific. I couldn't remember where I was headed, but some part of me seemed to know exactly where to go.

After a while I saw that I was approaching the house I'd lived in as a child from the age of seven onwards. I hovered outside my old bedroom window and was soon joined by my seven-year-old self. He was delighted to see me and I was delighted to see him. We flew together and he told me he was taking me to visit 'the grandparents'. I took this to mean a circle of tribal elders and I was very excited. I was all ready to receive whatever revelations they would give me.

Sure enough, we soon ended up flying over a forest and coming to rest on the ground by an indigenous-style circular hut. There was no electricity and I felt it belonged to people who were still in touch with the magic of life. I could smell the sweet smell of the fire and some incense that I guessed they were burning. My seven-year-old self was definitely leading and I followed him inside and sat down next to the fire with him on my right-hand side.

It took my eyes a while to adjust to the gloom of the hut, but when they did, I saw that we were sitting in a circle of people, all in magnificent and varied tribal dress. The colours and patterns were astonishing and it was difficult not to stare at the headdresses and beadwork. It appeared that there were a man and a woman from each shamanic tradition. I saw medicine people from all five continents sitting in the circle and they were all looking at me with serious expressions.

I had a moment of fear, but it was quickly replaced by the excitement of being with these extraordinary people. I wondered what marvels they were going to reveal to me. I have to confess, a part of me was already preparing to tell Arwyn and Batty about this wonderful meeting with the elders, and the prospect was giving me a glow of self-satisfaction.

I could hear music, and as I continued to scan the circle, I saw one man on his own playing a small oval drum and chanting quietly. I waited. The child beside me had become very still and I took this as a cue, though my mind was anything but quiet. Then the drumming stopped. The couple who appeared to be the leaders stood up.

Very formally and politely, they welcomed me to this council. I was instructed to sit still and listen to what they had to say to me. I was also told very clearly not to interrupt. I nodded my agreement. My heart was beating fast and I was glad of the fire and the child beside me.

And then the drums, more of them this time, began. As did a low rumbling chant that sent shivers down my spine. Smoke from the incense and from the fire was swirling around me and for a moment I was afraid I was about to lose consciousness.

Two by two, the elders stood and spoke to me. I say 'spoke to me', but the fierceness in their voices made it feel more like a lecture. They gave me the most severe telling-off I'd ever had. Who did I think I was, flying off to the States to work with some mask when I didn't even know where my own two feet were? They were certainly nowhere near the ground! And what about my finances? I was still in debt from my time at college and had no plans at all to bring that part of my life into balance. Why was I running away? What from? Didn't I know that my own ancestors had a rule about studying the mystical side of Judaism known as the Qabalah? No, I didn't. They were quick to fill me in. They made some more recommendations too.

'1) Get your life together in the material world by finding your work and making your contribution. 2) Get your family together and your home and learn to love in the material world and get your feet on the ground. 3) Gain some experience of life and maybe then, when you're 40[!!!], you can start to study the more mystical side of life.'

Basically, they were telling me to get a job, get myself out of debt, get real and take responsibility for my life.

Then they asked me about the benefactor that I was fantasizing would show up and pay for me to go to the States and study. Did I think I was so brilliant that I didn't need to work for my experiences? Did I think that it was okay to rely on someone else's hard work to get me where I wanted to go? Why was I even considering taking up Arwyn's offer of learning to fly when I hadn't yet learned to walk?

As they spoke, my insides turned to ice. I felt a gut-wrenching pain as my dreams of all the spiritual teachings they were going to share with me dissolved in the harsh tones of the lessons they were delivering. These could have been the voices of my own parents and grandparents, and I'd thought I'd managed to escape *their* opinions about the way I was living my life.

The child beside me sat perfectly still during all of this, breathing calmly. Becoming more childlike than him by the second, I couldn't understand his peaceful demeanour at all. He took my hand and gave it a squeeze. I felt like crying, but I wasn't going to show myself up. I could feel the pain in my muscles as I held on for dear life, praying that this would end soon.

And then I woke up, sweating, my eyes stinging with acid tears, my body sore and rigid on the narrow camping mat. I was so relieved to be awake and out of that grilling! And even though part of me knew that the power of that dream had already changed something irrevocably, I quickly quashed that awareness.

⁖

As I woke, I absent-mindedly reached for my bronze ancient Austrian goddess earring. I loved that earring. It was a symbol of the feminist man I was proud to be. God was over and it was time for the Goddess again. That earring was a symbol of the direction I believed my life to be heading in. I was on the track of the old ways. The current ones simply weren't working and a wholly spiritual life was the answer. I never took that earring out except to clean it and I'd cleaned it the night before as I'd been preparing for bed.

Now I was shocked to feel an empty space where it had been. I jumped out of my sleeping bag, woke Susannah as gently as I could and started a frantic search.

By the time we'd finished looking, I'd been through everything and the earring was nowhere to be found. I was in a foul mood. I did everything I could to calm myself down and gain some perspective, but my agitation was unmovable. I felt I'd lost something much more than an earring.

By now, I'd all but wiped the dream from my memory. 'It was just a dream. I must just be afraid of taking my power and going to do the work with Arwyn.'

That first night, I didn't even tell Susannah what had happened.

The day passed in a haze of mild irritation and agitation, and despite the beauty of our surroundings, as evening approached I had a growing sense of dread. Even the beautiful hoopoe birds that were hanging out round our tent were a source of suspicion and irritation for me. After all, maybe one of them had stolen my earring.

Eventually, it was bedtime again and I set my intention, as I usually did, to wake up in my dreams and see what came. I couldn't believe what did.

The first part of the night was filled with cameo dreams, short episodes of day-to-day activity with little or no meaning for me. But midway through the night I was amazed to find myself in exactly the same lucid dream as the night before. All the details were precisely the same. And even though I knew I was dreaming, I was powerless to change anything. I felt held in the strong energy of the dream itself and all I could do was go along with it and do my best to survive the powerful lessons that were repeated, almost word for word, from the night before.

This time there was no self-satisfied glee that I was being specially chosen by these people for some task. I felt humiliated by my own arrogance and ashamed to be so exposed in my pride. The same icy dread, now stronger, sat deep in my belly. I even thought I might vomit.

What made it worse was that the characters in the dream were all people I wanted to be close to. The only thing that was at all different from the night before was that some part of me was beginning to become aware of the care those elders had for me.

When I woke up, I knew I had to tell Susannah, and I did. She listened carefully to what I had to say and asked me what I made of it.

I wasn't willing to give up my dream of going to work with Arwyn in the States and I made that clear immediately. I was on the defensive, and even though Susannah was in no way attacking me or telling me to listen to the voices of these elders, I felt seriously under threat. I'd just found a place where my experiences could be understood, where I could learn about the things that really interested me rather than going through the rigmarole of an education that I felt to be a charade. This doorway had only just opened and these dream figures seemed determined to slam it shut in my face.

I've always had a strong will – sometimes way too strong for my own good. It's taken me nearly 30 years of journeying to see surrender as a positive thing. I used to think of it as an admission of defeat. Sure, in the years to come, I would learn to surrender to the spirit dance, but that was impersonal. Back then I wasn't going to give up on what mattered most to me because of a couple of lucid dreams. I was beginning to realize that my earring was lost for good and that something was happening that was beyond my conscious control, but one thing was for sure: I *wasn't* about to give up.

On the other hand, whatever part of my consciousness had taken the form of a circle of tribal elders in order to communicate with me wasn't about to give up either. Night after night that week, I entered the same dream. Each night I became lucid and was determined to achieve a different outcome and to hear a different message, but there was no give. The elders held steadfastly to their position, even though I tried reasoning with them, defending myself and even accusing them of being a rather bizarre expression of my ancestral fears. Throughout, they stayed constant and calm. They were as persistent as the sea that shapes the hard rocks on the shore.

So my nights were a battle between the different parts of my psyche, witnessed by the calm and ever-present sweetness of the seven-year-old me. My days were no better. I went from total resistance to full-on resentment, but slowly, slowly, I felt myself recognizing the truth in what the elders were saying to me.

On the sixth night of the same dream, a new elder stood up. He was as dark as the night and yet he shimmered with a strange light that seemed to come from inside him. His voice was like the sound of stones on the riverbed, guttural and watery, melodic and strong. He said, 'There is very little in this world that grows without strong roots. Your roots are weak. You are headstrong and impulsive and I warn you that if you do not heed our advice, each step you take will move you further and further from the self we are here to support you in becoming. Listen to us and what you dream will come to pass, but not in the way you think it will.'

There was something in his words or the way he said them that broke through my defences. I got that whoever these elders were, they were here for me each and every night, steadfast and constant in their love. That was it. A dam broke inside me and I started to cry. My tears were thick and stung my eyes and I felt my body shuddering. It felt as if something was truly dying inside me, and once the process had begun, there was nothing I could do to stop it. I stayed inside the dream, and the sound of the drums and the old voices singing kept a steady pulse to which I clung as I fell to pieces.

There was little or no thinking in my tears. A few images flashed before me of warriors dying in battles and of beautifully carved wooden doors opening and closing. And then I was on my knees, thanking the circle for showing up for me. I apologized for my stubbornness, swore never to fight their wisdom again and promised to sort my life out once and for all.

They laughed kindly in the way only elders can when they see the young pledging themselves to a pathway they know nothing about.

I awoke, exhausted but changed. When I told Susannah what had happened, she just smiled and gave me a hug. She had a confidence in me that I didn't have in myself.

Everything looked different that day. The freshness of the ocean and the sweet perfume of the wind seemed new to me. I knew my life had changed and I felt full of the hope that often accompanies such experiences.

We returned to London the next day, with the Portuguese sunlight on our skins. I had a new resolution in my heart. I was determined to find a more grounded approach to my studies and my life. I had absolutely no idea what I was going to do other than to contact Arwyn and let her know what had happened, but I hoped to find clarity and guidance along the way.

When we got back to the community, my post was neatly stacked up and I absent-mindedly started to open it. When I got to my monthly credit card statement, I found I was beyond my limit and had a demand for immediate payment.

At that moment, the fear I had felt in that repeating dream returned in full force. My guts turned to ice and I felt more lost and afraid than I'd ever felt in my life. All I could do was run upstairs and hide under my duvet.

I didn't know where to turn. I had no assured income. My dream of travelling to the USA and becoming Super Shaman was over. And my bills were red and demanding to be paid.

Terror is not a reasonable emotion. And terror had its claws in me. Lying there under the duvet, waiting for the night to come and swallow me in its darkness, I was lost and rudderless in the great unknown. I felt as if I was drowning. There was nothing Susannah could say to console me, though she did her best. What was so deeply terrifying was the experience of feeling utterly powerless as my direction and my hope were popped like some ethereal bubble by the harsh needle of a credit card bill.

As devastated as I was, there was still a quiet voice inside me that I could barely hear, saying, simply and without rebuke, 'Now you know, dear one, what you've been running from and it's time to grow up and learn to live well in this world. Facing this feeling of powerlessness that has been in you for a very long time is the beginning.'

I couldn't reply. I just curled up and fell asleep, taking refuge, as I always had, in the dark embrace of the night.

Chapter 3

A NIGHT ON THE MOUNTAIN OF FEAR

'There is no illusion greater than fear.'
LAO TZU

I got myself through the next few weeks, working with photography and massage clients and relying on the small business start-up benefit I was receiving from the government. In a way, I was still in shock from what had happened in Portugal. I had written to Arwyn to let her know that I wouldn't be coming and I continued with my daily practices trying to establish a sense of ground under my feet and doing my best to move through the dull blanket of fear that was greying my perception. It would take me more than a year to get to the bottom of it and to understand where it was coming from. Within that time, I did my best to learn to live with it in the night and in the day.

I was just about able to create enough work to live, but it was really touch and go and I was a long way from standing on my own two feet as the elders in my dream had demanded. I was having to face up to the powerfully negative relationship I had with money, which meant that earning enough was a real struggle. I wasn't afraid of work, but I didn't want to work just for the sake of money. I wanted my work to have some meaning and some connection to the deeper journey I felt my life was about. I was happy to make my offering, but I didn't want to compromise by just taking any job that was on offer. And so I continued with my sporadic ritual photography and with a few massage clients.

I got some high-level support for my photography when I was lucky enough to meet a wonderful woman called Jo Spence. She was doing something called photo-therapy, using the camera as a therapeutic tool to map her own life journey and that of others. By the time I met her, she was already fighting cancer. She was a magnificently brave woman and as well as continuing to develop her work in ways that didn't focus on her illness, she photographed and documented her journey with cancer in a profound way.

We were like a breath of fresh air for each other. I was using the camera as a shamanic tool, attempting to co-create images with my clients in which they could witness their own qualities of soul. Jo was using the camera to reveal the personally political issues of being a woman with breast cancer. She was attempting to get to the bottom of anything in her upbringing that might have had a bearing on her emotional wellbeing, which in turn might be affecting her physical wellbeing.

We shared some sessions together. I worked with her in the ways I was developing and she worked with me in her style. I loved the creativity that was sparked by our differences. I was poetic and imaginative in the way I approached the sessions. She was down to earth and gritty. Our conversations and sessions were deeply enriching for me and her encouragement was a godsend at a time when my confidence was really low.

Though the work with Jo was an exchange and involved no money, her encouragement to go further in the work I was doing helped me to take my work a little more seriously. I ended up with more and more interesting clients, the majority of whom were women who had suffered some form of sexual abuse. They saw this as a wonderfully healing opportunity to improve their self-image in the company of a man with whom they felt safe. I didn't go looking for this work, but it certainly found me. After the work I did with Jo, suddenly 90 per cent of my clients were women who wanted to move on from what they had suffered. I witnessed, again and again, personal work of the utmost courage and dignity, and it was my privilege to do so.

At the same time, every spare penny I had went on paying for my ongoing study with the Deer Tribe. I attended as many of their gatherings as possible, both in the UK and in Europe. Most of the gatherings took place in southwest England, in Devon, at weekends. Some of these were held by visiting teachers from the USA or Europe and others were held by local people who had already been studying for a few years.

The Deer Tribe had a system of study and initiation based on 15 gateways. In each gateway, the apprentice had several tasks to complete. Once they had done so, their teacher would confirm that they had passed through that gateway. Each gateway also had several rituals associated with it, designed to help students to face the past and be as effective as possible in the present.

One weekend, one of our teachers, a magically down-to-earth woman called Sue Jamieson, decided to hold a ritual for apprentices that was known as 'Night on the Mountain of Fear'. I'd continued to experience a lot of fear in my day-to-day life, which I put down to my financial challenges and the feeling that I might never be able to earn enough doing what I wanted to do. When I heard that the intention of this ritual was to spend the night out in nature, alone, preferably on a mountain, in order to face our fears, I thought, *perfect. That's precisely what I need.*

We were allowed to take waterproof gear with us, but no sleeping bag or tent. Devon is short on mountains, but there are plenty of rolling hills that offer seclusion and some height. We were to find our spot, gather eight rocks from as close by as possible and create a circle with each rock 'holding' one of the cardinal and non-cardinal points of the compass.

Once we had set up our circle, we had to invoke support from the four directions and the elemental powers they represented, our ancestors, our personal helpers in the spirit world and the spirit of the land itself. I was new to this kind of formal ritual and had no real idea of or conscious connection to either my own guides or my ancestors.

The invocation was to be made through a pipe ceremony. This involved loading the pipe with 20 pinches of tobacco, considered sacred by many traditions, each one holding a specific prayer. Smoking the pipe and offering the smoke to the four directions made our prayers visible to spirit.

Then we had to ask all our fears to come and show themselves to us and enter into a dialogue with them with the aim of becoming stronger than they were.

This ritual had been used over many generations to help students find and develop their internal strength.

After a day of preparations, we waited for dusk to arrive and then set out to find our place. It was forbidden to use any plants other than tobacco for praying and sage and cedar for purification. Sobriety is one of the qualities of a warrior and this was a ceremony in which we would need to access the warrior spirit inside us in order to have the courage to face our fears. This was the first time I'd heard the word 'warrior' used in this context. The ritual was a 'warrior task'. The 'enemy' was within and we were all intent on vanquishing it.

The camaraderie and humour amongst those of us doing the ritual was a strong part of our preparations, but when it was time for us to go, the high spirits of the day were replaced with a mixture of quiet determination and outright fear about what the night would bring.

It was early autumn and the ground was covered in early leaf-fall and wet from heavy downpours during the day. I headed off with a small rucksack containing a torch, a water bottle, a notebook and pen, my pipe, tobacco and lighter, and a small bag containing sage and cedar. Earlier in the day, I'd chosen a hill to climb and as soon as I went through the gate that led to it, the rain began to fall. I remember thinking quite clearly as I hurriedly donned my waterproofs that maybe, just maybe, some lunatic 1,000 years ago had managed to convince some folks in his community that doing this would be a good idea. For some reason they had listened, and here we were, several generations later, adding to the thousands of people who had already travelled this road. I almost got carried away with this thought stream and was sure that I could hear laughter as the 'sane majority' looked on in utter astonishment at the antics of a few ill-informed seekers who had fallen for the crazy premise of this ceremony.

The rain got heavier as I began to climb the hill. I was already tired from just the thought of getting no sleep, and with each step I found myself feeling heavier and more afraid. Maybe I was mad. Maybe this really was nonsense. Maybe shamanism really wasn't for me. For sure, I was no warrior. I heard these voices as I climbed the first part of the hill and my thoughts turned towards a nice warm fire indoors and a good hearty meal. We'd been fasting all day in preparation for the ceremony and the thought of food set my stomach rumbling.

But as much as turning back appealed, there were far too many reasons to continue. For one, how would it look to my newfound fellow apprentices if I gave up before I'd even begun? Surely this was the beginning of a real apprenticeship, and the hardships, whatever they might be, were just a way of confirming my intention to deal with my fears and find my feet in the shaman's world.

What happened next remains for me in the realms of the fantastical and inexplicable. As I continued to climb towards the summit of the hill, I went through a field of sheep, closed the gate behind me and found myself in a smaller field full of scrapped vehicles. There were all kinds of cars and vans piled on top of one another. I noticed an old Citroën 2CV with its roll-down roof ripped to shreds. What once must have been a beautiful old Triumph was sitting squarely on top of an old Ford van. I even climbed onto some of the rusting vehicles to get a good look at them. There must have been well over 100 of them in the field.

I wondered what they were doing there, halfway up a hill with no apparent roads leading there. I looked around for any clues as to how they'd got there or why they were there, but I didn't come up with anything. There were no buildings in the field of any kind.

Eventually, I found my way out through the gate and continued my climb to the top of the hill. Once there, I found eight stones, set up my circle, did my invocations with my pipe and began the night's work in earnest.

We'd been instructed to face each direction in turn, clap our hands loudly twice, bang our right foot on the ground, clap our hands again, bang our left foot on the ground and finally repeat the claps and stamp our right foot once more. We were told to do this with as much force and intent as we could muster, whilst at the same time calling to our fears to come and visit us from each direction.

I have to admit that I felt a bit of a fool making such a racket on top of a hill. I couldn't help but look around to see if anyone was out there walking their dog or bringing in their sheep. As I looked out into each direction and shouted to my fears to make themselves known to me, I'd no idea what to expect. Would images, feelings, ancestors or ghosts visit me?

At first, what happened was that I experienced an increasing level of fear in my body. At that time, I hadn't spent a lot of time out by myself in the dark and it's extraordinary what the mind starts to do with sounds and sights in an unknown situation.

Slowly but surely, I settled into the ritual. As the night went on, my concentration deepened and I started to get a feel for what entering into a dialogue with your fears meant. I realized I was in an altered state when I started to imagine Rasputin appearing in the clouds, bushes and trees around me. I used to have repetitive nightmares about him after being taken to see the classic film *Nicholas and Alexandra* by our childminder when I was seven. And now he was back, stalking me in the shifting shapes of shadows that were dancing wildly with the wind as the night went on.

At one point, I saw the figure of a plastic red clown coming to visit me. At first I found it funny and laughed. But as it came closer, the fear I was feeling in my body became almost intolerable. What was this? Was it a memory or a symbol of some sort?

And then it hit me. When I was around 11 years old, my father had caught me stealing. I'd been taking small amounts of petty cash from his wardrobe for years to buy sweets and magazines on my way to school. On this particular occasion, I'd taken a £5 note from his drawer. This was more than I'd ever taken. I hid the money in my little moneybox in my wardrobe. That Saturday night, my father asked me to go and get something for him from the car before he went out. When I brought it to him, he was standing in his bedroom with a fearsome look on his face. And then I saw it: he was holding my moneybox, a little red plastic clown! The fear I'd felt at that moment was like a sharp icicle shooting up my spine, and until that moment on the hill, I'd completely forgotten about it.

Not surprisingly, my father didn't react very well to realizing that his son was stealing from him. It was one of only two times in my childhood when he was physically violent with me.

As I stood there on the hill, I saw the whole scene again, not through the eyes of the child I was, but through the eyes of someone who was seeing all the characters in a movie. And more than that, I saw the effect that situation had had on my relationship with my dad and thereafter with authority and anything that smelled of masculine force or violence. I'd unconsciously let the fear of that experience shape my life.

All this came to me through a mixture of senses. I could smell the fear. I could see the tears. I could feel the silenced rage that had been eating away at my sense of self and power for all these years. I remembered making a choice not to utter a single sound as my father punished me. I didn't want to give him the satisfaction.

From up there on the hill, the darkness of the night helped me to see that my father felt he had no choice other than to beat some sense into me. Even more than that, I had the first inkling of how this experience had turned me away from my father and many of the things I associated with him.

He was an entrepreneur. He wasn't interested in money for the sake of it, but he loved the good things in life. He was a bit of a gambler and he loved his fine whisky. Sometimes he drank too much. Sometimes he took risks that didn't work out. He was often stressed about money. He worked hard to make ends meet and he didn't always manage it, but he was always trying to do his best for his family.

On the mountain of fear, I saw how I'd translated his stress around money and the tension that was so often created around family mealtimes into a reason to have nothing to do with money in my life. Money was bad. That was that. No wonder I was finding it hard to make a living!

I was amazed that the ritual had opened up this memory and given me such a deep insight into my fears. As the night went on, I settled into a more peaceful and connected state. Facing my fears in the rain and the darkness had given me a new feeling of strength and the courage to continue, and after I'd completed my ritual with prayers to the rising sun, I returned to Sue's house in a light and happy mood.

As I walked down the hill, I looked for the scrapyard that I'd stumbled across the previous evening. To my utter astonishment, I couldn't find it anywhere. I looked all around that hill, but couldn't find anything in the loveliness of the rolling Devon countryside that even remotely resembled a scrapyard.

My shock was intensified when I got back and asked Sue where the yard was. Surely I'd missed it somehow on the way down. She had no idea what I was talking about. Apparently, the cars I'd thought I was climbing on the previous night were a figment of my imagination. I simply couldn't believe it.

And then it hit me: my dad was a second-hand-car salesman. The scrapyard was a perfect symbol for my night on the mountain of fear. The conclusions I'd drawn from those early experiences with my father were like old cars, piled on top of one another in my psyche. And I'd just discovered that they weren't really there.

Chapter 4

ENTERING THE CAVE OF REMEMBERING

'It takes a huge effort to free yourself from memory.'
PAULO COELHO

I hoped that understanding some of my fears would help me to overcome them. But whilst that first insight helped me to put the strength of my emotions in context, I soon realized that my journey with fear was only just beginning. Memory is multi-layered, as is our relationship to it. I would have to spend many years finding the equilibrium to face the deepest places inside me, where fear lay quiet like a sleeping dragon. Later, I would travel deep into the Amazon rainforest, where I would finally meet that dragon and dance with him.

In the meantime I continued to offer my ritual photography and occasional massages and wonder how I was going to get myself out of debt and do what the tribal elders in my dream had told me.

Things looked up when I found some work at my local community centre, teaching photography to teenagers in an after-school club. They were interested in learning and we did some good work together. Emboldened by this success, I did an afternoon of training in something called Social Inventions, which was designed to prepare me to go into local schools and co-design creative projects with 14–18-year-olds.

My first school was a tough East End secondary school and the kids just saw me coming. I'd had four hours of training and it didn't even begin to prepare me for the classroom of an inner-city school filled with inner-city kids. They were used to a particular kind of authority that I wanted nothing to do with. I was still very much into non-violence and being a 'new man' according to the feminist principles of the time. The kids in that school simply chewed me up and spat me out, and I left with my idealistic ideas crushed and my tail between my legs.

So I continued to just about get by from month to month, from client to client, and to study on a shoestring with my teachers.

⁓

In the late summer of 1988 Arwyn was offering a seven-day intensive at a residential venue in rural Wales. She told us that it was time for us to face our karma and clean up our past.

We began with some dreaming practices that involved wearing small Herkimer crystals around our heads, holding other crystals in our hands and attempting to enter a lucid dream directly.

Before we went to bed, I was meditating in front of Arwyn's altar. At one point, she brushed past me and whispered, 'That's good, very good.'

I had no idea what she was referring to, but my attention was firmly drawn to one of her crystal skulls. Arwyn had two crystal skulls. They were symbols of Earth wisdom and the teachings from the stars that had been kept in the ancient South American traditions.

Then a bizarre thing happened. I heard a deep, seductive feminine voice saying to me, 'Take me to bed.'

I was startled, to say the least. I looked around to see if a fellow student was playing tricks on me, but there was no one there. I was further amazed when Arwyn came straight back to me and told me that the crystal skull wanted me to take 'her' to bed and wanted to help me dream.

I took the crystal skull and went to bed. I carefully placed the Herkimers in a headband around my head and lay on my back with a quartz crystal in each hand and the crystal skull on my belly. I lay there buzzing, unable to imagine how I could possibly fall asleep with all this energy zooming round my system.

I did the meditation that Arwyn had suggested, letting each part of my body relax as I attempted to walk across the bridge between wakefulness and dreaming without losing consciousness. I had practised this for years as a child, so I was quite used to it, but I'd never tried it whilst weighted down by a bunch of supercharged crystals, one of which could apparently talk to me!

I managed to calm myself and drop down through the layers of wakefulness until I was in that hypnagogic state where visions start to appear and a dream starts to form. Just as I felt I was going to cross the bridge, my hands suddenly became super-hot and the crystal skull on my belly started to vibrate. Before I knew it, I had the impression that I was moving at the speed of light through a long tunnel.

I had no idea where I was going, but I focused my thoughts on a good friend called Alan, who was still in London. We were both very interested in dreaming practice and had an agreement to try to reach out to one another whenever we became lucid in a dream. I saw the house where he was living coming into focus and I arrived in his room. I settled myself and tried to remain calm. I wanted to let him know that I was there and I reached out my dream hand towards him.

As I did so, I felt a violent tug behind my solar plexus and found myself rushing backwards through the same tunnel. I crashed back into my body and woke up sitting bolt upright. I was sweating, and the crystal skull, which had rolled into my lap, felt red-hot.

I tried to reorientate myself and I once again heard the voice of the crystal speaking to me.

'Oh no, you don't,' she said, 'you're dreaming with me tonight!'

I was alarmed and wasn't sure if I was awake or still dreaming, but the next thing I knew I was following a strange silvery woman through the forest and being taken to what she called the 'cave of memory'. There was a fire burning at the entrance. I was told to make an offering to it from a pot of herbs beside it. As I did so, it crackled and hissed. Then I was led into the cave.

Inside, a strange glow was coming from the ground, walls and ceiling. I couldn't locate the source of it, but it gave me a feeling of energized calm.

I was instructed to sit down and look at the walls. As I did so, patterns appeared and disappeared and pictures like ancient cave paintings went in and out of focus. I was told to keep looking and slowly an image took shape of rows of shelving full of books. They were all shapes and sizes and covered in dust and cobwebs.

The silvery woman told me, with a meaningful stare, 'These are your memories. In them you will find who you are.'

I was intrigued, but before I had the chance to explore further, I woke up. It was dawn and I was unable to sleep any more.

After a walk and breakfast, we all met up in the group room to share our experiences of the night. I was still holding on to Arwyn's crystal skull. I'd grown quite attached to it.

Arwyn started to talk about the need to look after our medicine items and treat them like good friends. As she spoke, I started to have a glimmer of hope that she was going to give me the crystal skull. The more she talked, the more certain I became that this was what was going to happen. In my mind, I was already preparing a little thank-you speech.

Suddenly Arwyn stopped in the middle of a sentence and looked right at me.

'No. No way. Time to hand that over.'

I immediately went red with embarrassment and sheepishly handed Arwyn her crystal. She laughed kindly and asked me to share my dream.

When I had, she smiled with recognition. 'Ah, yes, the cave of memory. We'll be going there later in the week,' she replied rather enigmatically.

She had that look in her eyes that I'd come to recognize, somewhere between mischief and 'I know something you *don't*.' We'd only been there one night and the air was already humming with the feeling that something momentous was about to happen. We didn't have to wait long.

⸎

The next day Arwyn told us we were going to do an ancient ritual called the kiva dance. This dance, she told us, had its origins in Hopi tradition; she had been connected with the Hopi for a long time and spent several weeks every year working alongside them. She told us we were going to do the ritual in a cave about an hour's walk from where we were staying. It involved each of us being painted with sets of symbols she had discovered on her travels.

We had a lot of faith in this wiry, canny medicine woman with a wicked laugh and a knowledge of other realms. She'd already shown us that we could trust her and so none of us were particularly surprised when she told us that these symbols and the ceremony itself would help us to remember the past, including past lives. I didn't know if I believed in past lives, but the thing I loved about the path I'd discovered was that belief was neither here nor there. These rituals were designed to give us direct experience of the mysteries that Arwyn was talking about. So either we would experience the past or we wouldn't.

Once painted, we were each to dance in the dark in front of the group. The dance was to be guided by the symbols on the body itself, a little like the 'possession' by the spirit of a mask that is central to many shamanic traditions.

Each person was then given their set of symbols to dance with. Arwyn told me that she'd recently come into possession of a set of symbols believed to be several hundred years old from the Qabalistic tradition, the mystical wing of Judaism. Since I was Jewish, she felt it would be good for me to dance with these symbols. They were very complex and she thought it would take around four hours to paint them on my body. She asked me to find a partner who would be happy to do this on behalf of us all. Ritual was a collective journey for our collective benefit.

It was late autumn and all the painting would have to be done inside the cave with only a small fire to keep us warm. I had a friend on the workshop who was happy to do as Arwyn had asked. We got to the cave at about 3.30 in the afternoon. We had water, body paints and torches for the painting and some blankets to keep ourselves warm.

I remember the strange and disturbing feeling that grew in me as my friend got to work on the complex designs. I was very aware of being in the cave and of feeling the cold water and body paints making shapes on my body. As each symbol found its place, it felt like a poultice, both drawing out and taking me deeper into memory. Images of medieval market places and secret meetings through the night to study Qabalah passed through my mind. I was meeting a side of my lineage that I knew little about.

As the process went on, I lost all sense of time. I no longer felt the cold. The fire of these ancient symbols was warming me, their power inviting me to travel deeper within. I was on a spiral stairway that took me way beyond my everyday awareness and led me into a dream of remembering. At the same time, I was very wide awake and full of energy. I was so ready to dance!

It was past 9 p.m. once we were all painted and the ritual began with drumming and a strong invocation of the spirits of the land, the four directions and a whole host of other helpers and allies whom Arwyn called upon to support the ritual.

The fire was put out and one by one we went up to dance. In the darkness, the only light came from the flash that Arwyn would set off at intervals to illuminate the dancer. The effect was utterly mesmerizing as it would light up the symbols on their body and sent them racing round the walls, floor and ceiling of the cave. We were instructed to sit still and watch the shapes and be open to what we saw. Arwyn also showed us a way of sitting with our hands folded together and our thumbs in our belly button to prevent ourselves from picking up anything negative that the dance might release.

Each dance produced a startlingly different effect. The shapes that flew across the cave walls and the sounds of the dancer's naked feet on the hard earth floor, alongside the insistent pulse of the drums, held us all in a deeply altered state. And as each person danced, Arwyn would name the things that she saw.

By the time it was my turn to dance, I felt as though my blood was on fire. My heart was racing. It was as if the energy of the symbols themselves lifted me up and started moving me. I was a witness, but it was clear I was not in charge.

Though it was perfectly dark, I clearly saw a blank screen. As my body danced, each time Arwyn set the flash off images appeared on the screen like previews from a movie. I saw battle scenes and I saw 'myself' dying many, many times in a whole host of circumstances. Sometimes I was the killer. Sometimes I was the killed. Scenes from different cultures appeared. I was in a market in southern India. I was a rabbi in Spain in the 1400s. I was a herbalist, a healer, an alchemist. These images moved across the screen of my mind and the witness in me simply watched, spellbound.

As I danced, Arwyn named the things she saw. Some made no sense at all, while others resonated deep inside me, as if I was hearing an echo from the distant past.

Just before the end of the dance, an image appeared that took my breath away. It came and went in a second, and it chilled me to the bone. I knew it was important, but just like a dream that retreats into the mist upon waking, it was gone in an instant and I couldn't recall it. Though I didn't even know what it was, it was the clearest sense of direct memory I'd ever had and I felt its effect very strongly in my whole body. When I stopped dancing, I was still shaking and the sweat that stung my eyes felt like old, old tears. But try as I might to bring it back, it was gone.

Afterwards, I shook for hours from the icy cold I had felt towards the end of my dance. The ritual continued, and as the dawn came, we each took turns to hold the blankets against the entrance to keep the early morning light out. It was a hilarious scene: people half naked, shivering with cold, their bodies a stream of colour from the paints that had run as they'd danced, working at keeping the light out so that all the dancers could have their turn.

By the time we'd finished, we were all exhausted. We walked back to the residential centre through a fine rain. Arwyn had this little game at the end of rituals where she would look into our eyes to see who was present and who was still in the wide-eyed after-effects of whatever it was we'd been up to. Whoever looked the most spaced out was sent to the shops to buy breakfast. That morning, it was me. Hunting for cornflakes, milk and loaves of bread is super-grounding, I can tell you. That breakfast was one of the best meals ever and the hot shower afterwards was about as holy an experience as I'd ever had in my life!

The day was given over to resting and to writing up our notes. I felt good after a rest, but I couldn't shake the icy feeling that had come unbidden in the dance and every now and again the shock of it hurt like a splinter, sudden and sharp. Try as I might, I couldn't remember what I'd seen that had provoked it. It was as if a window had been opened and a ghost from the past had blown into my mind like an icy-cold wind.

That night we were due to continue our work with a 'dark mirror' ceremony. Arwyn told us that this was a continuation of our ritual in the cave. I was both excited and deeply afraid. I knew something was coming into my consciousness, and like a moth to the flame, I felt inexorably drawn towards it. It was irresistible, and I felt as though I was about to die.

Chapter 5

A DARK MIRROR

'His thoughts inhabit a different plane
from those of ordinary men; the simplest
interpretation of that is to call him crazy.'
JULIET MARILLIER

As the day turned to dusk and dusk fell into the dark embrace of the night, my anxiety increased with each passing hour and I still had no idea why. I was so out of sorts that my normally healthy appetite deserted me.

After dinner, Arwyn gave us clear instructions for the evening's work, which she told us was called dark mirror work. We were to work in groups of three. Each group had a candle, a mirror that was large enough for us to sit in front of and see our face, and a bowl for burning copal resin. We would do an invocation as a group to open the ritual and then we would go to different rooms to work.

We were to sit in front of the mirror and start drumming. One person would be the focus and the other two would sit behind them and support them in their work. The purpose was once again to remember those aspects of the past that held energy for us or needed healing so that we could be stronger and more awake in the present.

This was a new concept for me, but one that is widespread amongst shamanic practitioners around the world. Stories from the past can have power over us in the present. Aspects of our being can be locked in the past by the emotional impact or trauma of what has happened and inaccessible to us in the present. Retrieving these parts is known as soul retrieval. It is a central theme in shamanic work. This ritual would be the beginning of my understanding of it.

Susannah and I decided to work together and a man called Nick joined us. He was tall and muscular and about 10 years older than us. He had a lot of experience in this area and I felt somewhat comforted and at the same time threatened by his presence. I didn't know him and here we were, about to look through the wide-open window of the dark mirror into the intimate details of our pasts.

We carefully set up the mirror against the side of a bed and placed the candle on the floor in front of it. We had a bowl with hot charcoal in it, on which we were to place the copal when we were ready.

We started drumming together to settle in and begin the ritual. Drumming was very new to me at that time. I had a beautiful drum with two blue snakes painted on it that I still have to this day. In the candlelight, the drumming echoed off the walls and seemed to take the roof off. I felt as if we were sitting under the stars and I sensed the wide-open spaces of South American deserts around us.

Susannah went first. Nick and I sat at her shoulders whilst she placed the copal on the hot charcoal and made her prayers and intentions known. Our job was to focus our attention on her left eye, and she was to do the same. As we did this, breathing evenly, the reflection of Susannah's face in the mirror started to change shape. It was like watching a kind of horror movie as the smooth lines and curves of her face started to melt and transform. Everything liquefied, and every now and again a new face would take shape and remain for a while. It was a truly extraordinary experience as person after person, from different times and places, appeared in the smoky mirror. Some were recognizable to me, some not. It was like looking into an old family photo album. The variety of times and places were bewildering, and every now and then Susannah would gasp with recognition or tears would come.

Nick went next, and although the images I saw then were very different, the same quality of quiet and sacred remembering filled the whole room. Magic was in the air and by the time it was my turn to sit in front of the mirror and make my offerings, I had lost any fear whatsoever. I was looking forward to revisiting the library of my dream and finding out more about who I was and where I'd come from.

I sat in front of the mirror with Susannah at my right shoulder and Nick at my left. Like them, I made my offerings of copal and said: 'Please reveal what it is time for me to know. I wish to change my relationship with the past and empower myself as much as possible in the present. I am ready to see what I need to see.'

I wasn't ready at all.

It all started off smoothly enough. Like Susannah and Nick before me, I saw my face melt and other faces appear one by one out of the smoky mist. I was calm, focused, very present and interested.

Then, out of nowhere, a cold wind blew into the room, almost putting out the candle. I immediately felt the same icy-cold shock that I'd experienced towards the end of my dance in the cave.

The flickering candle altered the reflection in the mirror. Everything went a little grey. An energy was rising in my body and I felt just as I imagine the shore must feel in the face of an oncoming tsunami. I was immobilized; whatever was coming was powerful and I was directly in its pathway and there was nothing I could do to avoid experiencing the full force of its overwhelming momentum. I knew I was going to drown.

The wind blew again, once more nearly extinguishing the flame. My body had gone rigid and I felt completely out of my depth. Susannah was still there, and Nick too. Suddenly I saw a gravestone and then a long concrete building. The feeling of fear intensified.

And then Susannah said the word that had been on the tip of my awareness since the night before. She whispered it, as if she really didn't want to say it out loud: 'Auschwitz.'

I was frozen. I was looking at a young boy I knew was me standing amongst a crowd of people both known and unknown to me. I was about five years old. I was wearing shorts and a black peaked cap. I was with my mother. We were being directed into a room with showers on the ceiling. A German guard was there in SS uniform. I looked into his eyes. He smiled at me, but his eyes were full of dread. And then the door slammed shut.

At this point, I lost any sense of witnessing the scene. I was there and I felt an animal-like fear bordering on panic. I heard a hissing and we all looked up to the showerheads. Then there was screaming all around me. I looked for my mother, but I could no longer see her. The panic took over and I realized that the screaming I could hear was my own.

In the room, my body had started to convulse and I was wildly flailing, desperately trying to put out the candle. I was totally out of control and it took all of Nick and Susannah's strength to keep me safe and keep the bed or curtains from catching fire. I wasn't at all aware of my physical body. As far as I was concerned, I was a five-year-old boy, suffocating to death in a gas chamber. Then I lost consciousness.

❦

When I came round, I was in Susannah's arms and Arwyn was in the room. My screams had been heard all over the house. Arwyn had a bowl of sage and a feather and was using the feather to move the cleansing smoke over my body. I was confused, between worlds and very embarrassed. I had totally lost control. I had abandoned my present-moment consciousness and been swept into a memory that had blown me to pieces.

Arwyn asked me what had happened. I struggled to find my voice. My throat was dry and sore. I was given water and told to sit up. Eventually, I got the words out. 'I was a child. I died in the gas chamber at Auschwitz. It was horrible.'

And now the tears came, hot and thick. There was little or no thought, just the flow of tears and the racks of a body releasing something I had no idea I'd been holding.

The tears and the presence of Arwyn, Susannah and Nick slowly brought me back into my body. I felt bruised from head to toe and my vision was unsteady. As I looked around, I felt myself slipping from one reality to another. The candle had been relit and any movement of the light seemed to shake the room. The warm ochre walls shifted to cold grey concrete and back again. I was on the edge of panic.

Arwyn told me to take a shower and get some rest and we would talk more about this the following morning. I did, and the water, more than anything else, seemed to bring me back to a solid sense of here and now. As I felt it on my skin, I coached myself through the shower: 'This water is pure and cleansing. I am releasing the memories I have had. I am here and all is well.'

I fell into bed and into Susannah's arms and quickly into a dreamless sleep.

‹ ✕ ›

When I woke the next morning, I had a feeling of dread in my belly. My mind went into overdrive. Why had I remembered dying as a victim in Auschwitz? Was this something that had actually happened to me or was it something that I was carrying from my ancestors or in my DNA? I'd heard that this was possible and indeed there is now a field of study called epigenetics that focuses on this. What did I have to do about it? Should I tell my family? What would they think? Was I likely to fall into that memory again? Could I learn to protect myself from losing consciousness like that…?

Question after question whirled around my head and I got a truly physical understanding of what it means to be in a spin. The ground seemed a very long way away. I was spaced out and confused and having a few doubts about the path I'd set out on. If this was the outcome of these kinds of ritual, maybe I should reconsider the whole thing.

Underneath it all, I was scared. I'd been hit by a tsunami and I just didn't recognize the landscape it had left behind.

One thing I did know: I was famished. My appetite had returned with force and I wanted food *now*! I ate a full breakfast and quickly felt better. A walk in the fresh air and some time with the trees in the garden helped further. After that, I felt ready to meet my companions again. I still felt embarrassed, though. Everyone in the house had heard my screaming and they were entitled to some kind of explanation.

Arwyn began the morning session with a meditation to help us all find a little more stability, and I was grateful for it. Then we had the opportunity to hear one another's experiences from the night before and a 'talking stick' was passed round. This simple ritual, which I first experienced with Arwyn, is a beautiful way to create more focused listening amongst a group of people. The talking stick is usually a decorated stick or something like an antler. It is passed around the circle. The one who holds it is empowered to speak and others are invited to listen. When working with material such as we were working with, we had all found that idle chat tended to diminish the experience, whereas the focus of a circle usually helped to deepen our understanding of what had happened. Hearing other people speak bravely from their hearts about what they had seen also helped to put our own experiences into context.

When it was my turn to speak, I felt the tremble in my body and in my voice. I also felt people's kindness and curiosity in equal measure in the way they listened.

In sharing what had happened, I found two things took place. First, I was able to regain a sense of witnessing the memory I had had. I was able to keep a healthy distance from it whilst still feeling the massive effect it had had on me. Secondly, as I spoke, I felt a new road opening inside me. It may sound strange, but I quite literally felt a pathway from my guts to my heart and I had a visceral sense that in some way, as yet totally hidden from me, this remembering was going to be a marker in my life's journey.

Arwyn spoke to me. She asked if I was willing to make a pledge and have it witnessed by the others in the room. Naturally, I wanted to know what the pledge was before agreeing to make it. She stood up and faced me. She told me that she had the strong sense that when I was ready I should go back to Auschwitz and dance there for the child whose death I had re-experienced and for all the thousands of children who had died in the same way.

As she spoke the words, I felt the pathway that had opened in my body fill with warmth and strength. It was a most peculiar sensation, but it produced in me the certainty that Arwyn's instinct was correct, and without hesitation, I stood up and said: 'I pledge, witnessed by my teacher, my companions, the spirits of the earth, fire, water and wind, by my ancestors and on behalf of all those children who died in Auschwitz, that I will go there, as soon as I am ready, and dance for them.'

The words tumbled out so easily and they rang so true for me. I was crying and yet I felt so strong. The tears were literally streaming from my eyes and yet I felt my vision was clearer than at any time in my life. I had a purpose. I had a direction. I had a task, a quest, something to work towards. And strangely, amidst the seriousness and tenderness of the moment, I felt joy rising up inside me.

As I look back on that pledge and all that followed from it in the nearly 30 years that have passed, I am astonished by the power of that moment. From here, that pledge looks like a laser beam that lit up the road for me. It was my first taste of phoenix medicine. I had no idea where it would take me, but out of the ashes of intense suffering had arisen a sense of direction that I could follow. The light that was born at that moment is still shining brightly in my life.

In fact it took me 13 years to prepare myself to follow through on that promise. Those years were full of challenges and awakenings, all of which I would need in order to be able to return to Auschwitz and fulfil my pledge. But I knew there was no turning back. I had to gather my strength to be able to go and do what I had to do.

Acknowledging what had happened at Auschwitz was the beginning of recognizing the ways in which I felt myself to be a victim of life's events. Paradoxically, what I saw in the dark mirror was also the start of recovering my strength and power.

✐

Part II

FIRE IN
THE BELLY

COMMITMENT TO THE PATH

*'You always have two choices: your
commitment versus your fear.'*
SAMMY DAVIS, JR

In my early encounters with shamanism I'd already met states of ecstasy, disillusion and terror, and I'd only just begun.

I was still in debt from my time at college and still just about eking out a living through a few massage and ritual-photography clients. I was spending most of my time either in ritual or on workshops or earning whatever I needed to attend the next event. I was still hoping that a benefactor might show up, recognize my enormous shamanic talent, pay off my debts and make it possible for me to study shamanism full time. In short, I was a passionate but irresponsible young man who thought the world owed him something.

I felt fine receiving government benefits. After all, I was on a mission to better society and save the world from the corrupt politicians and business people who were making a mess of everything. Life is so much easier when we have someone to blame!

My twenties were a paradoxical mixture of the over-excited arrogance and naivety of youth and recognition of my many insecurities.

⟨✦⟩

During that time, I attended my first sweat lodge ceremony, which was run by my Deer Tribe teacher Sue Jamieson in Devon. The sweat lodge is a traditional Native American ceremony that's something like an outdoor sauna with a good dose of alchemy, ritual and prayer thrown in. There are many cultures that use a similar structure as a place to get close to the Earth and the spirits and offer up prayers whilst cleansing the body, heart and mind into the bargain.

The leader of the Deer Tribe, Harley Swiftdeer, had quite a bad name amongst many of the indigenous peoples of North America. Many Native Americans, and specifically a radical and outspoken group called the American Indian Movement (AIM), were furious that not only had their lands been stolen and their people decimated, but now a bunch of white people and mixed-bloods were coming along to steal their spiritual traditions as well.

I can well understand this point of view and many years later I was lucky enough to meet one of the AIM leaders, a true Oglala Lakota warrior called Russell Means. I was in the United States to meet the Council of 13 Grandmothers, an international council of indigenous grandmothers set up to share and promote the common values of indigenous women the world over, when I was invited to the end of a Sundance ceremony, a traditional Lakota ritual performed around the summer solstice. It was being hosted by Russell Means in Wind Cave National Park, South Dakota, a place sacred to the Lakota people. It was his 30th year of Sundancing.

The Sundance done the Lakota way involves three days of fasting and dancing in the hot sun. Piercing the skin above the breastbone and inserting small pegs is common. The dancer is then attached from the pegs to a tree representing the tree of life and dances, leaning back until the skin breaks. This act is a 'give-away' – the dancer offers a prayer that their suffering will reduce the suffering for their family and tribe over the year ahead. It's a warrior's prayer.

The end of the ritual is a gift-giving ceremony. You might think that someone who had just been through such a gruelling ritual would be receiving gifts, but that is not so. In the old days, Russell told me, the dancers would give away everything they owned after the Sundance – their clothing, their horses, everything. So there I was, in the heat of the South Dakota summer, witnessing a Lakota warrior who had just fasted for three days and given his flesh and blood as a prayer for his people giving an enormous pile of gifts to everyone who had supported the ceremony.

I'd never heard of Russell Means at that point, but I soon got a sense of what kind of man he was. Even though I was only there as a guest, he still offered me a gift – a brand new torch.

'I've heard you Brits are afraid of the dark,' he said, with a wicked glint in his eye. 'This should help.'

I laughed. I knew a catalyst when I met one, and this was a man who had a sharp sense of humour and plenty of edge.

When we sat down to talk, he told me a little of his life. Like so many of his people who had been ripped away from all that they held sacred, he had suffered from alcoholism. He had fought on behalf of his people for his whole life. He had reserves of fury and was uncompromising in his views. I liked him very much.

I had with me a lovely leather shoulder bag made for me by a beautiful Italian dancer named Gigi. The leather was carved with exquisite patterns and the words of a famous Native American chief, Crazy Horse: 'A great vision is necessary ... the man who owns it must follow it like the eagle follows the deepest blue of the sky.'

The quote became the focus of our conversation. We talked for hours about the state of the Earth, people's loss of connection and the cruelty of those who felt they had the God-given right to take what didn't belong to them and kill anyone who stood in their way. He talked about his grandmothers and the wisdom they held. And he told me that he had lived his life committed to a vision of restoring respect, dignity and land ownership to his people.

I felt humbled by the strength of his commitment. Anyone who had Sundanced for 30 years had my utmost respect.

He sent me to a hill sacred to his people that was about an hour's walk away. He told me to go up there and listen to whatever the land had to tell me.

I sat on the hill in the late afternoon sun. Wind Cave National Park is magnificent territory. According to Lakota legend, the people came out of the Earth through the cave after which the park is named. The land has a rich heritage and has seen much bloodshed. As I sat there, I felt the power of that land and how it held the memories of the Lakota people. And as I watched the wind making patterns in the long grass, a lone bison came into view. I expected to see a whole herd following, but it was alone. It broke my heart. In an area that was once teeming with bison, just a solitary animal was walking the land.

Tears blurred my vision as I walked back to Russell's Sundance camp. I told him what I'd seen. He didn't need to say anything, and he didn't. Instead he gave me a book, his autobiography, *Where White Men Fear to Tread* (Antenna Books, 1996). He signed it and told me that in it I would find everything I needed to know about what I'd seen.

⌒⌒⌒

Russell's autobiography gave me a whole new understanding of what commitment meant. I remembered that first sweat lodge ceremony all those years before with Sue Jamieson. If Russell had been there, he would have done his best to have stopped it happening.

It's a lot of work to build a sweat lodge, and done properly, with reverence for the natural world around you, it's a very beautiful and powerful ritual. We arrived after lunch on a Friday and our first task as a group was to go out into the surrounding woods and gather enough firewood for the ritual.

The ceremony was taking place by a river and it was a warm day, so Susannah and I decided to take a little swim. We were in the water longer than we thought and eventually Sue came looking for us. She was furious to find us larking about in the water and gave us a bit of a lecture about the difference between what she called 'self-focus' and awareness of the needs of the group. She told us we were acting as adolescents, not as adults, by putting our own needs ahead of the group. Then she gave us time to think about what she'd said and about our commitment to what we were doing and to the people we were doing it with.

At that time I was very much the focus of my own attention. And though a large part of me rebelled at having to think about others as well as myself, I recognized the truth in what she had offered us.

⌐ ⌐⌐

Commitment includes the self but it also means having an awareness of our place in the wider circle of life. Russell had followed his truth to the nth degree. Despite the loss and grief he so obviously carried, his fury carried him forwards. When I told him my sweat lodge story, I had no idea that to him, the Deer Tribe was a symbol of some of that loss and fury. When I told him I'd been given a sacred pipe by my therapist, he nearly choked on his tea.

In happy ignorance of his ferocious reputation, I talked on, explaining that I felt that the pipe was a temporary gift that I'd been given to help me remember what I'd lost. I told him that the genocide that had occurred in North America had gone on in Europe centuries before. The Church had been a supremely successful 'ethnic cleanser', burning millions at the stake and nearly destroying the shamanic traditions of Europe.

I told Russell I didn't want to play at being Native American, I wanted to remember how to pray with nature. I wanted to reconnect to the world around me and to feel the presence of the Great Spirit here on Earth. I knew the mystery was out there, but the loan of the pipe and the teachings that came with it helped me to remember that the sacredness of life was all around me. I'd always known that there would come a time when I would give the pipe back and indeed that time had come just a couple of years before. But praying with the pipe and sitting naked on the earth, sweating and praying my heart out in the womb of the sweat lodge back in Devon had done so much to help me accept the reality and challenges of living in a body and being human.

Russell listened. He didn't tell me what he thought, but neither did he attack my experience. We parted in good spirits and I remain grateful for his kindness.

A day or two later, driving to the airport, late for my plane, I was stopped for speeding. The cop who stopped me was quite pleasant until he saw Russell's book on the front seat next to me. It seemed to send him into a rage and as a result I ended up spending the night in the South Dakota state penitentiary.

I remember sitting in the back of the police car with my hands in cuffs behind my back. On the one hand, I was freaked out. I was going to miss my plane and be late home for the workshop I was due to be teaching the following Monday. On the other hand, I had to laugh at how surreal life gets sometimes. I was allowed my one phone call and Susannah couldn't believe it when I told her where I was calling from.

It was the weekend and I now had the opportunity to meet the temporary community of those arrested on a Saturday night in South Dakota – a most interesting bunch! Nobody could believe I was in there for speeding, but when I mentioned Russell's name, wry and knowing smiles appeared.

'Oh, Russell Means! The police round here hate him. He's caused them so much trouble.'

In the penitentiary, I thought more about my time with Russell. He'd told me so much about how his people had had their freedom and their traditions taken away from them. A night behind bars South Dakota style gave me the tiniest of opportunities to experience what it's like to lose your freedom and showed me how enslaved I still was to ideas and dreams that didn't belong to me.

Russell Means died in October 2012. He was a man who gave his life to his people. My meeting with him, that lone bison and that night in jail lit the fire in my belly and sharpened the sword of my intention. Without total commitment and dedication to my path, I would be getting nowhere fast.

Chapter 6

WHEN THE STUDENT IS READY...

'Do you have the discipline to be a free spirit?'
GABRIELLE ROTH

It was July 1988. I was driving with a friend to work with Arwyn again, this time in the north of England, at a conference centre in Leeds. Duncan was a fellow apprentice in the Deer Tribe. He was also a social worker at the time and earning a reasonable salary. Hence he had a car and he had invited me along for the ride.

We were driving up the motorway talking about our most recent ceremonies when Duncan remembered that he'd brought along something for me to take a look at. He asked me to reach for a black-and-white brochure that was in the back of the car.

I picked it up and gave it a quick read. It was for an organization called the Open Gate. There was some blurb on the front about what the Open Gate was and then some information on a bunch of workshops. Nothing looked particularly special to me, but Duncan said, 'Open it up. It's on the inside pages.'

Some moments in life stand out like freeze-frames. This was one of those. I like to call them 'pearl moments' – shiny happenings that are seared into the memory. Whenever we call them to mind, the feelings remain fresh, the colours bright and the most arbitrary of details clear. Opening that brochure was one of those moments for me.

I remember a Toni Childs song was playing. It was a fine, clear day and the traffic was light. I was happy to be on the way to my next Arwyn 'fix'. I turned the page and saw the words 'Open Gate Training with Gabrielle Roth'. There was a picture of a rather beautiful woman with a leather jacket slung over her right shoulder, shining black hair and eyes that both fascinated and scared me. Who was she?

I read the short paragraphs describing the training. I couldn't believe what I was reading. If I'd sat down to devise the perfect course of study for myself, I couldn't have come up with anything half as good as what I was reading. Creativity, shamanism, ecstasy, trance – I was hooked. And then I looked at the price.

Like a balloon that is blown up and instantly popped, I moved from super-excitement to total deflation. I was certain it was well out of my reach. But next to the blurb for the teacher training course there was a short piece about an introductory weekend happening a few weeks later in London.

Later that day I called the Open Gate from a phone box in Leeds and booked the weekend.

When I arrived back in London a week later, I told Susannah about it. She looked at me quizzically and then laughed.

'I just booked the same course.'

The weeks went by and autumn closed in. I cooked, cleaned the stairs, went to my *t'ai ch'i* class, did my dreaming practices and bagged bags of sticky dried fruit at the wholefood store I was working at, went to my therapy … and day by day, my excitement grew.

The week before the course began, I was still short of money to pay for it. As much as I wanted to be there, I was on the verge of cancelling it. I prayed for help and guidance. Within 20 minutes, I had phone calls from three new clients wanting ritual photography sessions that week. I was elated.

I don't know what I expected from something called the 5Rhythms. I certainly wasn't thinking about dance, but when I walked into the Karate Dojo at the top of the East West Centre on Old Street at 6.45 on that Friday night and saw a room of people in leotards stretching, I was sure I'd come to the wrong place.

'Is this the Gabrielle Roth workshop?'

'Yes it is.'

'Oh!'

I hid away as best I could in a corner, wondering what on earth I'd signed up for. I didn't dance unless I was drunk or in an occasional ritual in a dark cave! How had I got myself in this mess?

Music was playing and the 20 participants were stretching and moving around as if they knew what they were doing. I didn't. I felt acutely self-conscious. And then that same Toni Childs song that Duncan had played on that journey to Leeds came over the speakers. As the words rang out, a woman entered the room in a full-length black leather jacket. She had long black hair and was wearing dark sunglasses. She waltzed through the space. As Toni Childs sang about power in her song *Hush!*, Gabrielle danced past me, lifted her glasses, looked right into my eyes and sang the words 'the power' right at me.

I didn't know where to put myself. I just had the feeling that there was nowhere to hide.

The rest of the warm-up was equally excruciating. I just hadn't realized that I was coming on a dance weekend and my mind was frantically thinking of ways to make my excuses and leave.

But then Gabrielle sat us down to introduce the workshop. She was funny – very funny. She seemed to recognize the turmoil I was in as she talked about how far from our bodies most of us were and how disempowering a state that was to be in. She talked about self-consciousness and how it was a step along the road from unconsciousness, and she promised us that self-consciousness would soon be replaced by consciousness.

I liked her immediately. She was sharp and sassy and those eyes shone mischievously and hinted at mysteries to come. She had 'New York' written large in her style and yet there was something ancient and compelling in the way she spoke and moved. Her words weren't static – they danced. I was hypnotized.

When she asked us to get up and started to guide us into movement, I was astonished by what happened. The music was percussive and her seduction was simple: 'Just focus your attention on different parts of your body and let them move. Don't *make* them move. Simply be fascinated by how they respond to the rhythm.'

Every now and then my mind tried to reassert control, but it was useless. I didn't feel as though I was dancing. I wasn't concerned with how my body looked. Nor was I drunk. I felt free, strong, totally fascinated, and within a few minutes, I realized I'd found my teacher.

I'd been studying with the Deer Tribe for two years and I loved my teachers, but this was something else. It's difficult to explain, but some part of me just loved Gabrielle right from the beginning. The feeling of coming home was overwhelming. And the feeling of energy and creativity that was unleashed in those next hours and days was immense. I rediscovered poetry. I rediscovered the creativity of my own body. I discovered for the first time that whatever I thought about it, my body loved to move, loved to dance, and that the deeper I danced, the more into trance I went. I could be *in* my body and in trance at the same time. In trance, the mind is quiet and still. My body spun and moved, seemingly with a will of its own, and my emotions just passed through me like the weather – one moment an autumn storm, the next a still summer's day. My eyes cried tears I didn't know were there. I raged and I didn't know why. It was if my whole psyche recognized an open window, took a deep breath, leaped out and flew.

By the end of the weekend, the impossible mountain that had been the fee for Gabrielle's training course had become an insignificant molehill. I knew without doubt that I had to be there and I knew without doubt that I would find a way.

Susannah was having a similar experience. When we'd got together in the late summer of 1986, we'd had the feeling that we had something to do together. There was a purpose to our relationship. At the time, I was known as Mikk and she as Opi, so we formed the MikkOpi Project. We weren't sure how, but it was clear right from the beginning that our project was to find or create a body of work that was focused on personal creativity, healing and creative approaches to conflict between people and nations. Our purpose was to create a deeper sense of balance and relationship between people and the Earth that sustains us all. We both felt that Gabrielle's work was a significant step along the way, and more than that, we both had a feeling of wanting to offer ourselves fully to her and her work. Although she used to joke about not wanting to be a guru ('Why sit on a pink cushion all day answering stupid questions?'), the devotion we both felt for her was intense. We were desperate to get a place on her teacher training and to start putting her work out into the world as soon as possible.

That first weekend, when a few of us went out for a meal in a restaurant in Hampstead, I felt awkward around her. She was dynamic, gritty and unpredictable. She seemed to have a radar for the part of me that wanted to be noticed and she ignored me entirely when I was feeling in need of her attention. Yet as soon as I settled down and relaxed, she was right there.

She also had an unearthly talent for making me and everyone around her feel special. When Susannah and I told her we both wanted to do her training, she just smiled and said, 'We'll see.' But she winked at us both at the same time.

We also told her, with the impetuousness of the young, that we were there to serve her and her work for as long as she'd have us. I was 24 years old.

I went home from the workshop changed. When I got back to the community, the phone rang. It was an old friend I hadn't seen or spoken to for a couple of years. We chatted and caught up with each other's lives. And then he asked me if I knew anyone who needed support with a project.

I asked him to tell me more.

He said that every two years, he gave a sum of money to someone who was starting out on a creative project and he asked if I knew anyone who needed that kind of support.

My heart leaped. I asked him how much he had to give. 'Four hundred pounds,' he replied.

That was the exact amount required for the first payment for the training. I told him about it and without hesitation he told me the money was mine!

I thanked him, we said our goodbyes and then I put the phone down and ran up the stairs shouting for joy. I couldn't believe it. The doors were opening and I was on my way. I rang the Open Gate there and then and asked them for an application form.

❧

Susannah and I were told that we would receive our answers from the Open Gate in a few weeks' time. In the meantime, my life continued. I danced every day and did my best not to think too much about my application.

On the day the letter was supposed to arrive, Susannah and I were house-sitting for a friend in Devon. It was a cold, damp day, almost gloomy. We were both agitated and doing our best not to let it show. We'd asked Lynn, a woman from the community, to call us when the post arrived. We were sitting at the kitchen table when the phone rang.

'There's a letter for you with "Open Gate" written on the front. Is that the one you're waiting for?'

'Yes.'

'Shall I open it?'

'Yes, please.'

There was a pause and I could hear the sounds of an envelope being opened mixed with the roar of my heartbeat in my ears. What if it said no? What if one of us got a place and the other was refused?

'Okay, let me see... Shall I read it to you?'

'Yes. Please read it.'

Lynn started to read: 'Dear Mikk and Susannah, I am glad to tell you that your applications for Gabrielle Roth's Teacher Training have been accepted.'

We both jumped up and danced round the kitchen.

'Are you alright?'

I heard Lynn's voice from the phone, which I had dropped in my excitement.

'Yes, absolutely bloody brilliant!'

'Should I read on?'

'That's alright, Lynn. We'll wait till we're home. Thanks so much for calling.'

'I'm happy for you both. Congratulations.'

I put the phone down and collapsed into my chair. I hadn't been aware how tense I'd been. I didn't know whether to laugh or cry. So I did both. We both did.

༄

The training was due to begin the following January and the next few months were a whirlwind. Our MikkOpi Project evolved into the 5 to Midnight Gaia Dance Project and we found our very first organizer to help us set up the five teaching assignments we were supposed to do between modules one and two of Gabrielle's training. She was a marvellous woman called Bee Quick. True to her name, she'd soon set up our first ecstatic dance workshops in London, Glastonbury, Dorset, Cambridge and Bristol. We were so ready to begin making our offering, even though we'd hardly even tasted the work we were about to train in!

When around 20 of us arrived at Gabrielle's training, we were supercharged and ready to rock. We danced and danced and danced in a small room at the delightfully named Grimstone Manor, Horrabridge!

Gabrielle did her utmost to pass on the spirit of her work to us. She was determined to teach us how to get people back into their bodies, out of their heads and into the extraordinary, creative and unique beings she believed everyone to be. She told us that she didn't mind how we taught. If that was sitting in a pub listening to people, creating theatre or teaching movement, she didn't care, as long as each of us was true to our own spirit and to the spirit of the work.

Over the 10 days we were there, she became more and more exasperated with us. It was clear we were beginners and had a huge amount to learn. She led us in a theatre exercise called the Meisner technique. In it, we had to sit in pairs in front of the group and name things we saw and felt in our partner. By the second afternoon, Gabrielle was so infuriated by how safe we were keeping our exchanges that she brought a pump-action water pistol into the room. As soon as she felt we weren't risking enough, one or both of us ended up with a soaking. It was a mixture of hilarious, humiliating and terrifying. It took us three days to get what it was she wanted from us, and by that time people had started to arrive at sessions in swimming costumes, wearing waterproofs or with umbrellas.

Gabrielle would use just about anything to get us to learn and in those 10 days I started to discover and to recognize the power of her work. It was revolutionary. It brought the body back into Western spiritual practice.

Gabrielle was a shaman of her culture and of her time. She saw the ways in which the dominant story of the time was throttling our true individuality and destroying our sense of community. She saw the devastating loneliness of spirit that we suffer from and she saw where our disembodied and totally rational and results-led mindset was taking us. And, just as a shaman must, she had travelled the roads of her own suffering and found that the dance was big enough to carry it all.

She implored us to throw our hearts and bodies into the rhythm and lose ourselves in the beat. She played wild and tender music and she gave everything she had to seducing us back into our own direct connection with the guiding force of life. She was a genius with a big heart and all the other complexities that often go with that territory. And, as dedicated to her as I was before I arrived, by the time we left that incredible initiation, I was totally devoted to the mission of both living her message and getting it out into the world. I was totally fired up. I had found my purpose and, strange as it was to someone who only a few months before had no wish to dance at all, I was now a movement teacher in training with a message to deliver and a practice to carry it.

As we left Grimstone, I was distraught saying goodbye to my teacher and to my new companions. I felt my heart breaking as we drove along the driveway. Even though I knew we would meet again in a few months, it was like leaving a womb. I knew that the harsh world of London wasn't exactly waiting for me to return. I knew we'd have to work like maniacs to get this work out there. And most of all, I knew that I had a huge challenge to deal with.

On the dance floor, I'd found a freedom and a power I'd never known I had. Every time I stepped onto the floor, I had no idea where it would take me. I didn't care. I was willing to go anywhere to find the healing, the expression and the freedom that those ecstatic states promised. And yet off the dance floor, even within the relative safety of Grimstone Manor, I still felt tongue-tied and awkward whenever Gabrielle approached. I still wanted her approval. I wanted her to see me as someone special. I wanted her to see the shaman in me.

Gabrielle showed me the difference between hiding my gifts by trying to get them noticed and what she used to call 'disappearing in the dance'.

I saw and healed so much in that training and I could see the challenge that faced me. How on earth was I going to bring the freedom I'd found on the dance floor onto the dance floor of everyday life?

As we left, the tears started to flow. I felt naked. The world seemed such a huge place and I felt so insignificant. I was carrying something precious. I had found something sacred. It was a blend of my own medicine and the medicine that Gabrielle was entrusting us to carry into the world. Was I worthy of such a task? Would I manage it?

Although Susannah and I had each other, we were both overwhelmed by the task that was in front of us. We knew there was no ready-made group of people just pining for us to get going and offer our new inspiration. Gabrielle, like Anna Halprin and Martha Graham before her, was a pioneer. And we were part of her first cohort of teachers in Europe.

The cold grey January streets of London did little to lift my mood. I could only see the loneliness and the disconnection that Gabrielle had so eloquently pointed out to us. I felt so small in that vast city, but somewhere deep inside I'd rediscovered the determination of the warrior.

It was January 1989 and our first workshop was in two weeks' time. We had work to do.

∾

Chapter 7

YOUR FEET ALWAYS KNOW THE WAY HOME

'Choose the paths which are not worn out by many feet!'
MEHMET MURAT ILDAN

One of Gabrielle's pithy invitations, which we heard her repeat many, many hundreds of times, was: 'Put your mind in your feet.' My own education, probably much like yours, had placed a strong emphasis on getting me to think. Actually, it wasn't even thinking, rather remembering and regurgitating what others had thought. Either way, the head was boss and that was that. In the conscious dance world that we were part of creating, 'getting out of our heads' was the new creed. It was a good first step and we all had the 'Dance first, think later' T-shirt.

We were both excited and scared by the prospect of our new careers as movement teachers. The week before teaching our first dance workshop was hellish. Although we had a full course, made up mostly of friends and friends of friends, I was super-stressed about the whole thing. I was about as far from my feet as I could get and my practice went to the wall. I've since come to learn that it is when life gets difficult that practice is most important. Without it, we tend to revert to the default mode that we learned early on to deal with life. As that week went on, that old phrase 'we teach best what we most need to learn' kept coming to mind.

Most of the week was spent trying to get our music in order. In those days, we had to teach using cassette tapes. That meant that if we wanted to play a song twice, we had to record it onto a separate tape, use a double cassette player and rewind one whilst the other was playing.

At night, I hardly slept, and when I did, every type of 'worst-case scenario' presented itself through my dreams. I wondered why I was doing this to myself. Surely there must be an easier way to make a living. Who the hell did I think I was to teach anything, let alone dance? *They'll all see through you immediately*, I thought. *The sound system will fail. Your music is rubbish. You only got a place on the training because there were so few to choose from. Walk away now, Mikk, before you make a total fool of yourself!*

My ego was having a field day. At the same time, I hung on to the thread of soul that was steadfastly keeping me on track. It wasn't a lot of fun and it got worse as the week went by. I could hardly eat. And I had no space to support Susannah, who was in the middle of a battle with her own demons. Nevertheless, come Saturday, 'Life Dance' was to be the first workshop offered by the 5 to Midnight Gaia Dance Project.

I remember driving the two miles to the venue with the car packed full of stuff. It was a bright day. I remember wishing that I'd been teaching for 10 years. I thought I might have something to offer by then.

In actuality, the event was much easier than all the fears had led me to believe it would be. The longer the weekend went on, the more we found our feet. Whilst I was teaching, I found that the ego voices that had plagued me all week were silent. There was just no space for them when I had people in front of me who not only deserved my undivided attention but to whom it was a great pleasure to give it!

By the Sunday evening, we were both elated. We'd taught our first movement workshop, the people attending had got something out of it, and, miracle of miracles, we were being paid for the pleasure of it. Witnessing some of our friends get the simple magic of the dance was an absolutely beautiful experience.

One thing we discovered rather quickly on the dancing path was that if you give yourself to the drums, move your body that deeply and let go that much, then you're in for some serious changes. Strange as it seemed to a young man who used to be too self-conscious to dance, this powerful meditation technique was opening up a deeper sense of self than I'd previously accessed. It was pure embodied shamanism.

Our second module of training was due in the early summer. During the months leading up to it, my daily practice was bringing me closer and closer to Earth. I felt as if I was landing in my life for the very first time. I was starting to have some choice about how much influence past hurts, fears and limiting self-concepts were having in my life. I was getting stronger and finding the beginnings of something I'd been short of – a very real confidence. For the first time, I started to see that there might be a way for me to stay true to my values *and* make a living. At the same time, I still had lots of attitudes about money. It took me a long time to work out that if I wanted to make a difference in this world, then learning to live in it was a prerequisite. And that meant paying off my debts and keeping up with my bills.

As my movement practice went deeper, so the unpredictability and spontaneous nature of what we were teaching started to find its way into my life. Change was soon the only constant as my sense of self went on a rollercoaster ride. Although things were going in a good direction, I'd often wake up with an underlying sense of dread. The unfinished business of my childhood and teenage years was starting to knock on the door of my psyche.

From the moment I'd left home to the time I'd begun teaching, I'd had a wild ride. Like most teenagers, I'd started to question everything. The rules and laws of my religion that had satisfied me as a child had become empty of meaning. I wanted answers to the deep questions that my life was bringing into my awareness. I'd seen ghosts, experienced psychic phenomena and had numerous out-of-body experiences. Sometimes I'd seen people's illness or heard their thoughts. What did it all mean?

I used to take our dog for long walks on the beach at Southport and sit watching the sea. I loved open vistas where there was nothing man-made visible to tell me what century I was in. I'd get lost in the rhythmic sound of the ocean and the shapes in the sand as the waves retreated, and I'd write angst-filled poetry. I asked my questions out loud just in case God was listening. And though I was alone in those places, I never felt lonely there. Nature's voice was always calming. Out in the open, I knew I belonged. Amongst people, things were more complex. Nature never tried to be anything other than what it was. People, on the other hand, so often said one thing and meant another altogether.

Nevertheless, I wanted to be cool and one of the gang. I got by with a blend of being good at sport, being a strong leader and going to football. Shouting and swearing both as player and spectator was wonderfully cathartic. I had an active fantasy life, replete with many a romantic episode on moonlit beaches, and a sweetness which had girls often wanting to share their hearts with me but not their bodies.

I developed a rather dramatic way of leaving any situation that I found too emotional: I would simply make myself leave my body. I can remember choosing to faint and watching from above as people went into action to deal with the supine body of a teenager whom I recognized but didn't identify with from my safe out-of-body place.

By the time I met Susannah, in May 1986, I was 22 years old, a serious peacenik and had adopted the feminist ideals of what it meant to be a good man in the 20th century: caring, unthreatening, emotionally literate and much more passive than the previous 9,000 years of patriarchy had been famous for. Of course, my friends and I felt responsible for that. So, theoretically, inspired by Gandhi, I was totally into non-violence.

In actuality, I was full of repressed impulses of all kinds. I was working for the Youth Service and had learned to be scared of saying the wrong thing. Political correctness was all-important. I learned later that telling people what to say or think doesn't change or even touch the layers of ignorance and insecurity from which all kinds of -isms arise. Real change demands real work with the body, heart and mind. But back then I thought it was enough simply to agree with an idea in order to live it.

My very first conversation with Susannah took place in her bedroom in the squat in Hackney where she and her women friends lived. We'd met earlier in the garden and though it wasn't love at first sight for either of us, it was definitely recognition at first sight. We felt we must have met somewhere before, but we didn't know where.

Later that day, I was at a planning meeting, and as it progressed, I found myself more and more distracted. I made my excuses and left. I wanted to find Susannah and talk.

I found her in her room. Our very first conversation was about whether it was possible to be completely free and completely committed at the same time. It was a time of grand ideas and high ideals. I was ready to explore the big wide world. Susannah's encouragement to do so was provocative. I felt a door inside me beginning to open.

I moved to the peace camp at Faslane. The camp had a serious mission: to protest against the building of further nuclear submarines and to highlight the damage done to the loch by nuclear leakage. At the same time, it was full of people who saw no paradox in blending serious protesting with serious partying. It was a wild summer of political action, partying and loving. In the day, we protested. At night, we were rarely sober. We smoked chillums standing on our heads, sang songs by the fire and talked about how to put the world to rights.

In my time in the peace movement I was arrested four times for non-violent direct action, twice in Scotland at Faslane nuclear submarine base, once in Belgium and once in Denmark. In each incident, my non-violence training, which taught me to resist arrest by going floppy and refusing to cooperate, worked well. I noticed on each occasion that the arresting officers were furious with our tactics. And I noticed how strangely superior that made me feel. *They* were the violent ones. *They* were the oppressors. My fellow protestors and I were the victims and we held the moral high ground.

I learned later that my passivity had actually been a form of indirect violence. And I recognized that much of the violence I'd met in those situations had been an expression of my own unowned aggression. After one of those arrests, alone in a cell for four days, I had nothing to do but look at the white wall and think. On that wall, I kept seeing the angry face of my arresting officer. And I saw how the more passive I'd become, the angrier he'd become. I started to get an inkling that the two things were related. But playing the righteous victim was part of my survival system and it would take me many years to see this clearly and be able to make the choice to step out of it. Back then, on the outside, I was sweet. On the inside, I was seething, with some justification, about the ills of the world. But being angry didn't fit my self-image as a Gandhi-esque non-violent activist. So I didn't notice. Apparently, my arresting officers did.

I learned a lot from the crowd of regulars and visitors who frequented the peace camp, but by the summer's end I was ready for something else. I moved into the Mornington Grove community in London in the early autumn of 1986. It was less than five miles from where Susannah was living. Having spent a couple of months courting by sending each other notes through mutual friends, we got it together. She was ready to find all she needed in one man, and though I'd enjoyed my summer of free love, I was ready for something deeper and more meaningful. We fell in love.

∽

When we met Gabrielle, the physicality and immediacy of her work was very different from the kind of shamanic work we'd studied until then. The deeper I went in the dance, the more I discovered the wisdom that was living in the extraordinary, complex and intelligent structure that is the human body.

Our second module of training was due soon after Susannah's 26th birthday. For her birthday, I decided to have a ring designed and made by a jeweller we'd met. When I gave her the ring, she thought that I was asking her to marry me. I was shocked. I hadn't thought about the obvious significance of having a ring made for her! It was an awkward moment as I apologized for any confusion and Susannah backtracked as gracefully as she could.

We went to our second module of teacher training with a lot going on. I was even feeling an uneasy sense of dread. Nevertheless, we were delighted to see everyone again and to catch up with our fellow trainees. And as far as I knew, I was there to do more training. But my heart had other ideas.

We were working in a new venue called the Karuna Institute, also in Devon. It was May 1989. One afternoon, Gabrielle was teaching us how to work with emotion through the dance. The central premise of her work was that the dancer inside us could move through anything if we got ourselves out of the way. She told us that the body was like clay. If you shaped it into a sculpture of sadness, sadness would fill that sculpture if sadness was present. If you made a sculpture that acknowledged anger and let the body bring movement to it, if anger needed to move, it would. She encouraged us to increase the body's vocabulary by working with different tempos, shapes and expressions. If we could remind the body of its capacity to move with emotion, when emotion was present in our day-to-day life, we would have a much wider vocabulary for moving with it.

I loved this way of working. It gave such freedom to express the heart responsibly without having to justify or explain any of it. That particular morning, though, I couldn't seem to find my dance. The further we went, the heavier I became. I was exhausted. I felt grey and sluggish. And by the time we reached the end of the dance, a time when I would have expected myself to be in a shimmering silence, I felt awful. The feeling of dread that had been creeping up on me for the past few weeks had truly landed.

As the dance wound to a close, I asked myself why. I was totally shocked by the answer that came back, clear as a lightning flash: 'You want to marry Susannah and you're terrified of how your family will react.'

Although my rational mind started turning somersaults in an attempt to obscure again what had become so clear, I knew immediately that it was true. I knew my parents would be deeply upset, as Susannah wasn't Jewish and I'd been brought up with stories of the terrible family consequences that had followed any decision to 'marry out'. Echoes of a distant great-great-uncle who'd been banished from the family for following his heart rang loud between my ears. Despite this, I couldn't ignore what had become obvious.

At the end of the session, I asked for a word with Gabrielle before we had lunch. We sat down and she asked me what was wrong. It was clear from my state that something was seriously upsetting me. I told her simply that I wanted to marry Susannah and I knew that my parents and grandparents would be devastated. I was scared and I didn't know what to do.

There were a few times in my 18-year apprenticeship with Gabrielle when light shone through her dark eyes and she spoke words that shook me to the core. This was one of them.

'Nobody is asking you to give up your family. Life is just asking you to give up your need for their approval.'

Boom! Time to grow up and take responsibility for your own life, Mikk. In an instant I went from fear of 'what if' to elation. Concern for my family and their responses didn't disappear, not at all. But Gabrielle had helped me to put it into perspective.

'I want to spend my life with this woman. I'm going to ask her to marry me.'

I went into the dining room to find Susannah and in front of my friends and colleagues I got down on my knees and asked her. She said yes and the dining room erupted. More than anything, she was relieved. The ring incident had been hard for her.

We both knew this was going to make things difficult with my family and we accepted that. But we were going to get married.

Life was good. My mind was landing in my feet and I was learning that the feet always know the way home.

⟨ ✗ ⟩

Chapter 8

TO YOUR OWN HEART BE TRUE

'To thine own self be true, and it must
follow, as the night the day, thou canst
not then be false to any man.'

WILLIAM SHAKESPEARE

We decided to get married that October, a few days before offering our first intensive workshop at a place called Springhead in Dorset. We found a beautiful house in Devon called Hazelwood House that we could rent for the weekend. They were just setting up as a venue and we were to be their first wedding. We invited 60 people to come and spend the weekend with us and we asked them all to bring an item of food suitable for a wedding feast. We asked our good friend Julie Devine to make the cake and the rest we left to a mixture of chance and our faith in our friends' generosity.

Telling my parents that I was getting married was, as I had feared, a terrible experience for them and for me. I decided the best thing to do was to write them a letter explaining that it wasn't my intention to hurt them in any way. I recently found a photocopy of that letter. Reading it, I felt the pain, strength and determination of that young man. He truly gave up the known road to follow his heart.

I hoped my parents could see their way to welcoming Susannah into the family, but my father told me that if I married her, he wouldn't speak to me for six months. I knew he would keep his word. He also told me that I would be cut out of his and my grandparents' wills.

There was nothing I could do. I loved Susannah and that was that.

As difficult as it was for my parents, it was also tough for her. Through no fault of her own, her love for me was seen not as something to celebrate but as something to mourn.

And for me, wherever I turned, I saw people in pain. There was nothing to do but dance, prepare for our wedding and keep on walking on the road we had set out on.

Nevertheless, I awoke each morning with a terrible sense of loss. And even though I kept coming back to Gabrielle's words that I was simply being asked to give up my need for my family's approval, it was a tough time for everyone involved. There was loss, and loss hurts. Learning to live with hurt is part of growing up, and life was giving me a crash course in just that. Everywhere I turned, I was being challenged to stay with my heart's choice, with or without the agreement of those around me.

Time and time again in my life, I've noticed that when I've had a vision and made a powerful decision to follow it, life sets up a little test for me to see how real and how deep that decision is. This whole process brought Susannah and me closer together. It made us more determined to follow the path we were on. And so we prepared for our wedding and continued to develop our work.

❧

That summer, we went down to Devon to work with Heather Campbell, one of our early Deer Tribe teachers. She was offering an Eagle Dance, a one-day ceremony in which we were invited to dance backwards and forwards to a beautiful large oak tree in the grounds of a lovely old country house. Originally built with stolen South American gold, the house was being used now as a venue for mindfulness meditation and Heather told us it was the perfect place for our ceremony.

Everyone had their own 'lane' to dance in, marked out by ribbon on the ground. As we danced towards the tree, we were supposed to bring our prayers to the 'tree of life', and then, as we danced backwards towards the edge of the circle, we were supposed to bring back blessings into our lives. The dance was going to continue for eight hours. We were fasting and we weren't supposed to turn our back on the tree. The music was provided by a tape recorder playing four Deer Tribe Sundance songs over and over again.

At one point, Heather had to leave the circle to go and pick something up she'd forgotten. I don't remember what it was, but I suspect she was just testing our discipline. We all continued to dance in our lanes for the next half an hour or so. Then at some point, one of us broke out of the form and within a couple of minutes we were all dancing wildly around the tree, following our own impulses *à la* 5Rhythms.

When Heather came back, she was furious with us. She sat us down and explained that this was an ancient ceremony that she had been given permission to hold. And we were not respecting the form, the tradition and therefore the ancestors.

A part of me felt annoyed. Here I was facing another set of rules and laws restricting my free movement and telling me my impulses weren't okay! But another part of me knew full well that she was right. We'd agreed to take part in a particular ceremony of our own free will. No one had told us we had to be there. And we'd broken the structure she'd clearly set out for us. I felt like an adolescent resisting the rules of the adult world. But again, a part of me knew that these weren't arbitrary rules. The structure was designed to bring us to a state of focused attention through disciplined repetition.

We got back into our lanes and danced on for the next six hours. I went through such boredom as I danced back and forth to the tree. I felt stuck in a rut, a routine. I felt imprisoned by the form, but I also felt that something was there for me, just out of reach. It was a strange state to be in. My internal dialogue was jumping between resistance and something new that I could sense but not quite name. I felt I needed the discipline, the form and the structure. At the same time, I hated it and felt restricted by it. Wasn't this the reason I got into free dance? To break the mould, to be wild and free? On the other hand, I felt that if I just kept going, I would break through some invisible wall.

We were blessed by the weather. It was fine with a strong summer wind to keep us cool, and the great tree provided us with welcome shade. We danced on and on, back and forth, the same four songs going round and round on the ghetto-blaster. I was hungry and thirsty, but after a while I found my stride. The more I danced, the easier it became. I felt lighter. On the outside, nothing had changed. But on the inside, a quiet revolution was taking place.

I was in two places at once. My body was dancing in this everyday consensual-reality world whilst my mind seemed to have opened or become momentarily illuminated. It was as though someone had turned the lights on. I could see the details of my life clearly as if I'd been looking down on it from above. I could see my family and my friends. I could see the road I had walked along and the road ahead. Everything had its place. The pieces of the puzzle suddenly came together as a single picture that made sense to me. It was so simple. I knew I was on the right road.

It wasn't the kind of knowing I'd ever experienced before – it was impersonal knowledge. Everything else was quiet. The normal buzz of my internal dialogue was gone. My breath was sweet. I could taste the summer sun and smell the light coming through the branches. Everything was in its place. There was a perfection beyond understanding and it was neither kind nor unkind, neither light nor dark. It gave me a feeling of incredible strength, and from that strength, I understood clearly that, like everything that lived, I had to follow the road that made the most sense to me. I understood that structure and fluidity were the yin and yang of the dance and of creation, and that if I wanted to create anything, I needed to honour them both equally.

⟨ ⟩

Back in London, I heard about a famous Jewish Qabalist called Z'ev Ben Shimon Halevi, who had married a Swedish non-Jewish woman. I wondered if I might be able to talk to him. So I found a way to get in touch and I wrote him a letter. Very kindly, he invited me to come and spend the day with him and his wife.

I arrived at his flat at 11 a.m. I was nervous, curious and unsure what to expect. I rang the bell and a man in his fifties answered the door. He looked as though he'd jumped straight out of a tarot pack. He was the archetypal wise man, all beard and mischievous shining eyes. I warmed to him straight away. He invited me in and we sat in his smallish kitchen. His wife came in, offered me tea and joined us.

He asked me about my situation with my family and I told him the story. He listened quietly and nodded. When I'd finished, he said, 'You know, God doesn't make mistakes. You've been born Jewish, and there's a reason for it. If you love Susannah, you must follow your heart and marry her. At some point in your life, when you need to know, you will know why being Jewish is a part of who you are. Until that time, follow your way, follow your way.'

Wow! What a gift. This very generous elder was repeating the message I'd received in the Eagle Dance – different medium, same message. I was beginning to get it.

After our tea and talk, he took me into his workroom. It had an eerie, magical quality. There were strange metallic sculptures like angels hanging from the ceiling and the walls were lined with religious books bound in green and red leather.

He led me on a meditation journey up through the spheres of the Tree of Life that are the basis of Qabalistic work. Amazingly, sitting there, I went into the state that I'd experienced in the Eagle Dance. That same impersonal and direct knowledge of how things are arose in me. To be clear, this wasn't a fluffy 'everything is perfect as it is' kind of revelation. It was much more straightforward than that. There was knowledge of suffering and injustice. There was knowledge of pain. There was knowledge of the unfairness of life. And simultaneously, there was the knowledge that everything was in its place, playing its role in some great drama in which all the characters had temporarily forgotten that they were on stage.

In that state, there was meaning to my life and I knew that I had to get down to work. I didn't feel righteous or religious. I had no 'I've got to save the world' story going on. I just knew that I had to commit totally to being the person I was and doing what I had to do. And I knew for sure that there were many, many truths and many, many ways to access those truths. And I knew that the ultimate meaning was magnificently shrouded in the mists of deep mystery. And I felt just fine with that.

❧

Strengthened by these encounters, a month before our wedding day Susannah and I took a cheap vacation to Tunisia in order to relax a little and dream the marriage we wanted. Gabrielle had suggested that we write our own vows. She felt it important that we didn't share them or discuss them until the ceremony itself. There was to be no negotiation or compromise. The truth in each of our hearts and the vows that matched that were all that was needed. Although we were scared ('What if I promise the universe and she only promises the Earth?'), we were up for the truth and having as real a marriage ceremony as we could.

In Tunisia, we camped and lived frugally until the penultimate day, when we went for a lovely lunch in a posh hotel overlooking the sea. After lunch, we sat on the deck and within minutes our marriage ceremony just seemed to drop out of the sky into the space between us. I got a piece of it, and then Susannah got one, and before long we had a perfect marriage ritual all designed and ready to go. It felt to both of us as though we had received a great gift, fully intact, fully operable and ready to rock and roll.

We were discovering the magic of creation in an everyday sense. The more we told the story that we were connected to spirit, the more we experienced that to be true.

This was the beginning of a more mature relationship to spirit. There was no God on a cloud. It certainly wasn't all about light and some kind of endless bliss, it was about something very tangible, a sense of feeling physically connected to the ground beneath our feet and, through that, to the life around us. I guess it's what the mystics call 'presence'. We were arriving, here, now, in our bodies, on Earth.

We were simply experiencing a sense of guidance that felt bigger than either one of us. The intensity of our practice was starting to open the door to a deeper experience of life.

In the light of this, we knew that if we were going to enter into this marriage and do justice to the ritual we had unearthed, we needed to enter it with a clean conscience. On our last night in Tunisia we had a painful night of confessions, each of us acknowledging times and places where we hadn't been honest with each other. There was nothing particularly enlightened about that night. Just as a storm can blow up out of a beautiful clear blue sky, the marriage ceremony that we had crafted acted as an immediate and very strong catalyst. Our intentions were clear. We both wanted to enter the space of marriage without hidden skeletons rattling away in the closet. Nevertheless, I think we were both shocked by what needed to be shared, and though we did our best to hear each other, the hurts we bring with us into our relationships from past experiences can blind us to the reality in the present and leave us shadow boxing for hours on end.

We hardly slept that night, but as the dawn lit up the sky, we found we had survived. We were emotionally bruised, cautious and afraid of what the future would bring, but we were learning, step by step, what it meant to walk the talk.

The day before our wedding day, my dear father called me to beg me not to marry Susannah. It was a painful call. I did my best to understand where he was coming from. He was doing what he felt in his own heart to be right, just as I was. But my understanding couldn't cover over the loss we both felt.

For years, I'd felt that at some point it would come to this with my father. We were very different in so many ways and very similar in ways we wouldn't have recognized at the time. It was clear we were both stubbornly on the road we'd chosen and neither of us was willing to pull out of the inevitable headlong crash. That was the last conversation I was to have with him for six months, and for years afterwards our phone calls were a predictable and repetitive dialogue: 'How are you? Where are you? Do you want to speak to your mother?'

It was only when faced with his death from cancer at a relatively young age that we truly connected again on a heart-to-heart level. There were many times when I missed having a father to talk to. I still do. But on another level, I feel that we played out an archetypal drama in which we both performed our roles to perfection. I couldn't be the son he thought he wanted and he couldn't be the father I thought I wanted, but love runs deeper than we know, and many times I've looked with wonder at what he brought out in me. He pulled the rug out from underneath me many times, and in so doing, he taught me to stand on my own two feet. He stayed true to what he felt to be right and didn't give in to me, and in so doing, he taught me to be strong. The older I get, the more I feel his presence with me.

He wasn't there on my wedding day, though. He felt he couldn't support our marriage and, quite rightly, my mother felt it necessary to stand by him. Gabrielle, however, was due to join us all at Hazelwood to lead the ceremony.

We awoke to a misty grey Devon morning, not at all what we were hoping for. And then we received what could have been a devastating blow. Just after breakfast, Gabrielle called from London to tell us she had food poisoning. We couldn't believe it. All our plans were suddenly high up in the air blowing in the early autumn winds. She talked about renting a helicopter to get to us, but we all knew that it wasn't going to happen.

We put the phone down and looked at each other. Maybe we both expected the other to break down, but we had fire in our eyes to match the sun that was just beginning to break through the clouds. We knew without words that this was spirit's invitation for us to step a little more into our own authority and, witnessed by a circle of friends and family, marry each other. If Gabrielle couldn't get there, then so be it. It was down to us.

In our ageing photo album of our wedding day, there is a photograph of both of us on that morning. I am barefoot in the misty rain, wearing a floppy hippy sweater and Susannah is in her black sunflower trousers. We both look so very young. And yet there is a determination there and a joy in each other. We had the chutzpah to design and hold our own wedding. And the strength of the ritual came both from that and from the presence of a loving community of family and friends.

A good ritual carries you through the hard times. Well done, it provides a river of strength that will be with you when it's needed. It was 5 October 1989 and we were beginning a new chapter of life together.

At the end of the day, after a beautiful ceremony that contained elements from the Jewish tradition, the Quaker tradition, a Native American pipe ceremony, singing, blessings from the assembled community and hours of great music and dancing, we were escorted to our wedding suite. Our crazily creative friends lined the stairs, singing to us as we climbed. Unbeknownst to us, they had been in the room and set it up. The bath was full of hot water. There were floating candles in the sink, champagne cooling in a bucket and beautiful fresh grapes and homemade chocolates by the side of the bed. And on the bed, painted in gaudy colours, there was a message.

'Go ahead,' it said, 'break *all* the rules…'

Chapter 9

ME, MYSELF,
MY ROYAL I-NESS

'But I will find new habits, new thoughts, new
rules. I will become something else.'
VERONICA ROTH, *DIVERGENT*

For several years before I committed myself to the shamanic road, I was an active member of the anti-everything brigade. Anti-nuclear, anti-apartheid, anti-racism, anti-globalization and corporate power, anti-factory-farmed mass-produced food industry and anti-the poor excuse for democracy that I was certain was destroying our future. Finally, I'd found a target for all my frustrations. Finally, there were some real and tangible faults out there. Finally, there was someone to blame! Those were such important times.

One time, locked alone in a cell over a long bank holiday weekend in Glasgow's Maryhill police station, I discovered meditation by accident. The cell was empty save for a bed and a toilet. The walls were white and I had nothing to do. I wasn't allowed reading or writing materials, so it was basically down to the walls and me. I sat and stared at those walls for hours. I went from fear to resignation, from pride to doubt, and from a busy, busy mind to a quietness and sense of being that I hadn't experienced since I was a child.

The reality of being in a police cell for four days was quite different from what I'd anticipated. For one, I was completely alone, save for the moments when a plate of food and a glass of water were delivered. No attention was paid to my requests for vegetarian food, so for the most part I was fasting. So, nothing to do, hardly any food, white walls and silence – my very first white-wall Zen meditation retreat!

I went over the action we'd done and my arrest many times. It was like watching a part of a movie stuck on repeat mode. My men's group had spent the late, late hours of a damp night traversing moorland and then cutting down over 300 feet of fencing around the nuclear naval base at Faslane in Scotland. This was in 1986 and security then wasn't what it is now. But as dawn came, we were arrested.

I kept returning to one moment again and again. As we were cutting into the fencing with the vague plan to get inside and spray some peace symbols on any Ministry of Defence vehicles we came across, I'd had an epiphany that had landed out of nowhere. I'd realized that all these fences that I was so enjoying cutting down with my super-funky bolt-cutters were in fact, mirrors of the fences inside myself.

The anarchic crew who were responsible for organizing all these actions and protests were in a deep and divisive dialogue at the time. There was a split between those who were into the inner work of healing the effects of the industrial age on our capacity to be who we were. And diametrically opposed, there were those who were only into taking action to change the outer world. I didn't want to be judged by this 'action only' crew. I liked their anarchic, ballsy approach to protesting. They criticized the process-orientated folk for their endless belly-button-staring approach to change. Of course the process crew were equally critical of what they called the patriarchal, masculine (which was a dirty word in those circles in those days) action heads who wouldn't know a feeling if it hit them.

The thing that unified both camps was a commitment to non-violence, but the split was a very real one. And in that police cell, I became aware of that same split inside myself.

As I sat there alone, I contemplated all the non-violent direct action I'd been involved in. It wasn't my first time in a prison cell. I'd managed to get arrested in Belgium and Denmark already. But it was my first time in solitary confinement.

I remembered my non-violent resistance to arrest and how a burly Glaswegian police officer had dragged my purposefully limp body along by my scarf. (Aha! that's why they'd told us not to wear scarves in our direct action training!) From my moral high ground, I hadn't seen the man at all. I'd just seen his uniform and his role, and I'd treated him accordingly. Now I started to question what non-violence actually meant to me. I kept coming back to the same image of my bolt-cutters and the fence and the deepening recognition that the fence was inside me. Somehow it dawned on me, with a mixture of shame and relief, that I wasn't quite the Gandhi I aspired to be. I was going to have to spend some time getting to know myself better.

I came to a crossroads in that police cell and I knew which way I had to go. I wanted to meet and challenge the ways in which I was acting in the very same manner as the external culture I was so intent on changing. This new road had been illuminated simply by staring at a white wall.

In that jail cell, I wasn't trying to get anywhere. I had no one to impress. I understood the need for the twin roads of inner and outer action. And I understood that I had some rebalancing to do. It was time for a little belly-button gazing, or what Susannah and I came to jokingly call 'me-myself-my-royal-I-ness' time.

The community in London I went to live in was well populated by therapists, many of whom were part of the same peace group that I was working with. It was at that time that I found Manas, the gentle, fiery man who became my guide on this inner journey for the next two years. He gave me space to explore a whole new world.

I never really knew what kind of psychotherapy we were supposed to be doing, but each week Manas would have a new treat for me. One time he was into bioenergetics, the next neo-Reichian therapy and the next something called the 'path of least resistance'. Whatever the form, I learned so much in the little garden room that was his practice space. One particular session stands out.

I'd spent the whole day thinking about my relationship with my father. I wasn't in a good space with my family, especially my father, who simply couldn't understand why I was wasting my life on things he didn't understand. There was also a growing sense of conflict within me between the kind of man I thought I had to be and the man I actually felt inside – a battle between the vegan, non-violent, feminist, peacenik, Gandhi-esque 'new' man and the fierce warrior who was fed up with being silenced. This sense of frustration and edginess had been growing for weeks.

When I arrived for my session, Manas was waiting for me with a tennis racket and a huge pile of cushions. He told me we were going to work with anger.

'These cushions represent everything and everyone you feel angry with, including your father. Every now and then, rage is a good thing. Begin.'

For the first five minutes, I struggled as Manas encouraged me to find my strength and my voice and beat the cushions. Nothing was happening. I just felt stupid and embarrassed. I didn't have the heart for it and I was certain that Gandhi had never had to resort to such methods. But I did what I was asked and Manas kept encouraging me.

'Go on, that's good. Feels good, doesn't it?'

He was beginning to annoy me and all of a sudden, something just snapped in me. I started to pummel those cushions, shouting and swearing. I was a raging, passionate red-blooded animal. I was a fury of fire, letting all those swallowed emotions pour out. I used every bit of strength I had to destroy the many things that this cushion mountain had come to represent.

I've no idea how long I went on for. But after a while, there was a calming. There were tears, a kind of exhausted sobbing that is the body's way of releasing old stories from the bones.

Manas encouraged me to lie down on my back and covered me with a blanket. He put on some Native American flute music and I lay there, panting. That fury had opened up my heart. It was as if I'd been anaemic and suddenly the red blood cells had just flooded back into me. I recognized how much I'd been shaping myself to fit in with the people I admired. I'd always done it. That knowledge landed as clear as the first light of dawn. I was certain I'd never forget. But, as Don Juan told Castaneda, transforming our emotional realizations into an everyday part of the way we live, act and communicate is a challenge for the warrior in us.

At that time I was devouring Castaneda's stories. His apprenticeship with the Yaqui sorcerer Don Juan and his group of exceptionally disciplined warrior-sorcerers was such an inspiration.

Don Juan had given Castaneda the task of recapitulating all the experiences of his life. In the sorcerer's world, the past is a storehouse of potential energy that we've left behind us on our journey through life. How can we possibly change in the present if most of our power and life-force is locked up in the stories from the past that we haven't digested or completed? My 'tennis racket meets the cushion mountain' session had shown me how much life-force I'd been repressing. I dreamed of finding someone to hold the space for me so I could do my own recapitulation. And so, when my friend Simon, a colleague I'd often met working with Arwyn, told me that Victor Sanchez was visiting the UK, I knew instinctively that this was my next step.

⁄

Sanchez had been asked to be one of the people to bring the work of the Wirarika people of the mountains of northern Mexico into the world.

The Wirarika, I was told, carried the medicine of the ancient Toltecs. That was enough to grab my attention and I signed up to work with Victor immediately.

I remember the moment I saw him for the first time. We were working at Gaunts House in Dorset. It was the first evening of the workshop. We had eaten and were waiting for Victor to arrive. He came into the room and took his seat. Strong and upright, with black hair, he had the air of a native warrior about him. He impressed me with his strong male presence. He was the masculine version of Gabrielle Roth. Where she circled, he straight-lined, where she added mystery to the simplest movement, he explained in structured detail. Whilst Gabrielle taught us simply to put ourselves in the wide-open embrace of the dance and let go, he demanded our focused attention for the precise details of his next exercise.

On that first weekend, he ran a simple fire ceremony. He explained that since he'd met the fire and come to know him as his grandfather, he'd never been lonely. Even in a hotel room when he was travelling, all he had to do was light a little candle and he could have a heart-to-heart with his grandpa.

He laid out a beautiful fire with a large log to represent the pillow that old Grandfather Fire could rest his head on. Each of us was invited to collect a straight stick, a 'prayer arrow' through which we would introduce ourselves to the fire and come to know him better. We all dutifully gathered our sticks, and after the fire was lit with a prayer of thanks and an offering of sweet herbs, we were invited to approach and speak to it. We did. Quietly, whispering our hellos and introductions with a mixed air of reverence and embarrassment. After all, we were talking to a fire.

After a few minutes, Victor stopped us. 'Watch,' he said, 'and listen.'

He and his assistant approached the fire with their prayer sticks. And then, one at a time, they proceeded to speak loudly with strong, clear voices, directly from the heart.

'Grandfather, do you know how glad we are to see you again? Thank you, Grandpa, for your warmth and light and for your company. I am here again. I am Victor. I come with a prayer…'

We were all so shocked. Our idea of a sacred conversation with the holy fire had been blown out of the water.

'He's old. He needs to hear you. So speak loudly. Speak from your hearts, not from your heads. You are too careful.'

And so we did. Several at a time, we approached and found our own way to connect the strength of our voices with the strength of our hearts and speak directly to the fire.

I felt an immediate connection to the fire, not as something that I just took for granted but as a being without whom I – and we – wouldn't be here. I felt connected to it in a way I didn't know was possible. It wasn't like speaking to some faraway spirit or all-powerful god. It was an immediate and immanent connection, a feeling of the most intense love for the fire and for life itself.

I was amazed what came out of my mouth once I got out of the way. I told the fire how much I wanted to learn. I wanted to recapitulate my past and be of use to life. I needed guidance and courage.

I felt accepted and I knew my prayers had been heard.

After everyone had finished speaking and offering their prayer arrows, there was an awed silence punctuated by the hisses and crackles of the grandfather's old, old voice.

Then Victor told us that tomorrow morning would be 'kicks to the ego' morning and therefore we ought to get some sleep.

As I lay down in my tent, I knew I'd met another teacher from whom I could learn. I was grateful, but I couldn't help wondering what he'd meant by 'kicks to the ego'. My dreams were full of my imagination's answers to that, and none of them looked like fun.

Chapter 10

THE SHAMAN'S DOOR

'If you do not change direction, you may
end up where you are heading.'
GAUTAMA BUDDHA

And so began my journey with the third set of teachings to which
I'd found my way. Although my relationship to the Deer Tribe
was close to coming to an end, my relationship with Gabrielle was
deepening. But however deeply I danced, once I stopped, my mind and
its incessant commentary were right there waiting for me. I needed to
find a disciplined and integrated way of working with my mind and
updating the self-concepts and stories I was unconsciously repeating. So
Victor's teaching landed in my life at exactly the right time. I began an
intensive period of study with him that was to last for three years.

Learning about my feelings in therapy with Manas and about a more
feminine approach to life with Gabrielle had supported me in engaging
the body and feeling the ground under my feet. And as I grounded
myself in the reality that being an honorary feminist was a story that
had no future for me, I started to find a new level of discipline.

The morning after the fire ceremony, we met outside on the lawn. Victor
explained to us that for years he'd met people who were using sorcery

as a way to escape the challenges of being human. He laughed about all the young folk he'd met who were desperately trying to find their Don Juan and escape into the magical worlds that Castaneda had described so beautifully. With some embarrassment, I recognized myself in what he was saying. I had to admit that I did spend a lot of time dreaming of meeting my allies and of exotic ceremonies with medicines that would blow my mind and open me to the mysteries that would finally make sense of my life.

Victor described the next exercise, which was known as 'Kicks to the Ego'. We were to line up and place our hands on the shoulders of the person in front of us. We were going to walk forwards and give our full attention to placing our feet in the footsteps of the person in front of us. We would be walking like this for a while and we were asked to listen to the sounds of nature around us as we did so.

Victor's assistant led the line and off we went. We walked like this for a good half an hour and I was amazed how much sharper all my senses became. Even though I was only looking at the footsteps in front of me, I felt I could 'see' nature much more clearly than ever before. It was such a pleasurable feeling that it was easy to maintain focus. I felt that I could have stayed in that state for a long time, but I also knew that 'kicks to the ego' wasn't likely to be focusing on supporting my bliss habit.

As we continued, Victor and his assistant started to speak. 'You all want to jump into the magical world, don't you?' they said. 'You want to climb out of this mundane place and experience the magic of the allies. You want visions, don't you? You want to leave this world behind you and travel to the sorcerer's reality, the second attention. You want to meet Carlos' teachers up there in the branches, don't you? Don Juan and Don Genaro, they're waiting for you up there in the trees.'

They were laughing now and they continued their litany of invitations to leave this world behind and join the sorcerer's world.

As they spoke, the strangest thing started to happen inside me. I could feel their humour and I could feel the sharp edge inside it. I sensed they were playing with something behind my everyday awareness. I began to feel as if I was split in two. Half of me was totally present in the footsteps of the person in front of me. The other half was listening with a growing sense of unease and irritation to the loud voices of these strange men from Mexico.

And then their tack shifted. They told us to slow down and to repeat every statement they made, and then, as we were doing so, to kick the backside of the person in front of us.

'Don't hurt them, but don't tickle them either.'

And so it began, a fluid litany of insults and scorn, which we all repeated while both giving and receiving a sharp kick.

'You are children, lost in fantasies you've read in a book, pathetic little children running away from all your fears. You want to live in a fairy tale. You want to fly and you haven't even learned to walk. Wake up, children! It's time to grow up! Open your eyes and see the illusions you've been spinning.'

My mind went into hyper-drive. *Am I really paying these lunatics to insult me and am I really agreeing to kick the guy in front of me and be kicked by this bastard behind me?*

'You are gutless. You are without courage. You are cowards. You are lazy. You are a bunch of good-for-nothing space cadets who want to run away from your responsibilities as human beings. The Earth is calling to you and all you do is ignore her and run to the stars. Pathetic! Gutless! Cowards!'

My emotions were all over the place. I felt fury, self-pity and astonishment in equal proportions. I wanted to lash out and defend myself. I wanted to justify myself. I wanted to prove to these idiots that while this might be true of some of the people in our line, it wasn't true of me! And on top of all that, I was getting a sore ass.

And then it stopped. Suddenly there was silence again.

I was breathless and my eyes were stinging with thick tears of anger and shame.

Then Victor and his assistant told us to stop moving and to lie down on the grass and listen.

I heard two soundtracks simultaneously. The first was the ongoing and repetitive internal dialogue of self-defence and justification. The second, sweet, strong and ancient as the Earth, was the sound of nature around me. When I gave my attention to that music, I couldn't believe I hadn't heard it before, at least not in this way. The birdsong, the leaves moving in the wind and the sheer harmony of nature around me was overwhelming. My heart was bursting with the joy of feeling so connected and the pain of feeling so disconnected. I saw that it was my choice where I placed my attention.

As I gave my focus more and more to the song of nature around me, I suddenly understood. The Mexicans were right. Despite having received this warning on many occasions, I was still running. I still valued a fantastical other world way more than the everyday world. I wanted as many far-out experiences as possible in order to prove to myself and everyone else that magic was real. And all the time I was seeking them out, I was missing the magic that was singing right under my own two feet. I was blind and deaf to the everyday miracle of life that was happening inside me and all around me.

Victor seemed to recognize what was going on for me and seemingly for many others too.

'Listen to the song of nature,' he said. 'Listen to the cacophony inside your head. And make a choice. This is the power of nature. And she is talking to you. She is calling you to be with her. All this seeking other worlds is to ignore the magnificence of the world around you, the world of your senses. The Earth needs you to listen. You are part of her and she is part of you.'

And so we lay there on the ground, listening. Sometimes I was caught up again in the voices inside my head. They were predictable and repetitive. They were like a wall between me and life, defending and justifying a sense of self that had rather rudely been exposed as an imposter.

And then Victor was talking again. He had blindfolds in his hands.

'Come, friends, it's time to run in the dark.'

As we joined him, he explained that we were going to do an exercise to place this experience firmly in the deeper intelligence of the body.

We were in a large field. He walked us to one side of it, all the time encouraging us to keep our concentration high. His assistant was standing on the other side.

'Each one of you,' Victor told us, 'one at a time, is going to blindfold yourself and stand with me. Two or three of you are going to join my colleague over there and you are going to chant, "Follow the sound of my voice! Follow the sound of my voice!" The one with the blindfold, your task is to orientate yourself towards where that chant is coming from and then look into the darkness in front of you. I want you to imagine the wall of sound that is your internal dialogue like a group of people standing between you and your true nature. I want you to focus on what may be on the other side of that and when I say "Go", I want you to run as fast as you can through that wall, following the sound of that chant. When the chant ends and you hear the word "Stop!" you must stop immediately. Your friends who are waiting for you there will welcome you into the new state of being that begins on the other side of that wall.'

I was both afraid and excited and decided to volunteer to run first. With the blindfold on, orientating my body towards the chanting, I crouched low, like a sprinter on the starting line. Victor had his hand on my lower back, helping me to focus and gain as much courage and power as I could.

'See that wall,' he said, 'and see what's on the other side of it. In between, see those characters, those old ego structures, separating you, giving you false promises about things that only get in the way of what you truly desire. See what you desire on the other side and then run full pelt through that wall.'

I felt supercharged. I don't think I'd ever felt the raw force of such fierce, wild animal power inside me. I knew that I was standing on a precipice of change. If I could find the courage to run through the walls in my mind, I would be making the choice to develop more awareness of the ways in which my mind chatter was separating me from the world around me.

As I crouched there, I felt fear, like electricity, shooting through the soles of my feet. My heart was beating faster and faster and I could hear it pounding in my ears. Then I felt a push in my lower back as Victor yelled, '*Go!*'

All at once I was running in the dark. I could feel the ground under my feet, the soft springy earth holding me. The air was cool on my face. I ran harder than I ever had before. I could see the shadows of my mind in front of me. They were shaped like wraiths, and as I ran through them, I saw a beautifully carved wooden door. The chant of my companions guided me to it, and as I ran straight through it, I felt a jolt of energy, like lightning, flash through me. Lightning again. I'd felt that twice before.

When I was 11 years old, the rabbi in my community, a wise and kind man called Michael Alony, had encouraged me to take on my ancestral heritage. I'd been born into the tribe of high priests. On the high holy days, the high priests have a ritual to perform as they offer themselves as channels for the Creator's blessing for the community. As a younger child, I'd loved watching this ancient theatre (even though I wasn't supposed to) as the men ascended the steps in front of the ark, placed their prayer shawls over their heads and waited to be called into service. Now the rabbi wanted me to do the same. He wouldn't accept the excuse that as a young boy, my mind was far from holy. And so I acquiesced to his request, even though my father, uncle and grandfather didn't.

I remember how nervous I was in the synagogue as the time for the ritual approached. I wanted to hide, but I'd made my promise to the rabbi. There was only two of us, me and an old man. We had our hands washed for us and then ascended the marble steps of the ark, turned our backs on the congregation and placed our prayer shawls over our heads. I'd memorized the prayer in Hebrew that we were to say once we were called to turn around with our hands spread and our arms stretched out under our prayer shawls towards the congregation.

As the call came from the chazzan, the singer who was leading the service, something inside me just took over. My body turned, seemingly of its own accord, and the words came out of my mouth as if someone else was singing them. And then a bolt of energy hit me through the top of my head. I felt as if I'd been lit up and slammed into the ground at the same time. Momentarily, I felt huge. I saw a bright light behind my closed eyes and I felt a force of love coming through me that was totally overwhelming. I could have collapsed, but instead I felt strangely held.

Once it was over, I returned to my seat, shaking and shocked. The rabbi smiled at me and I knew something in me had changed forever.

The second time I was hit by lightning, it was a physical reality. I was 22 years old and playing golf with a friend on a municipal golf course in East London, where I was living. At some point we saw an early summer storm coming. Without thinking, I got out my metal-tipped golf umbrella, put it up and stood holding it. My friend joined me under it.

The rain came down and the thunder rumbled. The next thing I knew, my friend had been thrown away from me and was on the ground a few feet away. And I felt exactly the same feeling I'd felt as a boy doing my first priestly blessing. I was electrified and my heart felt as if it was shining out like a lighthouse across the darkened golf course.

I realized with a shock that the metal tip of the umbrella had been hit by lightning and that it had passed right through me. I was shaking, yet strangely elated. I checked myself for burns, but the reality was that I felt fantastic and strong. I'd been given a gift. I'd survived a lightning strike. Death had paid me a visit and left his calling card.

Afterwards, as many people who have had a close encounter with death will testify, the simple things in life seemed that much more important. I also had a sense of urgency. I recognized, in a way that was equally frightening and thrilling, that death could come at any moment.

There are moments in life when the constant tick-tock of time passing in an orderly fashion dissolves momentarily, to be replaced by a much more circular and multi-layered sense of time. Those last seconds of running in the dark were like that.

After bursting through the door, I ran towards the voices of my companions. They were calling me to them, but time warped and shifted on its axis and I found myself in one of those moments where everything around me was moving very fast but I seemed to be entirely still. In everyday reality, I didn't have more than a second or two at most left to run, and yet in the world I was in, darkness had been replaced by a hazy brightness. It was as if my eyes had been closed and now they were open.

I could see a group of people from different ethnic backgrounds and cultures and they were welcoming me. I saw their faces, and though I didn't know them, I recognized them instantly. Some of the elders from the Portuguese dream were there. My own ancestors were there. And a group of other beings, some human and some more animal, and I knew them as my allies. The warmth and support I felt from them all was tangible and moved me deeply. I wanted to stop right there and be with them, to talk with them, to know them. I could also see the Earth beneath me and she was alive and conscious. I wanted to lay my heart next to hers and let go.

But the moment dissolved as quickly as it had formed. I heard the voices of my companions in the 'real' world shouting 'Stop!' and I knew I'd reached the end.

Time rushed back in and I was suddenly being welcomed by my incarnate companions with strong hands and pats on the back. My eyes were crying, partly from the sudden rush of sunlight when the blindfold was removed and partly from the intense emotions of the moment. I was back in the physical world, but a part of me wanted to step back into that hazy bright world I'd visited for a moment. I felt sad and yet elated too. I knew with absolute certainty that I was home. I didn't have to go anywhere. My allies and my ancestors were with me. The Earth was alive beneath me. Most importantly, I'd made a choice.

Castaneda's stories described a life lived with a sole purpose: to die consciously and bring one's awareness intact into the next great adventure beyond the gates of death. I have great admiration for the discipline, art and sheer crazy wisdom displayed so dramatically by his teachers Don Juan and Don Genaro. The truth they shared rang like an ancient bell inside me: sorcery invites us to leave the ordinary world behind.

Conversely, all the shamans I knew were family people who engaged with the day-to-day world. Gabrielle was very supportive of the family path and of the part of Susannah and me that wished to become parents. She was very clear. If we wanted to engage deeply in spiritual practice, becoming parents was going to offer the best ground she knew for checking out just how real our realizations on the dance floor were. Having a child, she assured us, would be like inviting a Zen master to come and live in our house.

I sat down quietly. All that I had seen still felt present around me and I spoke to my ancestors, my allies and my guides. I told them in a whisper that I wished to know them more. I told them that I felt inspired by the strength and dignity I'd seen within them and I hoped to do them proud. And I told them about the choice I'd made.

In that darkness I'd run through, I'd caught sight of a child. Maybe I'd seen our future child. I'd definitely known that mine was the path of family, of relationship, of finding the way to live from this new awareness and direct experience of the Earth as a living being. I'd fallen in love with life and I felt such a desire to honour and protect what I loved.

It was clear to me that I needed to let the sorcerer's world go. I wasn't on the sorcerer's path. I was on the shaman's path and I'd just run at full speed through the shaman's door.

⟨✦⟩

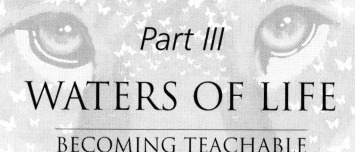

Part III

WATERS OF LIFE

BECOMING TEACHABLE

'The unteachable man is sentenced to being taught only by experience. The tragedy is he reaches nothing further than his own pain.'

CRISS JAMI, *KILLOSOPHY*

In those early days of study Batty said to me, 'It takes a very long time to become teachable.' I had no idea what he was talking about. In my own eyes, I was a model apprentice. I was dedicated, disciplined and always gave everything I had to whatever was happening. How could I not be teachable? What did Batty mean?

I had huge respect for my teachers. As a young man, I saw them as exotic road warriors. They appeared to have everything they needed, had a great sense of humour, were content in themselves and had reached a place of relative enlightenment. I remember Batty saying to us one afternoon, in his thick Austrian accent, 'Well, I travel the world, meet beautiful people, get well paid for doing what I love to do and the whole thing is one great adventure in spirit. Not a bad dream, eh?'

Not a bad dream indeed. At that time, I was awestruck by the possibility that life might have that depth of meaning and satisfaction. And I recognized how very far away from that I was.

Putting people up on pedestals and bringing them back down again seems to be one of the ways I learn. It's a messy business. It took me two decades of study and a lot of disappointments finally to land on my own two feet sufficiently to be able to stop playing the pedestal game. I had to learn that becoming teachable meant knowing who I was and standing firmly in my own ground, whilst at the same time remaining open to what life was offering me. It meant being willing to look my own unconscious behaviour in the face and take responsibility for my life. It meant recognizing that the more powerful I became, the more important it would be to have elders, guides and mentors who could provide me with accurate mirrors. Blind spots by their very nature are impossible for us to see for ourselves. Being teachable meant developing the capacity to take on feedback from those elders without feeling shamed or humiliated. That was what Batty was talking about.

In Western culture, we love to put our heroes and heroines up and then bring them down. That's why, when it comes to spiritual practice of any kind, it's so important to recognize what stage of relationship we are in with our teachers, and also why a strong teacher needs to be aware of the archetypal developmental stages that both they and their apprentices will journey through.

We bring our past experience with us into all our relationships, and our experience with power, authority and responsibility will probably be reflected in the journey we go through with our teachers. If we stay long enough and do our work, we'll arrive at the realization that, just like us, they are human. We'll acknowledge that they are further down the road than we are in the area of their expertise. And we'll be able to give them the appropriate respect. And then, as our journey develops and we make the choices to do whatever is necessary to stand at the centre of our own circles, we'll release them from the fantasy of perfection and see them as they are, both brilliant and flawed.

This is the beauty of being human. It's not our faults or blind spots that are the problem. It's the illusion that has us believing that we no longer have them and that we're over the need for guidance and supervision. The more powerful we become, the more important it is to make sure we're not surrounding ourselves with 'yes' people. Instead, we need people around us who aren't dependent on our goodwill and are willing to challenge us and keep us real.

I began my shamanic journey young. I was emotionally very immature. I needed the attention of my teachers and I did what I could to get it. Gabrielle taught through acknowledging the 'real me' and ignoring the 'false me'. It was tough to be around, but ultimately fruitful. As our relationship developed and I matured, I gained the capacity to witness my own behaviour and make different choices.

I was apprenticed to Gabrielle for 18 years and we shared many adventures over that time. She taught me to give everything in the dance, to let go completely and to surrender to the beat. She taught me to enjoy good food and wine. Susannah and I shared some hilarious and magical times with her in the coffee shops of Amsterdam, in the good restaurants she frequented in New York and on the many dance floors we shared. She was a beautiful and generous friend to our son and called herself his 'sha-mama'. She introduced me to the creativity and brilliance of the embodied soul and I will forever remain grateful for the life she lived and the beauty she shared. There were areas where the quality of genius shone through her. And, like all of us, there were others where it didn't and she remained blind to her own blindness.

For many years, 'power' was a dirty word for me. I made the mistake of thinking that because power had been so abused throughout the millennia of our human story, power itself was the problem. I had to learn that without access to my personal power, it would be impossible to make an effective contribution in this world. There came a time when I realized that I needed to put my relationship with power in the washing machine and give it a damn good clean.

~

Our dear elders and friends, Jake and Eva Chapman, taught us that self-awareness was the key to a responsible use of power, and that the quickest way to self-awareness was direct experience. In the spring of 1990 in a hotel room in Hampstead in London, I had one of these direct experiences in a spontaneous shamanic journey.

Susannah and I had been out to eat with Gabrielle and as we were all staying in the same hotel we decided to go back to our room for tea and to continue our conversation. Pleasantly softened up by the 1997 Valpolicella Amarone we'd been drinking, we all sat on the large bed in our room talking about what being a shaman meant in the modern world. Gabrielle had often told me I was a shaman. She used to call me and her son her 'baby shamans'. I didn't like the term very much, but nevertheless, being acknowledged in this way by my teacher was meaningful to me.

At one point in the conversation, she turned directly towards me and looked at me with her piercing eyes.

'What is it you want from me?' she asked.

'I want to share my experience of the shaman's world with you and know what it is for you.'

She didn't say anything, but her response was evident in the way she kept her gaze steady, and I realized that this was the moment. It was right now. Not tomorrow. Not at some future-maybe-time, but right now. The door opened. I remember that split second of decision-making. If I'd looked away, the moment would have passed.

Fear was present, as it always is when the door opens. I remember Don Juan saying to Carlos Castaneda, 'When the door to freedom finally opens and you look through it, you see the unknown … and the unknown just stares right back at you. Very few choose to walk through that door.'

The part of me that was afraid to enter tried to assert itself, but I'd already made my choice. I returned Gabrielle's gaze and fell into her shaman's eyes.

Susannah tells me that we were gone for more than an hour. She held the space beautifully for us, sitting in deep meditation, a fierce guardian for us as we travelled.

I'm falling backwards through time. I see a kaleidoscope of images of our recent human history. I see symbols of our collective wounding. I'm shown how the shamanic lineages that were once so strong have been torn down, cut to shreds and burned at the stake of dogma and superstition. And in this process, paths laid down by generations upon generations have almost entirely disappeared.

I see the damage this carnage has wrought upon the Earth, upon the plant, mineral and animal kingdoms. I see how for generations, as a species, the dominant mechanistic story we have been telling has led us to attack those who understand the delicate balance that we are part of. We have learned to ridicule the shamans, the medicine people, the witches and the midwives for their unscientific ways. We have waged war on the indigenous peoples of the Earth, those who know about the cycles of life, the plants, the importance of honouring the dead. And we still are.

We have created a world where power and wealth are concentrated in the hands of the few and we are taught the art of being distracted and disconnected from what matters most to us. We have created a world where our idea of intelligence is very limited.

And this all creates a deep lack of confidence in the very roots of our being. We suffer from a collective disease called 'not enough'. I am not enough. You are not enough. However much I have, I don't have enough.

All of this I see and hear and sense in my own experience. And it doesn't stop there.

I continue to fall backwards through the tumult and chaos of our human story on Earth. I witness wars, so many wars. I see genocides beyond comprehension and a baffling array of cultures and costumes.

Gabrielle's face is changing and I stay steady and with her as mask after mask of being appears and dissolves into yet more times and places I've never known. And yet each place feels like a memory. I see children playing by the river, women giving birth and warriors fighting and dying on so many blood-soaked battlefields.

Eventually, we reach a beginning of sorts and there we rest for a while. At the edge of the forest, as humankind first looks out over the open plains, I see our people, dancing, drumming, speaking to the spirits through the heart and power of the dance.

Eventually we arrive in the place that Gabrielle calls 'the silver desert'. In that empty space, everything is present. All possibilities swim before our eyes like the threads of the billions upon billions of stories yet to be told. In this place, we are beyond individual form, and silence hums with the potency of life itself. We are here, home again, at the beginning and at the end, here in this mysterious shining darkness, and here is where we stay. There is a feeling that is beyond bliss, quieter than silence and vaster than the night sky. There are no words, but there are tears of recognition. It's as if we have been here always, and at the same time there is a recognition that we will never return. I hear the words 'original essence' and then, as suddenly as when we left, we are back.

We are speechless. There is nothing to say.

I'm so grateful. I've seen something of the roots of shamanism, and for the first time since I was a child falling into the mystery every night, I am whole. I have returned. My backbone feels stronger. For a few moments, certain that I will never forget again, I remember who I am.

When we returned to the room, Susannah welcomed us quietly. I tried to put into words what I'd experienced, but it was pointless. My everyday language was useless for describing it. But I felt a newborn urgency to get down to work and later I wrote:

If I want to become teachable and find my own road to liberation, I need to find out what turns me on… Without the willingness to make mistakes, I will never be able to live from who I truly am, I will never change and I will perish in the wastelands of a soulless world.

Understanding that a shaman was a messenger for the voices of the natural world and the spirit world overwhelmed me with a terrible sense of responsibility.

Gabrielle looked at me and said, 'Now you know why being a shaman is known as a blessed curse.'

I carry the medicine of that journey with me to this day.

Chapter 11

REBIRTH

'There can be no rebirth without a dark night
of the soul, a total annihilation of all that you
believed in and thought that you were.'

HAZRAT INAYAT KHAN

My work with Victor had laid the choice between sorcery and shamanism in front of me. And I had made my choice. Both Gabrielle and Victor were clear that the purpose of their work was to support their students to live as creatively and as powerfully as possible in the world. And I had chosen them as my teachers.

I embraced a new level of discipline in my work with Victor. For me, there's nothing more satisfying than throwing myself totally into any creative endeavour that comes from the heart. I now began to apply this to my shamanic journey.

At the same time, the door to becoming a father had well and truly opened inside me. I was amazed. I'd always thought that it wouldn't. My awareness of the crisis that we as a species were in had always laid a dark cloud over that part of me that more than anything wished to father a child with Susannah. But when the spirit called, it was a choice-less choice to answer.

It was the autumn of 1990 and we were in another gathering with Gabrielle in London. We were due to be teaching ourselves over the same weekend, so we could only attend on the Friday evening. After the dance, Gabrielle led us into what she called 'trespasso meditation'. It was simple. It involved sitting opposite a partner and softly gazing from your own left eye into the left eye of your partner. Susannah and I ended up sitting opposite each other.

As I settled into Susannah's eyes, a doorway opened at the top of my head. My spirit moved up and out through that doorway and I found myself looking down at our bodies. My mind was quiet. And in that silence, I suddenly knew without doubt that Susannah was pregnant. I was astounded by how delighted I was by this knowledge. At the same time, I was certain that Susannah would be freaked out.

We discovered later that Susannah was having almost exactly the same experience, her own knowledge coming from the sound of heavenly bells ringing. Looking into my eyes, she had become certain that she was pregnant. She was secretly overjoyed about it and certain that I would be freaked out!

Neither of us mentioned this to the other until the next day. We were in a venue just outside London, preparing for our workshop, and were sitting under two huge cedar trees. It was late afternoon and we were talking about how to begin. I don't remember if it was Susannah or me who brought up our experiences of the evening before, but all of a sudden, we were acknowledging that both of us thought Susannah was pregnant. We both admitted we were certain the other would be freaked out by this news. But neither of us was. In fact, no sooner had we shared our experience than we both fell into a kind of trance. It was if our eyes opened for the first time and we could see each other in a new light. We were in a state of love that was beyond the two of us as the sun set between those two magnificent cedars. We were convinced that we were about to become parents. And we were ecstatic about it.

In fact it turned out that Susannah wasn't pregnant, but there came a moment in her next cycle when we both consciously opened the door to the spirit of the child we both felt we had already said yes to. Susannah said out loud, 'If you want to come in, baby spirit, now is the time and there may not be another.' The gate opened and in came Reuben, our son, who, as Gabrielle had rightly predicted, became our new live-in be-here-now Zen master.

I was both overjoyed and scared by the thought of becoming a father. My relationship with my own dad was still fractious. He had already cut me out of his will when Susannah and I decided to marry. He remained deeply concerned about how I was going to survive doing work that he didn't understand. And I was concerned about how much I would repeat the stresses and tensions I'd experienced growing up. I wanted to change the story, but I knew it was going to be a challenge.

The nine months of Susannah's pregnancy were quite an emotional ride for me. It was a cocktail of total excitement blended with a whole host of stressful questions. How would we survive? Would I be a good enough father? Would we still manage to follow the path we were on or would I have to get a 'proper' job in order to provide?

Reuben's birth remains the deepest ceremony I have ever been part of. Susannah's labour went on all night. She was magnificent. Our midwife was an angel and we were beautifully supported by our good friends David and Julie. The moment I held our son for the first time and he looked into my eyes was one of those shining pearl moments that will stay with me forever.

I was to discover that children bring their own fortune with them. And as our young son grew, so did the success of our work. As each day unfolded, I fell more and more in love with the beauty, strength and innocence of this everyday blessing called family.

I was working hard, setting the wheels in motion for our work, and as a young family, we travelled everywhere together in those early years. We taught with Reuben in a sling strapped to either one of us and we danced ourselves around Europe and the USA teaching and just about making a living from our work. When Reuben got too big to carry round all day and wanted to explore more, he made a beeline for one of our participants. Malcolm loved kids and was happy to take him out and play. And that's how he got the job and became part of our travelling band. We were on the road a lot, carrying everything in a good solid Volvo. Those were special times – lots of adventures, lots of laughter and the little miracle of being in a relatively well-functioning family.

At the same time, not everything was rosy. As those of you who are parents will know, parenting isn't all a joyride. And being a father brought out the worst as well as the best in me. There were moments when my emotional responses were so strong that I was unable to disentangle myself from them and witness them. Once fully identified with a feeling, perspective is limited to say the least. I found myself as irritable and unpredictable at times as my own father had been with my sisters and me. Susannah and I occasionally had blazing rows born of deep misunderstandings on both our parts, and our son was sometimes caught in the crossfire.

I have compassion for it now and can even laugh at some of those early parental memories. But the stress of being young parents and being young in our work, coupled with the ongoing need to pay the monthly bills and a lot of travel, made for some challenging times.

In fairness, the amount of laughter and play and love-filled moments in our household more than balanced out the moments of suffering. Right from the first moment I laid eyes on our son as he came into this world, the love I felt for him and his mama was the most powerful feeling I'd ever experienced. In contrast, the moments of losing the love and being overwhelmed by life that were part of our everyday experience of being parents were deeply upsetting.

I could see that the pain I was causing was an import from my own past and generations past. It was deeply rooted in both my own childhood and in the stories that came from the undigested experiences of my family line. I was never physically violent with either my wife or our son, but I kept finding myself being triggered by deep and unconscious feelings. I could see that I needed to get to the roots of these old emotions. I wanted to be free of the unconscious patterns that kept taking over my day-to-day actions. I wanted to be a better husband and a better father. I was 28 years old.

⸻

I was aware that my survival fears were more than simple present-day fears. I saw in my dreams that they were deeply rooted in being the great-grandson of refugees. I felt a growing urgency to do something to try and free myself from the weight of the past. I needed a way to heal this trigger-happy papa who was so full of love and responsibility and so apparently unable to handle the deep feelings that would arise over the slightest kitchen spillage or teabag left in the sink.

As is often the case, come the need, come the medicine. Victor had begun to talk about his new distance-learning course called 'The Art of Living Purposefully'. I signed up on the spot. Its purpose was to free ourselves from the learned habits of the past that no longer served us and, more importantly, wasted so much of our precious life energy. The most intensive of these ritualized processes was to be the recapitulation.

The recapitulation was the central practice of the Toltecs. The ancients saw that most of our available life energy was taken up in presenting our idea of ourselves to the world, rather like playing a character in an ongoing soap opera. We repeated the same mistakes again and again, as if the script we were living was cast in iron and we had no choice but to follow the inevitable expectations of this character to their bitter conclusion. We needed to change the dream, but the effort was doomed to fail since we lacked the spare energy.

They also knew that a source of high-octane energy was available to us in the undigested and unhealed experiences of the past, and they had a technique for accessing it: the recapitulation.

Each story that keeps repeating itself in our life has a root experience behind it. The ancients called this experience an 'energetic command'. It often takes place in childhood. Faced with shock or trauma, children have a massive capacity to survive. They do this by separating from the experience in order to protect themselves from the full impact of what may be happening to them. The result of this is that what Susannah and I have come to call the 'self's protective adaptive survival mechanism' (or spasm) kicks in and the trauma is locked away in much the same way as the body deals with physical trauma: it is frozen in the body. Each frozen experience is life energy that is no longer available to us.

The purpose of recapitulation is to gain access to each frozen experience, bring our present-day consciousness to it and change our relationship to the memory it holds. This releases the energy that has previously been used to keep the memory frozen.

The ancients did the recapitulation process in a cave. However, due to the lack of both available caves and South American warmth in northern Europe, we were instructed to construct a recapitulation box. The box was to be just large enough to sit in and was to be covered with black cloth on the inside so as to be completely dark once we got in.

At that time, Susannah and I had just bought our first home – a ground-floor flat on the outskirts of Totnes that happened to have a cellar. We had converted the cellar into a sauna room, and since it was below ground and mostly soundproofed, I thought it would be the perfect place to carry out my recapitulation.

Victor gave us precise instructions. We were to write a list of all the people with whom there'd been any significant exchange of energy in our lives, starting in the present and working all the way back to our parents. Next to each person, we were then to write down, in a bullet-point fashion, the nature of those events. This would leave us with a list of approximately 4,000 events. We were then to make time every day, or during the night if necessary, to sit in our recapitulation box and breathe through these events one by one using specific breathing techniques.

In the decades that followed, I refined the system that I'd been given to make it more effective in the modern world. I called it the SEER process (systemic essential energy retrieval) and it is described in my first book, co-authored with Susannah, *Movement Medicine: How to Awaken, Dance and Live Your Dreams* (Hay House, 2009).

In my own recapitulation, I spent between three and six hours a day in that box. I went on doing our admin, being a papa and teaching too. When I was working during the day, I did the recapitulation at night. When I was away from home, I sat in darkened hotel rooms with a blanket over my head to cut out the city lights and continued.

We had no source of income apart from our teaching, but Susannah saw the need for me to do this work and she literally held the baby whilst I did my work in the office and in the cellar. Even though we were on a low income, we'd decided we didn't want to receive any support from the state. We thought this was the best way to affirm our capacity to be self-sustaining.

I'd never been so determined or met so much resistance in my life. Every time I climbed down those wooden steps into the cellar to begin, I had that familiar feeling, *Uh-oh, Mikk, you've finally gone and lost the plot. Have you really got nothing better to do than sit in a black box and recapitulate the fine details of your personal history? Aren't you taking yourself just a little too seriously? Isn't this all just a tad selfish?*

But nevertheless, with Susannah's support, I went down those steps and into that box. And day after day, I went through my list. It was thoroughly boring at times and super-painful at others. And every now and again, a jewel would appear like a shining turquoise gem as I sifted through the sands of the past.

I was getting a deep insight into the themes of my life. As I recapitulated my relationship history, I was astonished to see the same stories repeating themselves – different times, different people, same stories. There I am feeling betrayed again. There I am playing the victim, and wow, what drama I can create! I witnessed myself choosing to faint several times as a young teenager when I was emotionally overwhelmed by a situation. I did it on a train to school, at parties, even in a small forest in Ibiza when my then girlfriend went off with another guy. To see myself with such naked clarity was embarrassing, challenging and sometimes really touching. In the Ibizan forest, I was found on the ground by a good friend, picked up and carried back to the hotel. But then my girlfriend showed up and I whispered in my 'oh so dramatic lost boy voice', 'See what you've done to me.' Oh dear!

I witnessed the hundreds of times I'd felt overwhelmed and lost and been unable to communicate clearly. I saw how the stories I had about who I was and what I could expect were remarkably self-fulfilling.

I witnessed my personal, familial and cultural wounds. I recapitulated the time my father caught me stealing and beat me and how in response I closed my heart to him. I recapitulated the time when my mother told me how my father had wept as he read the letter telling him that Susannah and I were getting married. I saw that he felt he'd failed in his duty to pass on the traditions of his forefathers. In some ways, maybe he even felt that he'd failed as a father. I felt such love for him then. I recapitulated the time when he called me on the day before my wedding to ask me not to marry Susannah. How painful it was to hear him in such distress and to know there was nothing I could do. And at the same time, I began to discover a certain compassion for the young man I'd been, and for the child, and for the father and husband I'd become.

I saw clearly that my experiences had created a deep separation from the ground of the body and through that a loss of connection with the Earth herself. I saw with sadness how these patterns repeated themselves in every area of my life and I saw the roots of my own disempowerment.

I began to recognize that the patterns I kept on repeating all had their roots in early experiences. Events such as a Caesarean birth or the trauma of ritual circumcision had set a default mode in me. This original setting had led to event after event that would simply confirm the underlying mistrust of life, and particularly human beings, that I had carried inside me for so long.

It became clear that each misfortune that I'd encountered along the road was a repetition of an earlier event, and as I kept mining through the rubble, occasionally I would find one of those 'energetic commands' appearing like a crushed diamond in the coal face. When I found a 'root event', it was like hitting the jackpot. One day, I found a young boy who was so in touch with spirits. Like everything that lives, he just wanted to be recognized in the magic, innocence and power of his soul.

Day by day and night by night, I continued. And day by day and night by night, the clarity of my focus intensified and I found more and more willingness to face the difficult truths about myself.

I witnessed the martyr in me, and the addict who could never get enough of anything. I saw how I wasted my energy by trying to gain kudos with people by sharing some amazing shamanic experience that I'd had. And most of all, I saw how much fear there was in me. I was afraid to really show up. I was afraid of doing my creative work for fear of it being judged unworthy. I was afraid of my power. And I was afraid that I wouldn't live up to my own very high expectations of myself.

I kept seeing the present through the filter of the past and acting accordingly. Often, I wasn't actually present at all, but acting my part in a movie with only one predictable outcome.

It was painful work, but step by step, the effectiveness of the recapitulation gave me the strength to step further into my past and change my relationship to it. Giving back what didn't belong to me and retrieving the life-force that had been locked in those stories enabled me to recognize that when those triggers were activated, I had a choice about whether I identified with them or not.

Slowly, my family and I began to experience the harvest of my work. My dreaming became increasingly lucid. I had more and more energy available for my wife and son and our work. I felt as if the work I was doing in that black box was giving me the millisecond of awareness it takes to avoid going into an old story. Just as my hand reached out to press the 'play' button on that old movie in which I'd starred countless times, a quiet voice inside me began to whisper the magic words, 'Choice, Mikk. Choice.'

I began to listen, and often (though not always) I was able to step back, take a breath, see another possibility and choose to change.

I was determined to let my past become my medicine rather than my excuse. But for a time, I found being with people excruciating. Everything that came out of my mouth seemed the voice or opinion of some imposter or other. As much as I was gaining energy, I had lost my old ground, and the new road was still under construction. I'd left the known and, like my refugee ancestors, I was a stranger in a new landscape. Learning to stay steady in the unknown is very much part of the initiatory journey, and it can be tough to do so. Only the love I had for my wife and our son and the love I received from them both kept me going.

Step by step, and story by story, I moved on. My recapitulation took me nine months, but eventually I reached the end of my list. I had finished. In my square, dark womb under the ground, with the support of those who loved me most, I had been reborn.

Chapter 12

AN AMAZONIAN DREAM INITIATION

'Yes: I am a dreamer. For a dreamer is one who can only find his way by moonlight, and his punishment is that he sees the dawn before the rest of the world.'

OSCAR WILDE

Through my recapitulation, I felt lighter, more focused and full of energy. I knew myself so much better and I'd seen the roots of the behaviour I wished to change. The next step on Victor's course, which I began immediately after my recapitulation, was to make an inventory of my energy expenditure.

The purpose of this enquiry was to learn how I used my energy every day and particularly to find out about the activities that wasted energy and those that enhanced it. Saving energy was one of the principal tools in becoming a 'warrior of the spirit', and even though I wasn't exactly sure what being a warrior of the spirit entailed, it sounded good to me.

So, every 20 minutes during the day and once an hour during the night, I was to stop whatever I was doing and write down the answers to three questions:

1. What am I doing?
2. What am I thinking?
3. What am I feeling?

I was to do this for one month. I spent that month carrying my notebook and timer everywhere. Susannah had to do all the driving. My nights were broken and my dreams were full of crazy repetitions as I witnessed all the ways in which I was wasting my precious life energy.

I loved the attention to detail that was Victor's trademark. The energy-wasting acts had to be placed in three categories: those easy to stop, those difficult to stop and those really hard to stop, such as longstanding addictions.

We weren't expected to go from average energy-wasting humans to being impeccable warriors overnight. In fact, we were warned that trying to go too fast would more than likely lead to failure and the abandonment of the challenge we had taken on.

After taking this inventory, as instructed, I went to a special place I often went to on Dartmoor in order to 'make an offering to power'. I had to spend the day in ritual in the company of the wisdom and guidance of nature. Once I'd seen the major ways in which I was regularly wasting energy, I had to make a commitment to life and to the Great Spirit to use my energy more purposefully. The underlying intention was to live an impeccable life dedicated to spirit.

With the help of the fire and my copious notes, I reviewed my daily usage of energy and compiled a list of 21 energy-wasting acts. These ranged from 'arrogance and boasting about my achievements' to 'not saying no when I need to' and 'an apparent need always to win, no matter what the game'.

The realization that so much of my life energy was wasted in trying to project an idea of myself into the world that didn't serve me or anyone was a stinging wake-up call. At the same time, I felt uplifted and focused. I worked hard. I poured out my heart to the river, to the trees and the rocks, asking for the courage to change and the strength to be who I was and to live a good life.

There were also moments when all I could do was laugh. Was my whole life just a piece of theatre? At other times, I felt deeply connected to the landscape and felt that my prayers were being witnessed by the nature all around me. And in that place, I made my commitment to be conscious of those energy-wasting acts and, where possible, make a choice to stop them.

The art of 'not doing' meant choosing to stop an energy-wasting act or even do the opposite. For instance, I challenged my apparent need always to win by finding a squash partner who was a better player than me. And I discovered that there really was more joy in giving everything in a game than in the tension of having to win.

⟨ ⟩

Looking back, I feel so much love for that sincere and dedicated young man who was giving everything he had as a father, a husband, a teacher and a student. He was disciplined, single-minded and intent on integrating all that he was learning into all aspects of his life. He was so passionate. And so impatient – another energy-wasting act!

As I see him from here, I recognize that some of the habits I spotted then are still present in my life. But there is a difference. At that time, I was at war with myself, with my habits and with my ego structures. These days, I have far more compassion for the ways in which I don't live up to the expectations of my own ego. The thing that has changed most is that most of the time I live in the acceptance of my own imperfections. I'm not complacent, just kinder. And, counter-intuitively, this relaxation allows for more focus, clearer choices and far less wastage of energy. Naturally, this has changed the way I am in relationship to others too. I've discovered a deep river of patience and an even deeper ground of trust in the process of life.

Gabrielle was clear that the ego would do anything to get attention and that if she had to acknowledge it at all, she would do the two things it hated most: 1) expose it; and 2) laugh at it. In her workshops, we would put our ego characters on stage and she would direct the shadow play. We gave our ego characters names, dressed them up and 'confessed'

135

them. In one piece of ritual theatre, a character of mine that I named Billy Busy skydived whilst doing his administration. He fell through the air at terminal velocity, making plans for his future success and entirely missing the moment.

Creative and funny as this method was, exposing the crazy patterns of our own egos in such a public way often had the effect for me of creating a backlash of shame. In order to step out of these destructive habits, I knew that I needed to go further.

Victor encouraged us to adopt a clear strategy when dealing with the patterns and repetitions of the ego. It was a relief to be able to engage my thinking mind and see what the back stories were behind these ego characters.

This robust approach was making a difference that my family and friends could feel. The ancient Qabalists talked about the body, heart and mind as being the three strands of the candle which, when woven together, ignited the light of the soul. Take one of them away and the soul was absent. With Victor, I'd found a missing thread.

Added to this, the importance he placed on being directly in touch with the powers of nature gave a whole added raft of support to this chapter of my journey. We went from ceremony to day-to-day strategy-led action and back to ceremony and so on.

⁓

Once we'd made our commitments to suspend the easier of our energy-wasting acts and replace them with energy-enhancing acts, we were provided with the next ritual in order to be able to take the next steps and suspend the harder-to-stop actions. We were asked to get up before dawn every day for a week and climb a hill to a place where we would be able to see the sun rising.

Arriving before sunrise and facing the east, concentrating on the feeling of connection with the Earth as dawn came and the sun became visible over the eastern horizon, we had to trot easily on the spot. As we warmed up and the sun rose more, we were instructed to raise our arms to the sky. As the sun rose higher and higher, we were asked to speak from the heart to the sun. If it was cloudy, we were told to begin to trot and trust the timing we felt in our body. We were to refer to the sun as 'father' and, speaking out loud, make our ongoing commitment to cease energy-wasting acts and replace them with energy-enhancing ones.

The purpose of this ritual was to align our intention with the great light of Father Sun and to connect the fire of purpose in our heart to the heat, light and divine energy of the sun. Victor often talked about us being children of Mother Earth and Father Sun. And rituals like these made this more and more tangible.

Hilariously, and somewhat typically for the intensity junky in me, I misread this instruction and set about doing this ritual every morning for a month rather than a week! Off I went, each and every morning, up onto the hill to 'run to the sun'. It was a new feeling to enter into this direct and personal relationship with the immanent face of the divine on Earth. As the sun rose, I would increase the intensity of my trotting, reaching peak intensity as the sun became fully visible above the horizon. At that exact moment, arching my body like a bow, as instructed, I would send an arrow of intention from my heart directly into the heart of the sun with a powerful yell.

On some mornings I took our four-year-old son up the hill with me and we did this together. To him, it was a fun early-morning adventure and it was a wonderful game to shout as loud as we could and imagine ourselves sending our love like arrows into the heart of the sun.

I felt strengthened by this dynamic way of expressing my intention every day. And I was getting some positive results. I found myself hearing that quiet voice inside me just as I was about to launch into an irritable reaction or boastful comment. I would then take a moment to feel the ground under my feet and the warmth of the sun in my heart. This reminded me of the choice I had and the commitments I had made, and more and more often I would acknowledge that voice and make a different choice. The powerful blend of this daily practice and the recapitulation was giving me new ground and supporting me in the art of living purposefully. I was beginning to get the whole warrior thing.

⟡

Next Victor invited us to ask ourselves the following questions each night as we were going to sleep:

1.   What marvellous act could I carry out in keeping with my father the sun and my mother the Earth for all that they have given me?

2.   With what true and simple act could I do something for my fellow human beings?

3.   What generous act would fill my heart with joy?

I was delighted by these questions. They were so spacious, and implicit inside them was the empowering acknowledgement that we all have something of great value to give.

We were encouraged not to analyse our answers or become obsessed with them, but to trust that they would come in dreams. And they did.

Dreaming has always been both an important refuge and a place of deep learning for me. For as long as I can remember, some of my dreams have had an oracular quality, revealing what has been hidden and illuminating the way forwards. Over the years, I've come to trust these dreams. They provide guidance that I've learned it's always in my best interests to follow.

After a month of sunrise rituals and dream intentions, I had one of these dreams. It was the early spring of 1995. For days, I'd felt that I was warming up for a major night-time adventure, and sure enough, it arrived.

I dreamed I was flying over the Amazon rainforest. It spanned out in every direction as far as my eyes could see. I was both excited and awed by its power.

I had no connection to the Amazon other than watching colourful TV documentaries about it. So I asked the dream, 'Why am I here?'

Immediately, I saw a very old hand emerging through the top of the canopy. It could have been a man's or a woman's. The bony fingers curled and beckoned me into the forest. I flew down, curious and afraid.

I landed in a clearing with some round primitive houses with thatched roofs by the side of a winding river. There were hummingbirds everywhere. I heard chanting coming from one of the houses.

That sound, combined with the music of the forest and the force of life I felt in the Earth beneath my feet, made the place electric and I found myself filled with nervous anticipation. At some point I'd realized that I was dreaming and the dream now had my full attention.

I heard my name being called from one of the huts. I went in.

I was astonished to see some of the elders from the repeating dream I'd had all those years before in Portugal. They were sitting in a circle and I was told to join them. There was also an indigenous shaman there who had some kind of leaf rattle and a plastic bottle with some brown medicine in it. He gave me a small gourd full of the stuff and indicated that I should drink it. I did. It was very bitter and strong.

I sat and listened to the old shaman singing, but within a few minutes, I started to feel nauseous. I tried to control the feeling or make it stop, but I couldn't. I was scared and looked to the shaman for help. He continued to sing and wave his leaf rattle, and then the visions started.

It was like being inside a kaleidoscope – everything was shifting colours and forms. A vast array of animals was appearing and dissolving. I was very disorientated. I still knew I was dreaming, but I wasn't in control. I felt as if the old shaman was. His singing became stronger and then I was spinning in an hour-glass, falling back through time, very much as I'd done with Gabrielle that night in the hotel in Hampstead.

The spinning, falling sensation went on for some time until I arrived once again at the edge of the forest, at the beginning of our journey as a species. I was standing alone under a huge sky.

I asked the dream one more time, 'Why am I here?'

I heard an answer, like a vibration echoing through the caverns of my heart. 'You and your people have forgotten where they come from. Remember! Your people are lost in the wasteland of the mind. Remind them where they come from. Remind them who they are.'

I looked around me and asked for more.

The answer seemed to come from a humming vibration in the air. 'Remember your true name. Ask your ancestors to remind you. Do not come to us before you have found your name. And do not come before we call you.'

I spun forwards again and was soon back in the ceremonial house, but it was now empty and the dawn was coming. I was heartbroken and lonely. 'We have forgotten where we come from.' Like a mantra, the words were repeated, and with each repetition, I felt my heart breaking. I wanted to find the old shaman, but I remembered the warning not to go back to them until I had found my name.

Then I heard a voice calling me.

I woke up suddenly in my bed. It was the middle of the night. My body was shaking with sadness and my face was wet with tears. Susannah asked me what was wrong and I told her what had happened.

I felt a mixture of desolation and amazement. I was amazed to have found those old tribal shamans again. After my last dream with them, I knew their appearance spelled some deep shift in my life. And strangely enough, we'd recently been set a new task as part of our Deer Tribe apprenticeship. It was to perform a ritual to ask our ancestors for our true name. I was now more determined than ever to find it. A few weeks later, whilst teaching in Spain, I did.

◦ ✐ ◦

We'd planned to stay on for a few days after the course to enjoy some early spring warmth. It was my birthday and, as always, I'd planned to go out into nature to do a little ritual to digest the last year, give thanks and focus on my intentions for the year ahead.

In the shaman's world, names have power. To know the name of one's own soul, we were taught, gives a human being a very grounded sense of self. I'd recently experienced the power of choosing my own name at a dance gathering where I knew no one save Susannah. I'd surprised myself in the opening circle by introducing myself as Ya'Acov, my middle name. I hadn't consciously been thinking about changing my name, but at that moment it seemed the obvious thing to do. Strangely, I later found out that my own father and grandfather had also taken their middle name as their first name at a similar age. Joseph had become Brian. Simon had become Robert, and now, following some deep unconscious calling, Mikk had become Ya'Acov.

However, finding one's 'true name' was not a matter of choosing. It was a matter of asking and hopefully, receiving. Before my Amazonian dream, I'd tried it three times with only partial success. The ritual involved calling my ancestors from each of the four directions and asking them to tell me my true name. We'd been told that once we'd received our name, we were to shout it out with full power to the night sky. If we immediately saw a shooting star, we'd found it. No shooting star meant 'Please try again later.'

The instructions were simple. However, suspending my disbelief for long enough to be able to ask my ancestors for my name was not. I was also more than a little sceptical about my ability to conjure a shooting star as proof of the veracity of any name I received. To be frank, I thought it was impossible.

Cynicism can be violence to the soul. On the other hand, blind belief can be violence to integrity and intelligence. These ceremonies were helping me to walk the thin line between the two, the place where curiosity meets possibility.

My birthday ceremony took place in the hills of the Alpujarras in southern Spain, looking out across a valley towards a low range of mountains directly in front of me. The morning star had just come out. My Amazonian dream and the uncompleted ritual came to me, and without thought, I stood up and started calling my ancestors from the four directions. I thanked them for my life, and once I'd gone around the circle, I asked them, as I'd done before, 'Please tell me my true name.'

Maybe it was the mountain or maybe it was the state I was in from all those gratitudes, but I knew before I'd asked that I would receive it. And no sooner had I asked than I had heard it. I can't exactly say where it came from. I heard it inside me in words and saw it at the same time as an image inside my mind. My body shivered involuntarily. I immediately shouted it out to the night sky, exactly as I'd heard it.

I didn't expect anything, but in the eastern sky, on that far mountain range, I saw a shooting star. It was travelling from south to north across the horizon. It was so bright that at first I thought it must be a meteor.

I was jubilant. I was jumping for joy and punching the air and shouting and crying all at the same time, thanking life and thanking my ancestors for answering my request. I couldn't believe it and yet it was undeniable. I felt the force of that name landing in my system like a large shot of tequila. I shivered and shook and my eyes were open wide. The space inside me felt like the desert as the rains returned. I was thirsty for that name. It seemed to bring my inner garden into flower. I felt so bright and whole, humble and grateful.

Sometimes crying hurts. It's as if the heart can't be contained in the rib cage and there's a feeling of bursting forth like the sun coming through the clouds. I was home. I had been given back my name and I felt whole.

I was aware at that moment of the old shaman in the Amazon. I wanted to go to the Amazon and find him, but I knew that I had to wait. 'We'll call you,' they'd said, and I knew better than to try to push this river.

Satisfied with my night's work and keen to begin another journey around the sun, I sat and watched the dawn spreading its deep orange warmth across the mountains.

Chapter 13

MEETINGS WITH DEATH

'Death is not the greatest loss in life.
The greatest loss is what dies inside us while we live.'
NORMAN COUSINS

Meetings with death are an important part of any shaman's initiation. I remember hearing with a fascinated horror that the Mayan shamans of antiquity had to go through nine ritualized deaths, each more terrible than the last, in order to serve their people.

My father was a powerful man. We didn't see eye to eye. He died in 1995 at the tender age of 56, just eight weeks after being told he had cancer. It was a shock to us all. He had hardly had a day's illness in his life.

The week he discovered his cancer, Susannah, Reuben and I were on a winter holiday in Norway. I dreamed about my father every night, and during the days I was unusually aware of him, but I didn't know why. One day I felt like stretching myself and set off on a snowboard down a steeper slope than I'd tried before. Once over the ridge, there was no way back. I suddenly felt very afraid. I sat down, looking at what was ahead of me. I felt paralysed and was berating myself for biting off more than I could chew. Suddenly, I was aware of my father. I felt him sitting beside me. I realized that the fear I was feeling was in some way his, not mine. I didn't understand it, except that I knew he was afraid of heights. No longer overwhelmed, I stood up, said goodbye to my father's fear and, leaning forwards into the slope, took off.

When I came to a halt at the bottom of the slope, I felt both elated and, strangely, inconsolably sad. It was only when I returned to the UK to hear the news of my father's illness that I realized that I'd been unknowingly preparing for what was to come.

I only saw him once during the short time of his illness. Over that weekend visit, I had the chance to both witness his extraordinary dignity as he lost control of his physical body and to thank and honour him for all he'd given me. The dignity with which he faced his illness made me so proud of him. He also did his very best to restore some peace with Susannah by welcoming her to join us for our last Friday night meal together as a family.

One very sweet moment from that weekend stands out for me. Reuben, following his own impulse, decided to massage his grandpa. He did it with such uncloaked tenderness and presence, and my father was visibly moved.

~~~

I got to him three hours after he died. I had been working in Antwerp and got back as soon as I could. I'd asked the hospital not to disturb his body until I arrived and they'd very kindly agreed. I entered his hospital room at 11 p.m. He looked more peaceful than I'd ever seen him. I took his hand and sat with him, sensing his spirit still close by.

The presence of death has always brought me deep calm. That day, my heart was full of feeling, like a wild river, fast and unpredictable, and I took the ride with my father's spirit all the way downstream to the deep stillness of the ocean.

After three hours of being with him, thanking him for his life and what he had passed on to me, I was in a deeply altered state. I saw my father's father, who had died a year and a day before, arriving in a beautiful old Rolls Royce. My father loved those old cars and had traded many of them in his time as an entrepreneur. In my late teens, I'd sometimes had the great adventure of delivering cars to customers in London.

Once my dad asked me to drive a bright yellow Silver Spirit Rolls Royce from Liverpool to London. Unfortunately for him, the customer didn't take the car. I had the weekend in London with it. I was only 18 and my friends and I decided we ought to use the opportunity to try and get into Stringfellow's nightclub.

We were all in torn jeans, long before they were fashionable. I parked up 50 feet from the entrance and watched as my friend asked if we could come in. He was rudely refused.

I slowly drove up, wound down the window and asked, 'Is there a problem?'

'This guy doesn't want to let us in,' my friend replied.

I looked enquiringly at the doorman. 'Why ever not?' I asked.

The doorman did a quick double-take and changed his mind. 'I'm sorry, sir. Of course you can come in. May I park your car for you?'

Appearances, it seems, count for a lot.

My reverie was interrupted as I realized my grandfather had come to escort my father. I let go of his hand and watched as his spirit stood up out of his body, took the keys from his dad and drove off.

The atmosphere in the room changed dramatically. I took my dad's hand again and was dismayed to feel its empty weight. It was more like an inanimate object than a human hand. I crashed back into ordinary reality and felt the shock of death's finality. My father's body, which when I had arrived had still seemed to contain him, had gone ice-cold. He had gone.

⸎

In the months that followed his death, I dreamed of him many times. Apparently he hadn't realized that he'd died. I can't tell you for sure that the father I met in my dreams was more than an apparition based on my feelings and memories, but my experience was that I was with him in real time.

The dreams went on for a whole year before one night, in a ceremony in a huge tipi out in the wilds with a shaman from Mexico, I saw my dad's spirit on the other side of the river that separates the living from the dead.

It was close to dawn and the drums had been going all night and the fire was artfully tended and shaped into the image of a firebird that flew, with the help of the fire keeper, from the west of the tipi at sunset to the east, just in time for sunrise. There the great bird rested in front of a moon-shaped altar, fashioned from clay and decorated with flowers.

The ceremony was an extraordinary and life-changing experience for me. Earlier in the night, supported by the mesmerizing effect of a fast-tempo water drum and songs from the shaman's tradition, I'd found myself wandering in another world, pristine and unpopulated by other humans. The buildings were ancient pyramid-like structures. Everything was red earthy colours and dazzlingly bright turquoise.

I wandered round and eventually came to a magnificent black step pyramid that was humming with power. I started to climb the steps. At that point, from far away, I heard someone calling my name. I looked around, but couldn't see anyone. The calling was insistent. I didn't want to leave where I was, but I felt compelled to follow the sound.

I suddenly found myself back in the tipi with Aurelio, the shaman, standing in front of me calling my name. I looked into his eyes. He smiled a warm smile and then pointed to the design on his belt buckle. The geometric shapes, colours and patterns that I'd been exploring were engraved and painted on his buckle. He laughed and I fell straight back into that magical world.

Eventually, I came to a river and sat down on the bank. I started to sing. I knew I was calling, but I didn't know to whom.

As if in response to my song, I saw a long line of people emerging from around the base of a hill on the other side of the river. We were all singing the same song.

And then I saw him. Amongst the thousands of people on the other side of the river, there was my dad. He looked so well and seemed so happy to see me. I couldn't speak to him, but for one precious moment our eyes locked. I knew immediately that he had arrived. He was okay. And the deep tension that I'd been carrying in my heart since he'd died seemed to dissolve.

I left the river and pyramids behind me and found my way back to the tipi by following the sound of the drums. I opened my eyes for the first time in many hours and I was with the fire. It danced, phoenix-like, smoking fiery blue and orange ash. The fast rhythm of the drums seemed to be inside my blood. I could feel the medicine vibrating in my cells. I couldn't contain the joy I felt. I felt my heart bursting like a star. Everything shimmered in and out of focus in the first light of the dawn. My heart had expanded beyond the canvas walls of the tipi. I could feel the rhythm of the Earth under me. I felt the wildlife around us. Everything was in its place. The love I felt for everyone and everything was totally overwhelming. I had no choice but to let go.

For some wonderful time out of time, my individual sense of self evaporated. There was no thinking. There was no body. There was only a humming vibration as ancient as the Dartmoor stone, as wide as the sky and as free as the wind. There was only love. But that love was a destroyer as much as a creator. It was death as well as life. It was all directions at once and nowhere at all.

And in the force of that love, at the centre of it all, the water drum and the rattles held the beat. As I returned to an individual sense of self, that rhythm was my life raft in the vast ocean of the unknown.

It was the shaman's song that brought me back. The traditional food that signalled the beginning of the end of the ceremony was being brought into the tipi; sacred corn, buffalo meat, fruit and grains, all beautifully prepared, filled the tipi with a delicious smell and my body's response told me I was ravenous. I was back, and I watched that firebird dancing in the flames, born again fresh from the warm grey ash.

Something had died in me during that night in the tipi. I felt lighter and the experience of meeting my dad's spirit and the dissolution of separation that had followed it left me looking at the world through different eyes.

In the overwhelming moments that had led to letting go, I'd seen my own body in a grave. In what was like a speeded-up nature movie, I'd seen my flesh being eaten by the worms and my bones nourishing the Earth. And, unlike the first time I'd met death in a shamanic ritual, I'd felt no fear.

⚋

It was 1988 when I had the opportunity to take part in a burial ceremony with Batty in the ancient land of the Cathars in a place called Lavaldieu in the Languedoc region of France. Death is considered to be one of the great teachers in shamanic cultures around the world and as soon as I heard about the burial ritual, I thought, *Those old shamans must have had fun dreaming up the rituals for us apprentices to take part in.*

The burial ceremony involved digging our own grave. As the sun set, we voluntarily entered that grave. The shaman 'drummed death into our grave' and then held our 'funeral'. This was followed by a night in dialogue with death.

It was midsummer and the ground was hard, dry and rocky. I'd spent the whole day with a good friend called Steve, digging that grave with a pick and shovel. It was hot and exhausting work and by the end of the day I was quite happy to get in there and die!

Our instructions were not to fall asleep, but to look at our lives from the point of view of having already died. What regrets did we have? What had we left unfinished? What did death have to show us about the effect of our lives on those around us?

After all that, we were to ask death to give us another chance. We were warned that death was a tough negotiator. What could we commit to if we were given another year to live? What would we change?

Assuming that we came to an agreement, at sunrise we would be 'reborn' and have the opportunity to declare our intent to the rising sun.

My grave was deep. I'd lit a fire using fast-burning wood and bracken and covered the embers in a layer of sand in order to stay warm during the night. The grave was covered by pallets and there was enough space to squeeze in at the head end and a breathing hole at my feet. Once I was in, a couple of logs were rolled into place one and a half feet from my face and the tarp was rolled over them. I then heard the sound of my friend shovelling earth on top of the tarp.

Batty began to drum. I hadn't thought that I would be afraid, but as Batty called, 'Benevolent Death!' into the grave, I became truly terrified. Benevolent Death is the name Batty used to describe death as a teacher, a conscious being, who we can come into relationship with before the end of our life.

I was on the verge of panic, but I was determined to stay put. Up above, my funeral was taking place, but I was too preoccupied to listen. As instructed, I began to talk to death. I asked him to kindly give me some time to arrive in the ritual before he came to get me.

Apparently death was listening and loosened his grip on my heart. I settled in, shaken and suddenly aware of what a serious business this was! Slowly, my fear returned and seemed to increase in intensity with each breath, as if someone was turning a fear dial. I was covered in a clammy sweat and my body was shaking. I began to think that I was genuinely dying. I remembered that I'd felt this fear of death once before.

Five years before, some friends and I had gone to Glastonbury Tor for a winter solstice ritual. I'd had a terrible night. I'd spent most of it in a kind of numb terror, certain that I was dying. It was truly a dark night of the soul. I'd felt beyond useless. I'd done nothing of any value with my life and now it was over. My friends had tried to console me, but I was lost in the mire. Everything seemed a threat. The hedges seemed wrathful dragons. The land was full of dark energy and I had no protection whatsoever.

I felt a fool. I'd expressed my doubts about doing a ritual on the Tor, but my friends had persuaded me, and against my better judgement, I'd gone along with them. Why had I been so stupid as to go against my own instincts?

It was the longest night of the year and the darkness seemed without end. When the sun eventually rose, the relief I felt was beyond words. I'd made it through the night and the sun was returning. And I'd been given a serious warning. I made a promise not to involve myself further in amateur rituals.

In the grave at Lavaldieu, here I was again. But this time, I was being held by a medicine man and I knew I could safely let go. Still, my fear reached fever pitch. My breath was short and fast and I was again close to panic. I talked to death, telling him about my life through my chattering teeth. But with each sentence, the feeling of death's presence became more and more intense until I felt as if I was being crushed.

At the peak of my fear, without warning, and strange as it may sound, I went from the most intense fear I'd ever experienced to the deepest calm of my life! I'd let go and travelled through the eye of the needle to the other side of my fear. My body seemed to spread out in the warm sand. I didn't recognize myself. I was being held in the embrace of the Great Mother and I felt totally at ease. I wondered if

I'd actually died. I knew I'd passed through the first gateway of the ceremony and I still had the whole night ahead of me. From this place, I was able to do my work.

As a 'dead man', I looked back over the life I'd lived. I had many regrets. I regretted the many times I'd played the victim and blamed the bastards who were 'oppressing me'. I saw how I'd actively played a full part in causing the situations in which I'd felt the most pain. I regretted how mean I'd been with my love for the people who'd mattered most to me in my life and how passive I'd been with my dreams.

So much became clear to me in that grave. I was so deeply involved that I hardly noticed that I'd fallen into a dream.

I was seven and was standing outside the doors of a great abbey, asking to study with the Cathar masters inside. I was told I was too young and to come back in a year.

A year later, again I knocked on those great doors. This time, a nun let me in and I was instructed to sit on a wooden pew and, whatever happened, not turn around.

I became aware of an old man in a dark cloak and hood sitting in the pew behind me. I couldn't see him, but I knew he was there. I so wanted to turn around, but I daren't do it.

The man spoke. 'Put your hands out in front of you, child.'

I did. The man passed an object over my head and placed it in my hands.

'Take a look.'

I opened my eyes. A short sword in a black leather scabbard was in my hands. I took it out and saw that there were inscriptions on the blade, written in a language I didn't understand.

'This is your sword,' the old man told me. 'It is your sword of power. We are all born with one. Learn to use it well. If you do not, its power will turn against you. Dedicate it to what matters most to you. If you do not, it will cause you untold problems.'

I thanked him and he told me his name.

And then I woke up again in my grave. I was shocked. The dream had been so real that I was amazed that the sword was no longer in my hands.

In the morning, after some final negotiations with Benevolent Death that involved making clear commitments to tie up the loose strings I'd seen during the night, I was welcomed into my new life by Batty and my companions. Around the fire, I shared the story of the sword. Batty told me that I should look out for that sword or even find a way of making it. It was a representation of my power, dedicated to the purpose of my soul.

That made sense to me. I thought I would find it quickly, but in fact it would take 10 years. It slowly dawned on me during that decade that the process of bringing visions into physical reality wasn't something I could rush.

Meeting death as a teacher was an invitation to mature. Gone was the 'I'm gonna live forever' certainty of my adolescence. Death's presence was real, and my life, imperfect as it was, felt like a precious gift.

I was well aware that I'd made promises in that first burial ceremony to clean up my act. I had letters to write. The perspective of the grave made apology a must. I apologized for blaming past girlfriends for our break-ups. I wrote to teachers from my schooldays to apologize for my behaviour at school. Death had been clear that cleaning up the past was important. However, the most important thing was how I chose to live from now on. The ritual in Lavaldieu wasn't a one-night stand. I knew that in order to go deeper, like any relationship, the one with death would require my attention.

In 1990, I did another burial ritual, this time with Victor. Having kept the pledges I'd made in that first ceremony, I found this one much calmer. Death had become part of my day-to-day life, and during that second burial, I found myself feeling much more at ease with the reality of mortality.

Burial ceremonies became a regular part of my own initiatory journey as my dialogue with death deepened. A year later, just before our son was born, Susannah and I dug a round grave in our tiny back garden at home. We covered it over with small hazel thinnings, and covered the trees with blankets and canvas. We lined the grave with sheepskins and, one at a time, we spent 48 hours in the dark in dialogue with death. It was the perfect preparation for becoming parents.

Naturally, we knew that our lives would change radically with the arrival of a child and this rite of passage gave us the time and space to pray for help. I prayed with all my heart that life would show me how to provide for my young family. I prayed for help from the spirits, from my ancestors and from life itself to find the way to be the best father I could be. And all the time, death stood over my shoulder, reminding me that all things are temporary and that one day I had to let go of everything and return my body to the Earth.

⸌⟋⸍

Death has taught me how to appreciate life. Death's invitation has been to be present, to taste my food, to smell the earth and to dare to love in the sure knowledge that I and all that I love will pass away.

Many people I've met along the way have assured me that death is as simple as taking off your shoes at the end of a hard day's walking and that our spirit lives on forever. But when I asked, death was clear: 'You don't know what's next and that's how it's meant to be and part of what makes life so very sweet. The best way to prepare to meet me is to commit fully to living your life in the way that makes most sense to you. If you do this, when I come for you, you will die as you have lived, with a smile on your face.'

⁓

Chapter 14

THE LITTLE MATTER OF POWER AND RESPONSIBILITY

'To say you have no choice is to relieve
yourself of responsibility.'
Patrick Ness

One of the great gifts that Western psychology and the many different schools of psychoanalysis and psychotherapy have brought has been a deep understanding of how our early experiences in life affect us throughout our lives. Without strong foundations, we are blown about by life's storms like feathers in the wind.

Healing means acknowledging the past, releasing any old emotion attached to it and doing the work of accepting what has happened. In doing so, we change our relationship to the experience.

There's often a misunderstanding about what acceptance means. To be clear, accepting that something has happened doesn't mean condoning it, it means accepting the reality of it and the consequences it has had. This is the first stage in being able to change our relationship to it. This is the path of the wounded healer. Our wounds, given time, become our medicine.

Rituals that connect us to the holding stability of the Earth and to the illuminating clarity of the sun support us in connecting with the Great Mother and the Great Father, and, through the direct experience of being in relationship with these archetypal forces, our foundations are strengthened. I learned that once the raw emotion of old experiences has had its space, rather than complaining about what should-have-could-have happened, I could look to the Mother beneath my feet and the Father above my head for all the blessing and support I might need. As I released my own parents from any ideas about what should have been different, my love and appreciation for them as people increased massively. Becoming a father myself had already changed my perception, and my recapitulation supported the process further.

Ever since Batty first told us that how we perceived life was rooted in the story we told about life, I'd been fascinated by the stories I and the people close to me were telling. Batty told all his apprentices that we might as well choose a story that came from the deepest place of soul we could access. He invited us to find a story about life that gave us a sense of purpose and dignity and he told us that it was a warrior's freedom to choose this story for ourselves. I was both thrilled by the freedom this promised and daunted by the responsibility it implied.

❦

Susannah and I were now teaching ecstatic dance full time and having to learn on our feet. We were getting more and more invitations to take our work to different countries and we were travelling several times a month for work.

One night after a workshop in west London, I came out of the venue high as a kite from dancing and discovered that our car, with all our belongings in it, had been stolen. My initial shock soon changed to fury, and without hesitation, I danced my feelings right there on the street. Having released the emotional impact, I could choose the story I told.

'It must be time for a change' was more interesting than the 'poor me' movie that was waiting to take centre-stage again.

I went to find Susannah, who was ordering a post-dance pizza in a nearby restaurant. When I told her the car had been stolen, she got up right away and physically danced her feelings of shock, fury and loss. I explained to the startled diners that our car had been stolen. After a short time, Susannah was done. We sat down and ate our meal, went to Paddington police station to report the theft, bought a couple of toothbrushes and went to bed. We slept well, both of us rather amazed that such a significant loss should be having so little effect on us. Step by step, the medicine was finding its way into our everyday lives.

I was beginning to find my own power and to understand the responsibility of my role. I remember the first time I found my original voice as a teacher. For the first four years of teaching, nearly everything I said was prefaced with 'Gabrielle says that…' Then in the winter of 1993 we were teaching in Den Bosch in the Netherlands. I was ill and had a high temperature, but we had to work. When we came back together as a group after lunch on the second day of the workshop and I introduced the afternoon's work, it was like watching someone else take over. I was simply witnessing what was being said as it was coming through me. I had no idea where it was coming from, but I felt calm and clear. It was my first experience in teaching of becoming the hollow bone that is such a universal concept in shamanism.

Over the years of their initiation, a shaman develops a relationship with helpers from non-physical reality. These are called a shaman's 'spirits'. These can be animal guides, archetypal teachers and healers. In order to heal or serve the community, the shaman must let go of their everyday self and become a channel for these spirits to communicate and work through – a hollow bone.

I only had a vague sense of this until Bikko Máhte asked me about my spirits. Becoming curious led me down the path of exploring the specificity of the guides and helpers who had always been around me and brought me into deeper relationship with them.

Obviously, there are dangers associated with becoming a hollow bone. There are all kinds of energies and frequencies floating around looking for a way to be heard. Learning what to listen to and what to ignore is an important part of a shaman's initiation. Mistakes are inevitable, especially early on in the journey. The biggest danger is to take what spirit says as the gospel truth or to irresponsibly hide behind the certainty that because spirit says something is true, it must unquestionably be so.

I often made these kinds of mistakes. I would even use what I heard to bolster my own position in arguments with Susannah. Luckily, Susannah and our mentors were not afraid to challenge anything that felt unreal or unhelpful.

I remember one session with our long-term movement mentor, Helen Poynor, around this time. In our work with her, we would move without music and she would give us simple instructions to help us to become more aware and integrated on a physical and emotional level. That day I was moving strongly and 'getting into contact with my spirits'. My eyes were rolling around and I was a long way from an awareness of my own body. I dimly heard Helen saying something to me I was pretty sure I didn't want to hear.

'Ordinary eyes, Ya'Acov, ordinary eyes,' she kept repeating.

Eventually, I heard her as I landed with a bit of a thump back in my body. We all laughed.

I was aware that I'd entered a new territory. My power was growing and I was becoming aware of the responsibility that went with it. I was on the tipping point between an old way and a new one. Part of me was still playing the 'please recognize me' game whilst another part was determined to stay as grounded and matter-of-fact about the whole thing as possible.

Just as the choice to become a father had made me aware of the necessity to provide for my family, so the recognition that people were listening to what was coming through me made me aware of my responsibility to stay simple and deepen my own work as a student. There were still times with my own teachers when the child in me would take over and I would find myself in the same dance of seeking approval that I had performed with my own father. A smile here and an acknowledgement there could inflate my sense of worth. Conversely, a frown or a turning away could quickly have me doubting myself again. How much of this dance was going on inside my own head, I don't know. But I recognized it as a major waste of energy that got in the way of simply being myself. To a degree, my power was still outsourced and dependent on what others thought.

As our success grew, more and more people were asking me, 'Are you a shaman?' I continued to have ambivalent feelings about the whole thing. I was aware of how fashionable shamanism was becoming and there were (and are) many people calling themselves shamans with whom I didn't wish to be associated. I was also well aware of the deep mistrust that existed in the modern world about all things shamanic. Some of this was rooted in bad experiences, bad practice or misunderstanding. And some was the fallout from the 'shamanism is evil' spell cast by the Church and the inquisitions of the early modern era.

A shaman's initiatory journey involves the seeking of power. To be effective in your work and capable of staying steady in the middle of the chaos of healing work, personal power is a necessity. Having spent my twenties deeply immersed in the personal politics of eco-feminism, I was totally signed up to the idea that power corrupts therefore power must be bad. But my training was now at directly at odds with this belief system. With the help of Victor and Bikko Máhte, I was step by step coming to the understanding that power was neutral and it was down to me to make a choice as to how to use it.

I started to explore the drama triangle both inside me and in my work. This is a social model that was conceived by Stephen Karpman, MD, in 1968. He was a student of Eric Berne, the father of Transactional Analysis. It is the vicious circle that is at the heart of so much of the trouble we face as human beings. It describes how the Victim, the Persecutor and the Rescuer keep us locked into a destructive cycle that keeps the wheel of suffering turning at maximum speed and with maximum pain for everyone involved. The Victim is not intended to represent an actual victim, but rather someone feeling or acting like a victim. Their stance is 'Poor me!' The Rescuer's line is 'Let me help you.' The reward of this role is that the attention is taken off their own issues. The Persecutor insists, 'It's all your fault,' from a position of superiority. Karpman's understanding was that in conflict, all these roles are present and can even shift from person to person.

I kept on seeing this triangle in my own behaviour, in my marriage, in our students and every time I watched or heard the news. In both my own world and the larger world, we were all caught up in this blame game, declaring our own innocence whilst casually and unconsciously inflicting our revenge. I knew I needed to find a way to work with this. I asked for help in my dreams.

I dreamed about an archetypal energy called the Dancing Warrior. The Dancing Warrior has the strength to step out of the vicious circle and make another choice. They are committed to using all the force at their disposal to remind us that in every situation we have a choice about how we respond. So I'd found a positive archetype for power and, as always, life responded by providing me with situations in which I could check if I was willing and ready to walk my talk.

⌒⌒

It was timely that in my next encounter with Victor, he had just the medicine. He invited us to participate in a ritual called 'Make a Choice!' My fellow students and I stood in a warrior pose, a strong stance designed to help us feel grounded and awake at the centre of our own circle, all facing towards a fire. Victor explained that he and his helper, with drums going full power, were going to walk amongst us. Victor would take on the voice of the critic, whilst his companion would take on the voice of acceptance and praise.

Victor was obviously enjoying himself. 'Stay in your centre and stay in your power, no matter what happens,' he said. 'When the silence returns, shout out the first thing that comes into your heart. You will be making your choice. And you will be communicating with the Great Spirit, so be clear about what you say. Don't hesitate or censor yourselves in any way.'

Once we had made our choice, we were to stand silently and feel in our body the power of the decision we had just made. I had no idea what to expect.

It was a powerful experience to have these two strong men shouting totally opposing self-concepts into my ears at the same time. One would be shouting out ridiculously exaggerated praise: 'You are the strongest, kindest, most spiritual being ever to walk the face of the Earth!' whilst the other would simultaneously be shouting, 'You worthless piece of shit!'

All kinds of chaos ensued around me, but I kept a steady focus on my breathing, my roots and my body.

When the silence suddenly came, I found myself shouting with full power: 'I choose to live my life as a warrior! I choose to let go of seeking my father's approval! It is done!'

It wasn't just my father – I was choosing to let go of seeking approval from anyone to whom I had given power and authority. I felt a tremendous rush of freedom at that moment and knew that the decision had been made on a fundamental level within me. The words I had shouted were true.

I felt such love for my father at that moment, as if I was seeing him for the first time. He was the stone against which I had sharpened my sword. He had given me life and so much more.

I knew in my bones that it was time to redefine my relationship with power. I was finding my medicine and trusting that I knew exactly what it was for. Susannah continued to be fully alongside me in this search and she supported me with such deep understanding of the fire that was burning inside me. She too was on fire and finding her own clarity and strength as a medicine woman. And as a mother, she went on working, studying and making her offering in the world.

We were being given more and more responsibility to offer the different levels of Gabrielle's curriculum and we went quickly from being Associates of her Moving Center School to being asked to set up the Moving Centre School UK. This was in 1996.

We had a close relationship with Gabrielle and were often in touch. We talked a lot about shamanism with her. At times she was very happy to be known as an urban shaman and at others, like us, she wanted to distance herself and her work from so much of what was being offered as shamanism. Nevertheless, she described our relationship as a modern form of a traditional shamanic apprenticeship. I was delighted.

It was a good time. For the first time, I was making a living, and it was through doing what I loved. I had done what the elders from my dreaming had asked of me. I was a husband, a father and a teacher, and now I started to wonder what would be the next stage of my initiation. Would I be allowed to fly now that I had my feet on the ground? Over the years to come I would find out that as wide as the branches of the tree of life might spread, the roots must spread wider.

In the rituals I was running at that time, I was finding some of the essential ingredients that would later form the bedrock of the work that Susannah and I were unknowingly creating.

Before a workshop in Norway, a friend had offered to take me to her mountain cabin in the wilderness near Geilo. As we arrived at the parking place from which we would begin the hike to the cabin, I asked her if she minded if I shouted out my greeting to the forest and all the beings who lived there, in true Victor style. She had no objections, so I began to shout out my joy at being there and to communicate my intentions.

As we were walking to the cabin, we met a rather irate hunter on the way. He asked if we'd been the fools shouting. I said yes. He told us that he'd been stalking a deer for hours, had had it in the sights of his rifle and had been just about to pull the trigger when my shouting had startled it and he'd lost the moment.

I didn't know what to say. He was carrying a rifle and I didn't want to make him more upset than he already was. I apologized for having unwittingly startled his prey, but I was quietly overjoyed. A couple of weeks before with Victor, I'd been part of an exercise in which we'd imagined ourselves hunting a miraculous blue deer. The blue deer was sacred to the Wirarika people and was said to be the messenger of the Great Spirit. In the guided journey, we were hunting it with a bow and arrow. At the moment when we had it in our sights, it had turned around and looked us straight in the eyes. In that moment of meeting, we'd been invited to receive the message that the deer was carrying. That, rather than killing the deer, was the purpose of our hunt.

It had been a very strong journey for me and the gentle power in the deer's eyes had touched me deeply. The message I'd received was simply that life was sacred. Now here I was in the mountains of Norway in a real-life version of the shamanic journey we'd taken. I felt so close to the deer whose life I'd unwittingly saved. I was going to do another burial ceremony to mark my 39th birthday and I resolved to put an offering next to my grave.

The whole night in the grave was a deep conversation with the spirit of the deer. The innocence, agility and grace of the animal and the fragility of life were also the focus of my conversations with death. At dawn, when I came out from my grave, I noticed my food offering was gone and there were deer tracks over my grave.

Was it that I was now present enough to notice these synchronicities? Or was it that I was learning to take responsibility and therefore beginning to trust myself with power and play a more active part in creating them? I'd thought that I was hunting power, but it was now starting to feel as if I was the one being hunted. The invisible strands that weave the tapestry of our lives were making connections way beyond my control.

Chapter 15

BEYOND IMAGINATION

'I am enough of an artist to draw freely upon
my imagination... Knowledge is limited,
imagination encircles the world.'

Albert Einstein

I had invited Bikko Máhte to come and join us for the Norwegian
workshop. At his request, I'd also invited a Cherokee medicine
woman named Rainbow Medicine Walker. They knew each other from
a gathering of shamans in Finland some years before and I'd spoken to
her after my dream ritual in the Amazon. When I'd woken up in tears,
broken-hearted by the remembrance that we'd collectively forgotten
where we came from, I'd followed an instinct to call her. It was 4 a.m.
in the UK and 8 p.m. in Washington State, where she lived. We hadn't
spoken before.

I explained that Bikko Máhte had given me her number and asked
me to call her. After some courtesies, she asked me why I'd called. I told
her about my dream and I heard her gasp at the other end of the phone.

'That's quite something, Ya'Acov,' she said. 'I've been walking in the
mountains today and I found myself weeping. The trees and the spirits
were telling me that we'd forgotten where we'd come from and that I
needed to remind my people.'

I was stunned to hear this. Our connection had clearly already been made and I immediately invited her to join us in Norway.

The workshop was a wonderful gathering. It took place at Nissedal, by a beautiful fjord. The focus was on shamanic trance – we were intent on following the beat of the drums to the deepest place we could journey together and, in that place, seek a vision for the next chapter of our lives.

We spent four days preparing to go into ceremony and on the first day we were deep in our dance when Bikko Máhte decided to join us. As he walked into the room, the sound system blew a fuse. Everyone turned to look at him, but he just threw his hands up in the air as if to say 'Nothing to do with me' and gestured to my drum. 'Best use that,' he laughed.

Laughing with him, I picked it up and for the next hour we all danced to the beat of the drum. Bikko Máhte joined in, playful as a child and clearly enjoying himself immensely.

Chris Luttechau, a good friend also on the shaman's path, and I were sharing a small wooden cabin on the shore of the fjord. Bikko Máhte was staying a short distance away in a similar cabin. One early afternoon after lunch, we were all standing at the water's edge together. The fjord had been covered by a blanket of grey cloud all day. Bikko Máhte called me over to him. He explained through a translator that some *yoiks* (spirit songs) were very old and were handed down from generation to generation. He said he knew a very old one for the sun. He started to sing in the quiet, guttural voice that was his way. As he sang, a remarkable thing happened. Right above us, the clouds momentarily parted and a shaft of milky sunlight bathed the jetty on which we were standing.

I looked at him wide-eyed and he smiled his cheeky smile and laughed. 'Tell me a story,' he said.

This was how our conversations happened. He never sat me down to teach me anything, but when I was with him, I was always learning.

On a recent visit, I'd asked him to share his knowledge of healing work with me. He'd agreed and we'd gone into his living room and cleared away the coffee table to make more space. He'd then lain down on a blanket on the floor.

I'd looked at him, taken aback and certain he'd misunderstood my request. I told him so, but he just smiled and invited me to go ahead and do my work. Nearly all the healing techniques I'd learned had been through sitting beside other shamans and medicine people doing their work. But when the teacher feels you are ready, you are thrown in at the deep end. Bikko Máhte clearly thought me ready.

I was nervous, but I took a deep breath, called my spirits, did my best to get out of the way and get down to work. He was satisfied. There was no need for feedback. Either the healing would work or it wouldn't. I was so grateful for his trust and the chance to repay a little of the debt I owed this humble and powerful man for the manifold ways in which he'd helped me. And the confidence and implicit support this traditional mode of shamanic training gave me allowed me to start my one-to-one work as a shamanic healer.

Back by the fjord, now grey again, since the sun had disappeared almost as soon as Bikko Máhte had finished singing, I wondered which story to share with him. Then an event that had happened several years before, just after our son was born, came to mind.

I'd been working with my drum, attempting to guide myself on a shamanic journey through the roots, trunk and branches of the tree of life. Even though I'd owned my drum for many years, my relationship with it as a shamanic tool was just beginning and its efficacy and my own skill were very hit and miss. All I knew was that repetitive rhythm was good for trance and trance was good for journeying. So I wasn't expecting much, but on that particular day the doors of perception opened wide.

In my vision, I find the tree of life and enter into the root system through a beautifully carved door in the trunk. There is a circular staircase going down, lit by smoking torches. After climbing down several hundred steps into the darkness, I emerge in to a poorly lit mechanic's workshop. All the tools of the trade are lying around and there are several work benches. There is a faint smell of oil and rust and an air of organized chaos.

What happens next happens very fast. Several mechanics in overalls enter the workshop, pick up my body and get to work. They are almost gnome-like in appearance. I feel no sense of alarm and nobody speaks. The mechanics take my body to pieces. On one work bench, they work with my arms, on another my legs; on a third, my organs are spread out. The mechanics are cleaning, oiling, stretching and tweaking these parts in all manner of ways. I am clearly not in my body, as I am able to watch as it is entirely dismembered.

Each part is worked with and then put to one side. Once the mechanics have finished the cleaning, they insert 63 tiny crystals of varying colours into the different parts before putting the whole thing back together again.

I am then back inside my body and before I have a moment to ask anything or even feel what they've done, they lift me up and throw me with huge force into the Upper World (also known as the branches of the Tree of life).

I emerge from the dim light of the Lower World into the bright light of the Upper World and land on a gossamer carpet that is swirling like cloud beneath my feet. I look around to try to get my bearings.

Huge beings are moving silently about. They must be 30 feet high and they are swirling like the ground beneath my feet. I walk amongst them, feeling awe and peace in equal measure. All I can hear is the sound of air moving through the leaves and the melody of the wind grabs my attention totally. I feel rather than hear the words that are then spoken to me. They are like a tender caress inside the chambers of my heart and I sense their resonance shimmering throughout my body.

'It doesn't matter what you do, Ya'Acov. How you do it is what matters most. Intention is everything. It steers the mechanism of your fate. The dreams you carry inside you have many origins. Some belong to your spirit. Some are handed to you by your ancestors. Some you will bring to Earth. Others you will pass on to the next generation.'

I have so much to ask, but I'm not given the chance. Instead, the carpet beneath me dissolves and I fall back into my physical body.

As I opened my eyes after that journey, I was amazed to find myself still drumming. I gradually slowed the tempo, spoke my gratitudes and came to a stop. There was a humming in the room and inside me and it took me several hours to recover my normal perception.

Bikko Máhte had been listening quietly while I told the story. Then he said just one word: 'Shaman.'

For the first time, I felt neither shame nor pride. I simply felt that my vocation and my journey had been accurately named and I nodded quietly.

I had my drum with me and Bikko Máhte picked it up and asked me if he could play it. I agreed. He looked at it, then listened with his hands to the contours of the wood and the skin. Afterwards, he lifted it up to the sky and held it out to the four directions. I sat on the shore and watched, fascinated. After a while, he played one note. Then he waited. He watched the sky, the birds, the wind and the water. Then he hit the drum again, just a single beat, and listened. One beat, listening, one beat, listening. I wondered what he was doing. I think I even fell asleep at one point. Eventually, he was done.

He then told me that each sound of the drum had a different quality and therefore spoke to different parts of nature and the spirit world. He told me to practise playing the different areas of the drum and watching the effect it had around me and inside me. I'd never been taught about the drum, and in these hours with this beautiful Sami elder, I recognized how very much there was to learn.

Chris and I had been planning to take a little rowing trip out to a small island that was about 600 feet from the shore. It was now too late for that, but later that night I dreamed I was there. I climbed a tree that was in the centre of the island and found myself once again in the Upper World. I walked along a wide tree-lined path until I came to a set of huge golden doors, guarded by two black dogs. I asked for permission to enter and I found myself in a throne room. I sensed a great force and I sat and waited for the dream to unfold.

Sitting on the throne was Odin. Although I'd heard his name, I didn't know who he was. Somehow I knew that I wasn't allowed to look directly at him, but I could see his feet and I could hear him speak.

'The shamanic traditions of your land have been broken,' he said. 'The threads have been cut.'

Much as I respected the Druids who still held to their old traditions, and even though Celtic shamanism was beginning a renaissance, I knew this to be true.

'You and Susannah will continue to be given opportunities to learn from the traditions of other lands and you must find ways to distil and translate what you receive. Your medicine is coming.'

Disturbed in a way that I couldn't quite put my finger on, I bowed and thanked this old force of nature for his words.

I woke in my bed and lay there, unable to get back to sleep. Weren't we already offering our medicine? What could the old Norse god have meant? In the years that followed, I would find out, but for now, there was an indefinable discomfort deep inside my belly, like an itch that I couldn't scratch.

My time working with Victor was coming to a natural close. But before I completed my training with him, I went to one more gathering, at a venue in Wales called Spirit Horse. The final ceremony we did was a medicine walk through the night to visit and pay our respects to the *podorios*, or elemental powers associated with each direction.

We worked in groups of four, carrying smoking coals from one fire to the next to connect the four directions. Walking through the wind and the rain in the dark, keeping the coals alight and praying at each fire made for a tough night. By the end, as we reached the central fire, I was soaked, freezing cold and exhausted. The rain had finally stopped and there was a misty silence. The very first light of dawn was beginning to appear in the eastern sky.

I was sitting quietly, alone, close to the fire, finding a way to complete the ritual before I went to bed for some well-earned rest, when I heard a noise behind me and turned around.

I was more than a little surprised to see a beautiful woman standing there, dressed in buckskins with flowers in her hair. It was hard to tell her age, but she was clearly Native American. I was certain that my smoke-sore eyes were seeing things through the mist and changing light, but the image stayed steady.

The woman began to walk towards me until she was standing right in front of me. I was on my knees with tiredness and it seemed appropriate to remain there. My heart was racing, but at the same time, the closer she came, the calmer I felt.

I would have to use poetry to describe her beauty. She was physically beautiful, but much more than that, she was beauty itself. She looked at me with kind, wise eyes, and as she did so, the world stopped. She didn't speak, but I heard her with every cell of my being.

She told me she'd come because of a promise I'd made some years before about the pipe I'd been given. I knew precisely what she meant. I'd promised that when I'd remembered how to pray, I would return the pipe to its own culture. She nodded as if she was hearing my thoughts.

'That time has come. I am White Buffalo Calf Woman and I have come to reclaim what is mine. It is time to return what you were loaned.'

Her message given, she turned to leave.

'Wait! Please wait.'

There was a pause and then she turned again to face me.

'How will I know who to give it to? And how can I thank you?'

'You will know and you can thank me through the way you live.'

And then she was gone. My heart burst. There were tears streaming down my face. I felt at once blessed and alone. We'd sung songs to White Buffalo Woman many times. I knew that she was the spirit being who'd originally brought the pipe to the Lakota people. To have an encounter with her was beyond my wildest dreams.

I knew Victor had his elders, and even though they were in Mexico, I quickly made up my mind to ask him to take the pipe to them as my thanks for what I'd received through his lineage. I asked him and he agreed. After the workshop, we said our goodbyes and I solemnly handed my pipe, wrapped in its beautiful black and white blanket, over to him.

I thought that was the end of it, but a week later, while working away from home, I dreamed that my pipe was being handed to a Native American grandfather for a blessing. I woke up, confused. The grandfather I'd seen in my dream was clearly not a Wirarika person. Had something happened?

I called up my friend Simon, with whom Victor had been staying after our ceremony. Before I could ask him anything about my pipe, he said how glad he was that I'd rung because he'd been trying to get in touch with me. He told me that Victor had decided at the last minute not to take the pipe, feeling that it wasn't supposed to go with him.

'After Victor left,' he told me, 'a medicine woman came to stay with me. Her name is Dina. She's a Native American teacher. Something remarkable happened. She told me that she'd been without a pipe for some years but that recently she'd had a dream showing her it was time to work with a pipe again. In her dream, she saw the pipe that she'd be working with. It had two buffalos carved into the bowl and a very specific black and red pattern burned into the stem.'

Simon knew my pipe. We'd sat in ceremony together many times.

'I knew immediately it was your pipe,' he continued, 'and I knew it would be okay with you, so I showed it to her. When she unwrapped it, she smiled and told me it was the very pipe she'd seen in her dream!'

I was delighted. 'Is she still with you?'

'No. She left two days ago. She said she was going to take the pipe to her elder and ask him to bless it for her.'

I was speechless. My pipe had found its way home and spirit had taken care of it.

My imagination had always been strong and for most of my life my everyday reality had been struggling to keep up with it. Now the scales were shifting. Synchronicities were increasingly common and now it was my imagination that was struggling to keep up with my everyday reality.

Although I felt clearer than I ever had before, it had become obvious that the part of me that liked to think I was in control clearly wasn't. At the same time, I felt how important it was to continue to refine and sharpen my intention, communicate it precisely in ceremony and, most importantly, live it through my day-to-day actions.

I was learning how to connect with the powers of nature and the spirit world in a more grounded way. I was beginning to find my feet in the shaman's world.

I had already discovered that one of the best ways to learn something was to teach it and had created an exercise called 'Flying with Both Feet on the Ground'. It was clear to me that I was teaching what I most needed to learn.

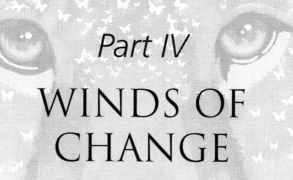

Part IV

WINDS OF CHANGE

THE INITIATION OF
AN EVERYDAY SHAMAN

*'Go out in the woods, go out. If you don't
go out in the woods, nothing will ever
happen and your life will never begin.'*
CLARISSA PINKOLA ESTÉS

The next few years would see some massive upheavals in my life. New teachers would appear in both human and plant form. And my relationship with Gabrielle and her work, which I'd believed would last for my whole life, would run into painful difficulties.

These changes challenged me on every level. I would be humbled again and again, both by the everyday magic of life and by recognizing how much I'd swept under the carpet to maintain an unhealthy status quo.

The winds of change were strong, and they needed to be as they blew away the old and made space for the new.

I finally met the primal force of the Amazon rainforest, where my shamanic training entered a whole new realm. In the forest, I discovered new levels of terror, strength and healing in equal measure. More than that, through my work with the Pachamama Alliance, I found family. Over the years, I have learned so much from our indigenous brothers and sisters in their unyielding and passionate struggle to protect their lands and cultures on behalf of us all.

And throughout all of this, I continued to be blessed by the steady presence of Bikko Máhte alongside me.

In a visit to Bikko Máhte's house in the winter of 2007, I was again doing ceremony on his land. It was bitterly cold. The sun doesn't rise at all in the Arctic winter. At one point, I came back into the house to drum with him. As we drummed together, I looked out of the window and saw a massive reindeer running towards the house. It was only its size that helped me to discern that what I was seeing was a vision and not a physical animal.

My eyes were wide and Bikko Máhte turned slowly to look out of the window too. He raised his eyebrows a little and then laughed. He stopped drumming, pulled a chair up to his wooden dresser, stood on it, reached up and pulled down two large reindeer antlers.

'Since the King of the Reindeer came to see you today, I want to give you this so that he can always travel with you.'

He handed over a nine-pointed reindeer antler. It was absolutely beautiful. Since that time, I've always travelled with that antler. More importantly, Bikko Máhte's ability to share in my vision had us both laughing.

'Either we're both shamans or we're both lunatics!' he said.

*

Over the years, life has shown me time and time again just how important initiation is. Initiation is a ritualized acknowledgement of the ongoing process of change. Most significant changes throughout my life have been greatly supported by rituals that placed my personal experience into a much wider context. So many of the challenges I have faced have not been just personal but archetypal.

As well as excellent human support, from time to time I've been greatly helped by taking an honest look in the great mirror that is nature. Just as an old tree must expand into a new circle of growth each spring, I've often been shown and told how I have to expand beyond the known again and again if I'm serious about finding my freedom. And I've learned that, like a tree, strong roots and a good connection with the Earth are the medicine I need in order to grow in a good way.

Not long before I became a father, at the height of my apprenticeship with the Deer Tribe, I went out onto Dartmoor for a five-day vision quest. I fasted and spent the whole time alone, praying for a vision. Many things happened. I got lost, my compass stopped working and I was visited by ponies, sheep and cattle, but by the last night, I was still without a vision.

The moon was up and nearly full. I was in my circle made of eight Dartmoor quartz stones representing the eight directions. I was hungry and cold and thoroughly disappointed that a vision hadn't arrived. And after all that effort too! I was singing, creating rhythm with two pieces of wood I'd found for the purpose and praying with everything that I had to receive a vision.

Eventually, I had one. It was simple and mysterious. All I saw was a nine-year-old child playing the saxophone. That was it.

I came down from my quest and, in an attempt to stay true to my vision, bought myself a second-hand saxophone. I got lessons, but it was soon clear to everyone within earshot that the saxophone really wasn't my thing. I was disappointed and disheartened. Eventually, I had to let it go. There was nothing else to do.

Ten years later, I was returning home from teaching a workshop. As I came into the lovely little house we were living in, I heard the sound of music. I took off my boots and went into the living room to say hello to my family. As I entered the room, I stopped dead in my tracks. Right in front of me, there was a nine-year-old child playing a saxophone. It was our son. I couldn't believe it! What a lesson! The vision I'd worked so hard for wasn't even about me. Through my tears and laughter, I hugged my wife and our rather bemused son.

Something fell deeply into place for me at that moment. I'd been told many times that some of the things that we hold most dearly are dreams that belong not to our time but to future generations. I remember seeing a quotation that touched me in this way. It read: 'We know we have become fully human when we start to plant trees under which we know full well we will never sit ourselves.'

More and more, I came to see that the challenges that life presented me with were perfectly designed for me to discover who I was and what was mine to give. Through time and attention, wounds that had been so painful to me in earlier times became the source of my deepest medicine.

I've often pondered what it is that makes the difference between being crushed by our challenges and polished by them. What was it that made it possible for me to change my story whilst others with similar experiences remained lost inside theirs as if there really was no choice? I've come to the conclusion that it's a blend of personal empowerment, the love and support of someone, anyone, who sees us as we are and a sprinkling of good timing and good fortune. What I do know is that I've witnessed far deeper happiness and fulfilment in people who have really suffered and worked with that suffering than in people who seemingly have had all the privileges and blessings of an easier life.

In nature, it is diversity that creates health. I believe this to be true in our human community too. When we all end up aiming for the same goals and dreams, hypnotized into believing that what really matters is something that is outside us and always just out of reach, we land in the kind of trouble we now face collectively as a species.

I've witnessed in myself how attached I can become to my idea of reality, to the point where some part of me thinks it's my divine duty to impose my reality on everyone and everything I come into contact with in the name of faith. I've learned that's not faith. It's fear. My own lack of tolerance only reveals my own lack of security in who I am.

Having said that, one of the stages of awakening I've witnessed in myself and seen in others is a loyal and sometimes rigid adherence to teachings or practices. I've been through 'the religious phase' many times with each new discovery I've made. I've noticed that part of finding my ground has been a need for external security, so I've bought the T-shirt, worn the colours and carried the feathers that made my allegiance visible. For me, this rigidity has always been temporary, and as time has gone on, I've learned not only to tolerate but to celebrate the many paths up the mountain that lead to the same view.

Our Movement Medicine work, which initially took shape behind the veil of our conscious awareness and was finally brought to birth in 2007, is rooted in a magnificent mandala composed of 21 gateways. In Gabrielle's work, there is the artful simplicity of 5 rhythms. In Buddhism, there are the four noble truths. At best, these descriptions are beautiful works of art, vessels in which we can sail on the ocean of the unknown. They are maps and stories. They are not the truth. In reality, there are an infinite number of gateways, rhythms and noble truths. We humans seem to have a need to create perspectives through which we can better understand our place in the Great Mystery. This is a beautiful thing until we start to think that *our* truth is *the* truth.

The third and perhaps most challenging stage of a vision quest is called incorporation. Incorporation means living the vision and bringing its gifts to the community. Once we find a vision, it is our task to incorporate it into every area of our lives.

I wonder if this is particularly true of the time we live in or whether it has always been true, but I've met so many people who are running from one vision to the next and never getting down to the task of incorporation. It's a 'vision addiction' that gets in the way of bringing what we care about to Earth.

After the Ecstasy, the Laundry (Rider, 2000) is a great book by Jack Kornfield that speaks to this. For so many seekers, it's more like 'after the ecstasy, more ecstasy please'. After all, it's hard work and risky to make the attempt to bring what matters most to us from pristine idea into messy reality. If I have a vision of a beautiful garden and then return home to see uncared-for chaos outside my back window, I have two choices. The first is to trash my vision as being unreal or not quite perfect, give it up and go out and seek a better vision. The second is to pick up my shovel and start digging, and do the work year by year until my vision becomes an everyday reality. In my experience, it takes years and years of dedicated work to bring a vision to Earth. Thomas Edison's '1 per cent inspiration, 99 per cent perspiration' is about right.

Most of us in the modern world have been raised in a fast-food have-it-all-now culture. Permanent growth is the economic model we call healthy. This is the dominant story of our time and it has also found its way into the world of personal growth and spiritual awakening. Chögyam Trungpa is extremely articulate about this in his book *Cutting through Spiritual Materialism* (Shambhala, 1973).

As dominant as this story is, it is not nature's story. And we are beginning to discover that our attempt to dominate nature is about as wise as the idea that the builders of the tragically doomed *Titanic* had when they described their masterpiece of modern technology as 'unsinkable'. Nature works in cycles of life, death and rebirth, and like it or not, we are subject to that very same dance. In order for us to grow, ideas, habits and even relationships sometimes have to die.

⁓

Having done all the work I'd already done, I thought that I'd arrived. But I still had to learn that being real is a lot more challenging than displaying one's virtues. Life was making it clear to me that if I was genuinely interested in waking up from the daydream we call reality, I had to face my own shadows on a whole other level. I didn't want to, but the apprenticeship that was just over the horizon in the Amazon rainforest would show me both the consequences of not having been real and, as our dear friend Eva says, of continuing to place large quantities of sugar on large quantities of shit.

The powers of nature that I'd declared my allegiance to had some powerful and humbling lessons to teach me. Before I could accept the mantle of being an everyday shaman, I would have to make some fundamental changes. I would have to learn that the most dangerous thing I could do with my power was to deny it. I would have to own it, see its shadows and dedicate it again and again to love. Not the love of a New Age fantasy, but love that is fierce and determined to cut through illusion and denial. Love that cares passionately for life and acknowledges death. Love for my wife, for our son, for the land we live on and for the people we work with. Love rooted in action as well as being.

And I would have to learn how to live with the paradox between my intense desire to protect the wild places of this Earth that the balance of life itself depends on and the knowledge, which has always been with me, that I have absolutely no idea how this whole 'life on Earth theatre piece' should turn out.

Chapter 16

OUT FROM THE ASHES

'Sometimes even doing the right thing will leave you
with scars. But beauty comes from ashes, too.'
NATALIE LLOYD

Throughout the whole of my journey, I'd been aware of the pledge
I'd made all those years ago to Arwyn, my ancestors and my
companions to go back to Auschwitz and dance to honour the children
who'd died there. I'd made it clear that I would only go there once I felt
ready. That time had arrived.

It was 2001, 13 years after I'd made that pledge. One of our German
students, a fine young woman called Julia, had told me that she and a
group of psychotherapists she was working with had decided to visit
Auschwitz. She'd overheard me telling someone that I was planning to
go there myself and she thought it might be interesting both for me and
the group she was travelling with to have a Jewish man with them.

I was surprised to hear myself saying yes. I told her that I wanted
to travel to Auschwitz by train so that I could retrace the steps of the
horrific journeys that so many of my people had had to endure. She
and the group agreed and we planned to meet at Frankfurt station a few
weeks later.

I did ceremonies to prepare myself and ask for the support of
everything that guided me. I gathered all the tools of my practice that

I'd put in place over those 13 years and I also asked that my family and friends be aware of me on my journey. I felt well prepared.

I flew into Frankfurt airport and as soon as I got off the plane, I started to have flashbacks. As I walked through the customs hall towards the exit, I was acutely aware of the armed police in their uniforms. I felt as if I was in two places at once. Part of me was in the present, calm, collected and in control. Another part of me was on the verge of panic. I felt icy flashes of fear and the colour draining from my vision as if I was suddenly in a black-and-white movie. This part of me was on high alert and ready to run.

I did everything I could to stay in the present and to reassure the child in me who had had the memory of dying at Auschwitz so many years ago. I took a taxi to the train station and met up with Julia and the group. There were five of them in total – two older men, and two women in their thirties who were friends of Julia.

I'd booked myself a single cabin for the overnight train journey so I'd have time alone to prepare myself for the next day. On the train, my fear levels went through the roof as my flashbacks continued. I called my good friend David Rose and told him I was on the train to Auschwitz. As I said those words, the floodgates opened inside me and I was crying and remembering. The two worlds of the past and the present were colliding inside me and there was nothing to do but let the emotions flow and do my best to identify with the warrior in me who was choosing to make this journey. David helped me to remain in the present as much as I could.

Eventually I slept. My dreams were fitful, full of the ghosts of the past and the very recent genocides in Rwanda and the Balkans. The terror of the victims and the violence of the persecutors were very present aspects of our collective human capabilities then and now.

As the iron wheels of the train took me closer and closer to Auschwitz, in my dreams I shifted identities between the harmed and harmer. I awoke, adrenalized and on high alert, to the sight of the early spring landscape of Poland rushing by. I did my practice in that little cabin, dancing myself back into my body and doing my best to connect with all the support that I knew was there for me.

We got to our hotel in the early morning. Our plan was to eat breakfast and then meet to share our intentions before visiting the Auschwitz museum. I told the group about the night I'd had and listened to my companions as they shared their feelings of guilt and anger for what their families had allowed to happen in the Germany of the 1930s and '40s. I hadn't thought at all about what it would be like to be the only Jewish member of our group and I was shocked that I felt I was being asked to forgive them for the actions of their ancestors. I told them that I didn't hold them responsible for the actions of their forebears any more than I held myself responsible for some of the more reprehensible actions of the Israeli government in the modern day. As far as I was concerned, as truly horrific as the Holocaust had been, our human capacity for genocide is a story that belongs to us all as a species. My primary reason for going was to retrieve the soul of the child I'd become in the dark mirror ritual I had done with Arwyn all those years before. Alongside that, I intended to do my best to offer whatever I could to the children who had died there. It had become a basic truth for me that given different times and circumstances, any one of us could have been in any role in this terrible tragedy. My sharing had an edge to it. I didn't want the group's pity or their guilt.

It was a cold and blustery day. We spent it being taken round the well-organized museum that is Auschwitz concentration camp today. We were also taken to the Birkenau section of the camp and visited the ruins of the gas chambers. I'd been told that no birds flew over that eerie place, but it wasn't true. I saw and heard the song of many small birds and saw the first signs of spring, and I took solace in that.

As horrific as the day was, there was a strange sense of peace about the place, rather like that found in any large graveyard. It was as if the terror of what had happened there couldn't be felt in the light of the day. I realized early on that dancing there then was out of the question. I would have to return at night.

⚮

Back at the hotel, my companions' feelings had been exacerbated by what they'd seen and several of them were grey with shock. Their voices were quiet but full of emotion as each of them shared what they'd felt. I was moved by their courage in facing the horrors of the past and I felt a great sense of shared humanity. At the same time, I knew I had work to do. I told the group that I would return to Birkenau once it was dark and try to find a way into the camp so that I could do my ritual. I asked if any of them wanted to join me, although I made it clear that I had no expectations. The three women said yes immediately.

I went to my room to gather myself. I felt calm and focused, in the way that I often did in the storms of emotion that were catalysed by our work. I tried to rest, but soon gave up.

As soon as it was properly dark, I called my companions and we met in the lobby. We walked through the cool night air to the edge of the town, where the Birkenau camp was located. The iconic train tracks and guard tower that signalled the end of so many long and bitter journeys stood like silent sentinels of shame in the misty landscape. The gates were locked shut with a rusty old chain and padlock.

There was light coming from the guard room and I knocked on the door. A soldier opened it and looked at me, rather surprised. I don't speak Polish and he didn't speak English, but I managed to make it clear to him that I wished to enter and to say some prayers for my ancestors who had died there. He nodded and without further ado opened the gates for us.

Once inside, we stopped at the end of the train tracks where new arrivals would be met by the Nazi camp doctor who, with a nod to the left or right, condemned the prisoners to hard labour or immediate death in the gas chambers. That was where I began my ritual. I said

Kaddish, the Jewish prayer of remembrance. My prayer was laced with fury and defiance. Over and over, like the rising cadence of a storm, I found myself dancing, my feet pounding on the ground, my voice chanting: 'You failed! Fuck you! You failed!'

I needed the strength of my anger to give me courage, for as quiet as the camp had been during the daytime, I could now sense a painful clamouring, like the echo of much suffering. My companions quietly accompanied me as I followed the thread of the ritual I was in.

We went into what used to be a women's barracks. In the darkness inside the hut, I stepped over the boundary of time. Without warning, I felt the spirit of an old Russian woman enter my consciousness and I started to speak in Russian. In normal states of consciousness, I don't speak a word of the language. The woman was worried to death that the guards were going to discover a little baby that had been born in secret just a few days before.

I could feel panic rising in me like claustrophobia and my throat constricting with the terror and helplessness of the situation we were in. As Ya'Acov, I was just about holding on to my capacity to witness what was happening and I sat down and once again began to pray. I prayed for the release of this suffering and for the energy of these appalling memories to be cradled and composted by the power of the Earth underneath us. I felt nauseous and faint and knew it was time to leave. Out in the night air again, I gasped for air and steadied myself.

It was time to move on. I was walking between the worlds now, aware of the ground under my feet and a high-pitched humming that I'd come to associate with the presence of the non-physical world. We walked between the row upon row of long huts that had housed those waiting to die. Right at the end of the line were the ruins of gas chamber 1. Its form was still visible amid the concrete rubble and it was here that I found him – the boy in his shorts and black peaked cap.

He looked both happy to see me and terrified that we would be caught. My heart opened to this lost soul who had brought me here.

And he wasn't alone. Soon, there were hundreds of children around him and suddenly I knew exactly what to do. I just said to all of them, 'Follow me.'

'What about the guards?' they asked.

'Don't worry, they're sleeping.'

I felt like the pied piper leading a long line of children back between the rows of old barracks and the guard towers spaced evenly along the fence on either side. At this point, I'd lost all awareness of the women who'd come with me.

As we approached the gates out of Birkenau, the guard who'd originally let me in came out with the keys. At that moment, he appeared to me as the boatman over the river Styx and I walked right up to him, taking all the money I had out of my trouser pockets, and said to him in English, 'This money is to pay for the souls of these children. Do you accept it, boatman? Will you take them across the river to the land of the dead?'

I have no idea what he thought of this crazy Englishman stuffing money in his hand, but he nodded and that was good enough for me.

The gates were open and then we were out. I could still see the children behind me and at precisely that moment, a gap in the clouds opened up and the light of the moon shone down.

'Go, children,' I said. 'Now! Catch the light. Go home. This nightmare is over. You are free.'

I watched as one by one the children walked into the moonlight and dissolved. And then it was done.

❧

I was exhausted, relieved, emotional and very sensitive. The women were there now and they helped me to find the way back to the hotel and back to my room.

As I lay down in bed, shaking from head to toe, I gave thanks for all the protection and guidance I'd felt with me. After all this time, this nightmare and my personal connection to it was over. Or so I thought.

I fell into deep sleep and woke up in the middle of a dream. In it, I was walking around a festival. I found a poster on the floor. On it, there was a beautiful mandala, a little like a medicine wheel. At the centre of it was a phoenix. It was magical and compelling. After I'd seen it on the poster, I saw it everywhere. It was printed on the side of the marquees. There were altars made of flowers and stones, and all of them were set in exactly the same shape. I'd never seen it before and yet I recognized it as something familiar.

I looked around more. There seemed to be workshops going on using theatre, movement and other healing modalities. There was also a large stage and musicians were playing powerfully emotive music to a large audience.

I found an information desk and asked the smiling woman behind it what was going on.

She looked at me as if I was crazy. 'It's *your* dream,' she replied. 'You cooked this whole thing up.'

'What is it?' I asked.

'It's the Phoenix Festival. You created it.'

She picked up one of the leaflets and began to read it to me: 'The Phoenix Festival is a celebration of every human being's capacity to rise from the ashes of their suffering and create a new story. Through theatre, dance and other healing modalities, people who have suffered the terrible wound of genocide come together to tell their stories and transform them into medicine.'

I was both astonished and overwhelmed. A part of me intuited immediately what this dream would mean for me and for our work.

I woke up, sketched out the image of the mandala and wrote down all the details of the dream I could remember. And I saw that the leaflet in the dream and the whole dream itself was the way that my unconscious had found to tell me: 'This is the journey you have taken. You have risen from the ashes of your own suffering and chosen a new story. And now, Ya'Acov, it's time to offer that medicine to others.'

I got it. This was my work. Phoenix medicine was my thing. Creating the Phoenix Festival was my life's task. First in Auschwitz, and then in other places that have known similar suffering. In the stream of consciousness that was flowing that early morning in my tiny hotel room, I saw that the first step would be to take our work to Israel and Palestine and make the connection between the unhealed traumas of the Holocaust and the ongoing traumas that Israelis and Palestinians were inflicting on one another.

I was both excited and daunted and suddenly I remembered the words that Z'ev Ben Shimon Halevi had said to me all those years ago: 'You know, God doesn't make mistakes. You've been born Jewish, and there's a reason for it… At some point in your life, when you need to know, you will know why being Jewish is a part of who you are. Until that time, follow your way, follow your way.'

I'd done what he'd advised and now I knew. I'd thought that my work with Auschwitz was over, but now I saw that it was just beginning.

And those children? I'd given up asking if these experiences were real or not. For me, they were real enough.

Two weeks later, while teaching a movement workshop in Stuttgart, Germany, I saw the children again in a dream. The workshop was taking place in a gym with high windows all the way round. In the dream I was teaching there when something caught my attention out of the corner of my eye. I looked up and then I saw them, hundreds of children with their faces outlined against the window, the sun shining behind them, waving and smiling. I knew then that they were free. And in their freedom, I saw my own beckoning to me with the bright, unguarded smile of a child.

Chapter 17

IN EVERY GENERATION

'Deep under our feet the Earth holds its
molten breath, while the bones of countless
generations watch us and wait.'
ISAAC MARION, *WARM BODIES*

In the summer of the same year as my trip to Auschwitz, I met
Merilyn Tunneshende, a Toltec sorceress and *nagual* woman who
had been taught shamanic dreaming, energetic healing and sorcery
during the course of a 20-year apprenticeship in the Mexican desert
with Don Juan Matus and Don Genaro, none other than the teachers of
Carlos Castaneda.

In the Mesoamerican traditions in which Castaneda was studying, the
tonal is all that is material and can be known. If we talk about a tree, the
tonal is the leaves, branches, trunk and cellular structure. The *nagual* is all
that is non-material. It is the essence of that which gives life to that tree.
A human being known as a *nagual* is someone who is in touch with this
force, a man or a woman who has learned through disciplined practice
to perceive life from that point of view.

There is some dispute about whether the stories from Castaneda's
books are true or fictional. Either way, as a young man, they'd blown my
mind wide open to the reality that there are many ways of perceiving the
world and our place in it. Those stories and the wonderful characters

in them were my early guides. I was never really interested in the debates about whether Don Juan and Don Genaro were real people or figments of a brilliant imagination. To me, their knowledge, humour and magnificent discipline in the face of life's troubles were real enough to inspire me and countless others.

As you know, I'd made the choice some years before to study shamanism, not sorcery. However, there was something that drew me to Merilyn and I ended up working with her for three years.

I knew that I needed further support to develop this new sense of work that had been brought forth by my time at Auschwitz. I was fascinated by the mandala I'd seen and I asked an artist I knew to draw it for me. When I saw it on paper for the first time, I felt new life quickening in my blood. It was a beautiful symbol for the Phoenix Festival project. It had the feeling of an ancient story written in symbols.

At the same time, Susannah had a commanding dream in which she was visited by a luminous presence who spoke with a voice of immense depth and authority and said simply, 'Your work is to be called Movement Medicine.'

Neither of us realized the connection between the name and the mandala at that point. What we did realize was that things had become intolerably difficult with Gabrielle. There were differences in how we perceived our work and, more than that, fundamental differences in our way of being in relationship.

In many ways, I'd unconsciously become the bearer of the masculine shadow in our 5Rhythms world. I'd allowed myself to be cast as the ambitious one, the competitive one, the territorial one, and none of these aspects of masculinity were considered beneficial to anyone. I was therefore labouring under the misapprehension that being an ambitious, competitive and territorial man meant that I had a serious problem to deal with. I hadn't yet recognized the passion and strength in those characteristics. They were simply waiting for me to dedicate them to my highest purpose as a human being.

We had many conversations with Gabrielle in which we acknowledged the different tempos that we were moving at. We were approaching our forties and we wanted to know Gabrielle's plans for the future so that we could orientate ourselves and move forwards with full power in alignment with her. She was in her sixties and was needing to go slowly and carefully in thinking about her plans for the future. The vision she'd shared with us, of passing on her work to the small group of us who were her inner circle, had subtly shifted. We questioned her about this many times, and each time we did, she was clear that we were in a paranoid fantasy based solely and entirely in our own minds. So we danced as deeply as we could, did rituals, spoke to our friends and mentors and did our best to get to the bottom of our fear. And there was always something to find. We would do our inner work and our concerns for the future would lift for a month or two and we would see clear sky. But pretty soon the clouds would start to roll in again.

Eventually we found ourselves in a dilemma. We needed to know where to put our energy and it seemed that within Gabrielle's world, we'd reached a very real glass ceiling.

Maybe Gabrielle really didn't know the consequences of telling us her plans. Or maybe she was afraid to do so. I will never know. Whatever was true for her, we went round and round in circles with this dilemma for the last seven years of our relationship. There started to be 'no-go' areas in our conversations. We knew that at some point we'd have to speak our truth, but we felt that if we challenged what we saw to be some fundamental problems in the structure of the organization, our relationship and therefore our professional work would be endangered. As it turned out, we were right.

Despite all this, the love between us and Gabrielle remained strong. And, strange as it seems to me from where I am now, I kept the obvious possibility that our ways were diverging well hidden from my conscious mind. I assumed that somehow love would carry us through, we would work it all out and we would all live happily ever after.

That was the landscape in which I met Merilyn.

Merilyn and I quickly made a strong connection. I loved the way she talked about life. I loved her total dedication. And she was a master dreamer. In this way, working with her was a 24-hour-a-day thing.

Three major things happened in my three years of working with Merilyn for which I will be forever grateful. First, she helped me to find Bikko Máhte, even though at that point I'd no idea that he was anything more than an internal guide. Second, it was at a gathering with her that I found the sword that I'd been given in my first burial ceremony in Lavaldieu. And third, she supported me fully in recognizing the beauty of the fiery masculine energy in me that up until then I'd accepted was not okay. All three of these gifts were absolutely necessary for me to survive the apprenticeship which spirit was cooking up for me in a ceremonial compound deep in the Amazon rainforest of Peru.

On the first night of the first gathering with Merilyn, I dreamed that we would work together for three years and then our paths would diverge. It felt important to tell her that. She accepted it in a very matter-of-fact way.

At the end of the gathering, Simon, my friend and the organizer of the event, invited me to go out for dinner with him and Merilyn. But I'd been away from Susannah and Reuben for five days and, difficult as it was for me to say no, it was clear where my priority lay.

Back home that night, I dreamed a strange dream in which someone was asking me to deliver an important message to Merilyn. The whole landscape of the dream felt threatening and I woke myself up as soon as I could.

I called Simon the next morning and asked him where Merilyn would be staying that night. He told me the name of a hotel in Oxford that he'd booked her into. So later that day, I called the hotel and asked to speak to her. The receptionist was very sweet, but told me that nobody by that name was staying there.

Confused, I put the phone down. Then I remembered that Merilyn had told us that part of her training had involved becoming very different people in different situations in order to break the hold of her personality on her 'mysterious self'. For instance, one time her teacher had insisted that they spend three months living in a small fishing village in Mexico where he was known as an old drunk. She would be his hardworking niece. For the whole time they were there, they played these roles 24 hours a day, both in public and private. Given that Merilyn was a well-to-do academic from the west coast of the USA, she told us that the exercise had achieved the desired result!

I was familiar with this strategy from my earlier work. Indeed, on two separate occasions I'd become someone else just for a day. One time, I'd travelled to Cornwall on the train dressed as Madame Yacoushka, a clairvoyant cousin of Ya'Acov's who was visiting from Lithuania. She was a barefoot gypsy with rings on her fingers and toes. In order to pull this off, I had to totally become her. It worked so well that she ended up giving several psychic readings to her fellow passengers on the journey to Penzance.

On another occasion, when I was living in Nottingham, I'd asked a friend who was a professional make-up artist working for the BBC to make me up as an old man. When she was doing my make-up, there was a moment when I felt that I became that old man. My eyes went milky, my voice changed and my posture too. I spent the day in the city getting on and off buses, visiting the library and doing my shopping.

Both roles had helped me to loosen the hold of my personality and shapeshift into someone else. And, paradoxically, becoming another person had helped me to connect to the part of me that existed beyond style or presentation.

I guessed that Merilyn was now travelling in one of her alter egos, so I needed a strategy in order to get a message to her. I called the hotel back, this time pretending to be an American who'd met a stunning woman on the train and had a profound interaction with her. Embarrassingly, I told the receptionist, I'd forgotten her name. If I described the woman to her and she recognized one of the guests in the hotel, would she mind passing on a fax message for me?

The receptionist was quite taken with the romance of the situation and kindly agreed. So I sent a fax saying:

Dear Friend,

It was such a pleasure to meet you. I had a dream about a friend of yours called Carlos. He asked me to pass on a message to you, so please get in touch. Here is my number.

That night I had the very practical dream that I had to get on the 10.19 train to London and go and find Merilyn. I woke up and told Susannah that I needed to go to London. She was fiercely supportive of me in this strange adventure and simply smiled. So I booked my seat (sure enough there was a 10.19 train to London) and called the hotel in Oxford, again posing as the love-struck American.

'Did you manage to get my fax to the woman I described?'

'Yes, I did.'

'Is she still there? Can I speak to her?'

'No, she's just left for London.'

'Do you know where she will be staying?'

'I'm sorry, sir, but we are not allowed to give out details like that.'

'Yes, of course. Thank you. You're sure she got the message?'

'Yes, sir. I gave it to her myself.'

I came off the phone and wondered how on earth I was going to find Merilyn in London, a city teeming with 12 million people. Nevertheless, I had the feeling that I was in one of those dreams that had a mind of its own, so off I went.

I arrived at Paddington at 1.30 and sat down on my bag in the concourse. I called Susannah at home to see if Merilyn had left a message. She hadn't.

I had no idea what to do next. Sitting down, I felt invisible amongst the travellers going to and fro. It was as if I was in a dream. So, just as if I was dreaming, I asked the dream for help. I focused on a simple question: 'What should I do now?'

The answer I heard was simple and direct: 'Go to South Kensington.'

I had nothing else to go on, so to South Kensington I went. When I got there, I just started to walk. I didn't have a direction, but I decided to let my feet lead the way.

I was walking over a flyover when I had the feeling I should turn around. I retraced my steps and then I saw a hotel with a conservatory restaurant at the front. Suddenly I knew that was where I was heading.

I walked into the restaurant and there, to my utter astonishment, was Merilyn.

She calmly got up and greeted me. 'Hi, Ya'Acov, good to see you. I've just ordered lunch for both of us.' I must have looked shocked, because she continued sharply: 'Ya'Acov! Don't act surprised!'

'Don't act surprised?' I stammered. 'I *am* surprised.'

She whispered urgently that I should calm myself down and steadily held my wide-eyed gaze.

'Don't act surprised, Ya'Acov, or the spirits will give you something to be truly surprised about.'

That was enough of a warning for me. I forced myself to calm down, accept the situation and sit down.

For the next seven hours, we sat at that table and talked shamanism. She asked me about my healing way and maps. She told me about her time with Chon, the name she had for Don Genaro, and the healing methods he'd taught her. The time flew by and I learned so much.

We'd written notes and drawn diagrams on the paper napkins that the restaurant provided and suddenly, with a little shock of recognition, I remembered a story that Gabrielle had told me. One time, she'd been stuck at an airport in the USA after her flight had been cancelled. In the airport, she'd met a well-known Native American teacher. She told me they'd spent hours together sharing their stories and maps and writing notes on white paper napkins just as Merilyn and I were now doing.

I told Merilyn about it and wondered aloud if this was a dream that each and every generation of shamans dreamed.

She looked at me and laughed. 'Yes, it is,' she said. 'Yes, it is.'

∽

Just before we left, she asked me, 'Who are your allies? Who are your spirits?'

I told her about the spirit animals that I'd worked with, about the elements and about the Old Man of the North.

'Tell me more about him,' she said.

I told her how since I'd begun teaching, he'd always been at my back and in my dreams, supporting me and guiding me on my way.

She became silent for a while and closed her eyes. When she opened them again, she had a strange look that held my attention.

'He's calling you. He's no spirit. He's a living man. Find him.'

As I heard those words, a shock of electricity travelled up my back and my whole body jerked.

'See, your body knows it's true!'

∽

Day was now night and we said our goodbyes on the pavement outside the restaurant. Once again, life had revealed a little more of its mystery and my heart was bursting with gratitude.

I began to walk away, wondering where I was going to spend the night. Then I heard a voice behind me. It was Merilyn. I turned around.

'We said hello twice – once in the body and once in dreaming. So now we will say goodbye twice too – once in the body and now in dreaming.'

She had that shaman's look in her eyes again.

I went towards her to hug her, but just like a dream, she was no longer there.

∽

Chapter 18

CALL OF THE HUMMINGBIRD

'Manliness … consists in daring to do the right thing
and facing consequences whether it is in matters social,
political or other. It consists in deeds not words.'
MAHATMA GANDHI

Our next meeting happened back in Devon at Grimstone Manor. We were there to take part in a Quetzalcóatl ritual. Quetzalcóatl, from the Náhuatl language, meaning Feathered Serpent, is a Mesoamerican deity associated with the wind and wisdom. Sometimes known as Kukulcán, it is associated with many myths and stories. In our work with Merilyn, it represented the coming together of opposites that, when joined, become more than the sum of their parts.

The ritual took place at night, in candlelight, with copious amounts of copal incense filling the room with thick sweet-smelling smoke. Our intention was to bring some healing and a new sense of balance to the relationship between feminine and masculine inside us. Our work was personal, but Merilyn was clear that it was designed to bring benefit to everything to which we were connected. An imbalance between feminine and masculine rooted right in the very core of our creative sexual energy, she explained, was a major part of our weakened connection to our spiritual power. We talked at length about the repercussions of this for both women and men and for the web of life itself.

We began the ritual dancing a repetitive step in two parallel lines. Merilyn and I danced side by side at the head of the feathered serpent, drumming out the rhythm of the dance. All of us were moving together into trance. Merilyn was very disciplined in her focus and attention. She was aware of how easy it was for us to become distracted and fall out of the power of the imaginal world we were attempting to enter.

The rhythm and the smoke-filled twilight soon had us passing through the veil into the magical world of ritual. We chanted, the men finding a repetitive chant and the women weaving their voices around it. From time to time, I've witnessed what I've heard other shamans call 'the lines of the world' and in my altered state, they became visible to me. They are like radio waves that have become perceptible to the naked eye. Each frequency gives access to a particular station or story along which our ideas or dreams flow into reality. When we see or sense these patterns, as in a lucid dream, we become conscious in the realm that normally belongs to the unconscious. In that state, we are capable of making changes in the way we perceive and therefore co-create the world we live in. In every shamanic tradition I've worked in, the story we tell is primary. From it, individually and collectively, we give birth to the dream that we call reality.

As we danced through the room and the swirling smoke, the way in which I'd agreed to consign much of my masculine power to the shadows became visible to me. It was as if the characters from a theatre piece were practising their lines and waiting for my direction. I saw how I had massively limited the expression of the warrior energy in me, and how unless I freed him and gave him his place, his dignity and his purpose, he would end up causing havoc. I saw specific times when I had silenced myself with Gabrielle in order not to rock the boat or risk my position. I had folded my wings and bowed my head. In that moment, I got the first glimpse of my own complicity in the very things that upset me most in the organization I was part of. Susannah often says that when we dare to ask for hidden truths about ourselves to become visible to us, they appear like the fleeting shadow of a deer in the forest at twilight. And that's just how it was.

Acknowledging what is true is the first step to changing it. In that dark room, the warrior in me woke up and found his voice. I felt such power humming inside me. I sang and my wings opened. For a while, masculine and feminine were each distinctly themselves, each power supporting the other to shine as if the Earth and the sky were embracing through our dancing bodies. The power of each supporting the other to be itself and shine was a revelation to me.

We danced our prayers for harmony and a balance of power within us and in the world, and when we returned to ourselves, we brought back with us the knowledge of a new dream. I'd seen a new possibility and I was determined to bring it into my life, into my marriage and into our work.

When something that deep changes in my foundations, I'm usually in for a ride. This was no different. Every area of life where I'd submerged and buried the force of my masculine energy became uncomfortable. With Susannah, things were difficult for a time, as the balance shifted again between us. When I make a change inside myself, everything in my system has to adjust. And I'd been critical of and suppressed the force of my masculine energy for years. It was time for a rebalancing.

A year later, back at CAER in Cornwall, I worked with Merilyn for the last time. Our subject matter was the four foundational elements of healing that she'd been taught, which were likened to the four corners of a pyramid. The points were:

1. Masculine or yang power

2. Feminine or yin power

3. The dance between them

4.   4.   The manifestation of that dance in physical reality

Once these cornerstones were in place, we could safely access the fifth point at the peak of the pyramid, where it was said we could be in direct communication with the power of creation.

In our dreaming, Merilyn encouraged us to find the place that needed our attention most. I dreamed about the men's group I had belonged to in the 1980s. We were all proud new men, feminists and peace activists. We had gladly emasculated ourselves and, with a sense of irony, named ourselves 'the Wee Willy Wimpos and the Wailing Wizards of Gondwanaland'. That tells you all you need to know about where my relationship with masculine power had been hanging out! Like many of my contemporaries, I'd made the mistake of making masculine power the problem. I hadn't understood that power itself is neutral and it is entirely our choice what to do with it.

In the morning, before our dream sharing, I went to visit a friend, the same David Rose who'd been so supportive of me on my train journey to Auschwitz. He was staying in a bender in the gardens of CAER with his wife, Julie, and her son, Tig. (A bender is a dwelling made from bent hazel saplings and covered in tarpaulins.) I don't know how David knew what was going on for me, but he was clearly deeply tuned in to the energy we were working with in the group and, specifically, my own journey within it.

I entered the bender and sat down. I don't remember any initial conversation, just David asking me to close my eyes and put my hands out in front of me. I did as I was asked. He sat behind me and passed a short sword in a leather scabbard over my head and into my hands. He asked me to keep my eyes closed and told me that the ceremonial sword he'd just given me had been with him for many years. It had Sanskrit-like markings inscribed on the blade and David told me that pledges had been made across it and it was now mine if I was able to honour those pledges.

'The purpose of this sword,' he told me, 'is to cut through illusion with compassion, protect and honour the feminine, and protect and honour the children.'

When I opened my eyes, I gasped. There in my hands, in physical form, was the sword that I'd been given in the burial ceremony dream many years before. Finally, it had come to me. And what perfect timing! It was a beautiful symbol of the true use of masculine power.

I was so grateful for David's generosity, clear-seeing and friendship. He'd seen my need and found a perfect way to meet it.

I formally agreed to honour those pledges and, still deeply touched by the brilliance of life's choreography, I returned to the group, clutching this precious 'dream come true' object in my hands.

I was still visibly moved when the group gathered and Merilyn asked me to share my story. When I'd finished, there was silence. Eventually, it was broken by the sound of Merilyn's laughter. As so often when faced with life's majestic artistry, she simply laughed the laugh of the free.

We'd planned to end our gathering with an all-night ritual that would involve ingesting psilocybin mushrooms that had been preserved in mead.

It had been in 1989, at the Glastonbury Festival, that I'd first felt the power that teacher plants have to support us in directly experiencing our place in the web of life. 'Teacher plants' is the name given in shamanic traditions to entheogens, a particular set of plants that are said to have consciousness and the power to heal and open us up to a direct experience of the divine. They are in no way recreational. They are connected to traditions that go back thousands of years and are often part of initiatory practices. Where used properly and with guidance, they can open the windows of perception so that we can see ourselves and our place more clearly. Like anything, they can be abused, mostly in the way that people become dependent on having as many experiences as possible rather than integrating what they have been shown into day-to-day life.

At the festival, a good friend and I decided to take some psilocybin in a ritualized way. Our intention was to connect more to the Earth as a living being. I'd never taken anything like this before and I was both nervous and excited.

At first, nothing seemed to happen. But after a while I became supremely fascinated by the leaves of a tree in front of me. I was describing them to my friend when he asked me, 'What tree?'

I looked at him as if he was an idiot and replied, 'This tree here, right in front of us!'

I turned back to look at the tree and to my utter astonishment, nothing was there. The nearest tree I could see was about 1,500 feet away. As soon as I gave it my attention again, I fell back into an all-encompassing fascination with its leaves and the patterns in the bark. I was completely discombobulated, but my friend, much more experienced than me with these things, was laughing hard.

The mushrooms *spoke* to me. They instructed me in how to work with them and told me not to work with them again until I'd fully integrated what they were about to show me.

It started to rain and the sun was shining at the same time. The light was a physical presence and I felt the Earth and all the plants drinking in this holy gift of rain. I saw and felt the Earth breathing and my own body became part of that long in-and-out rhythm. I couldn't believe that I'd forgotten the beauty and sanctity of nature. I remembered that as a child, being connected to that was the greatest joy I'd had in my waking hours.

I felt so grateful to those little mushrooms that seemed to have a consciousness all of their own. They'd honoured my intention and showed me what I'd most needed to see. I was part of the land and the land was part of me.

In the ritual with Merilyn, we took the medicine in the woods at night with a fire burning and the sound of owls all around us. After a while, listening to the fire and the sounds of the night-time forest, it became clear that the parting of the ways I'd always known would happen with Merilyn had arrived. It was time for me to leave.

I had a quiet conversation with her. With the equanimity of the medicine woman she was, she let go. I left quietly and went to bed.

The group ended the next day and I said my goodbye to Merilyn and thanked her for all we had shared. There was sadness in our parting, but no holding on. We had played our roles for each other and it was time to let go. That was the last time I saw her.

✂

I returned home with my sword and all that I had received. That week, Susannah and I watched the second of *The Lord of the Rings* trilogy, *The Twin Towers*. In it, there is a huge battle called the Battle of Helms Deep. It's an epic battle and as Susannah and I watched, I felt something stirring inside me. By the time the movie ended, I was really emotional. Susannah asked me what was up. My frustration came to a head: 'I'm a warrior and there is so much to fight for! What am I doing living my safe little life in this safe little house in safe little Devon?'

I didn't know what to do with myself. I was certain that I didn't want to be at war. At the same time, the masculine energy that had been awakened in me and that I'd come to see as really positive was jumping at the bit to find some useful expression.

It turned out that my post-movie question was more of an invocation. Quite soon, life would give me an opportunity to experience my very own battleground.

The door opened in my dreaming. I was due to go to California in a few months' time to work on the next module of Gabrielle's professional training. In the dream, I met the old spirit whose bony finger had drawn me into the Amazon rainforest a few years before. The medicine people I'd met that night had been very clear that I shouldn't go looking for them but wait for them to contact me. This time, the dream spirits told me very simply, 'It's time. You will meet us in California.'

When I woke up, I immediately wrote to some colleagues in California and asked them if they knew of any Amazonian shamans working in the area around the time of the training. They didn't. I was a little surprised, as the dream had been very specific that I should ask them. But a day later, I was relieved when they wrote back telling me they'd just heard of a gathering that was due to take place three hours after my work had finished. I contacted the organizers and booked a place immediately.

⌖

A few months later, in the early spring of 2005, I arrived at the private house in California where the ceremonies would take place. I didn't know a soul there. We gathered in a large, wooden purpose-built room at the bottom of the garden, surrounded by trees. It was a beautiful spot. I'd no idea what to expect. Everyone was dressed in white and we sat in semi-circles with the musicians and ceremonial leaders at the front. I was given a seat near the front, a cushion and a songbook. We weren't told much, but I met somebody who kindly asked if this was my first time. He gave me some advice: 'Whatever happens, just keep on saying thank you.'

His words were a great help during those two nights of ceremony and have been in many situations since. We were told that during those two nights there would be a marriage, an Umbanda ritual and songs from many different spiritual traditions around the world. In the Angolan quinbundo language, Umbanda means 'the art of healing'. Umbanda is a religion blending original African traditions with Roman Catholicism, Spiritism and other indigenous American beliefs. The songs are powerful invocations of spirits, and the dancers and singers regularly experience possession in a positive sense.

We were told that 'getting well', or purging, was a normal part of these kinds of ceremonies and that we shouldn't be concerned if the effect of the medicine was to cleanse us in this way. Small white buckets and boxes of tissues were liberally scattered around the room. Most of the people there were very experienced and there were nervous murmurs from around the room. And then we began.

Prayers were said and a whole host of beings were invited to join us. I felt at ease, though my stomach was churning, partly from fasting all day and partly, I was to discover, from the presence of the Amazonian medicine that we were given one by one from a small cut-glass tumbler. The taste of the medicine was extremely bitter. After drinking it, I sat down and the singing began.

It was an extraordinary two nights for me. I reached the edge of my capacity to expand many times, and each time that happened, I thanked the medicine and was given support to breathe, let go and take another step. I asked questions and was given direct answers. I felt as if I was in the presence of an absolute *maestra* whose power I could trust. There was nothing in the way. I was given so much and I experienced divine presence through her guiding hand. The music was the most beautiful I'd ever heard. And all the time, like a green thread that pulsed and weaved its way through the rivers of my blood, the sounds and creatures of the Amazon rainforest filled me.

At one point, I asked, 'Please show me creation.' The roof of the building disappeared and I rose up into the sky. I was shown divine forms of creation and destruction, an ongoing dance of structure and fluidity merging and dividing like cells, each cell a world unto itself. Stars and supernovas came into being and disappeared in huge bursts of light. And behind it all was the vast and endless darkness from which everything was emerging and to which everything returned.

Throughout the journey, the lush, fertile wetness of the Amazon, the anaconda, the jaguar, the blue morpho butterfly and the life-force of billions of trees providing oxygen for us all sang their ancient song of remembering through the still night air. I saw the people of the forest too. I could only see them out of the corners of my eyes. If I tried to look at them directly, they were gone. But they watched and listened, and I tried to thank them. I also tried to understand what they were saying to me. All I could sense was a strong calling.

From out of the kaleidoscope of forest-dwellers, one single being emerged, its wings a dazzling array of dancing colours, bringing nectar from the heavens and delivering it, drop by drop, into the centre of my heart. The hummingbird hovered in front of me and I heard, in the hum of its wings, an invitation delivered in the form of the primal language of the uninterrupted force of creation that is the Amazon rainforest.

And then I knew that the forest, and its medicine, was the teacher I'd been waiting for. Right there and then, I made a pledge to go. I asked the hummingbird to open the way and lead me to the place where I could learn and the people I could learn from.

❧

By the morning after the second night, the English language was still worlds away. When I managed to work out how to call Susannah back at home, all she could hear at the other end of the phone was the strange twitterings of a hummingbird trying to convey his love and share the total joy and miracle of being alive.

❧

Chapter 19

HARDCORE OLD SCHOOL POPS THE BUBBLE

'This is the true joy in life, the being used for a purpose
recognized by yourself as a mighty one; the being a
force of nature instead of a feverish selfish little clod
of ailments and grievances, complaining that the
world will not devote itself to making you happy.'

GEORGE BERNARD SHAW

I joined a third ceremony later that week with the same group. This time I was asked to sit at the back, as my hummingbird twitterings had been quite a distraction for the musicians!

At one point I went downstairs to go to the bathroom. The small hallway was dark and had a beautifully soft white shagpile carpet. There was a picture of Osho on the wall. Like a photograph in the Harry Potter stories, he appeared to be fully alive and moving.

I asked what he was doing there and he looked back and replied, 'No, what are *you* doing here? I *live* here.'

I laughed.

I liked being in the dark. I felt a door opening to the Amazon. I felt a large cat close by and for the first time I briefly experienced the raw animal power of the jaguar in my body. What a force and what intelligence! I wandered through the invisible pathways of the forest, following the scent of my prey, before I was rather sharply brought back to a different reality by one of the assistants insisting that I come back to the light of the ceremony. I didn't want to leave, but I respected their request and left the forest for another day. My hunger to be there was growing.

∽

Soon after that experience I taught a workshop at our sister Moving Center School in Sausalito, California. The experience of that first medicine journey had already changed my inner world and the opportunity to bring some of what I'd received straight into my work was a blessing.

What I remember most from that workshop is how bright and strong the new energy coming through me was and how restricted I felt by the form of what I'd been teaching for the past 17 years. I could see the sky above me, but I felt as though my face was pressed hard against a glass ceiling.

For the first time, I could see the possibility that we were going to have to let go of the community we'd played such a strong role in creating. But I was still afraid of admitting to myself that there was a growing soul need for Susannah and me to step out of Gabrielle's circle and have the space to offer the medicine that was trying to find its way into the world through us. I was afraid of what that might mean.

∽

On my return home, there was the small matter of finding the right place and the right teachers to visit in the Amazon. I followed the trail and found a friend who knew someone, a young American man called Hamilton Souther, who'd been an apprentice of an indigenous shaman in the Peruvian Amazon named Don Alberto for the past five years. Don Alberto was considered to be one of the most powerful healers in the Ucayali region of the Amazon.

I sat alone in ceremony with my drum to ask whether this was the right place to go. This was all the more important as we'd decided to go there as a family. Our son was now approaching 14 and was showing signs of being interested in exploring other states of consciousness. We'd given him a powerful initiation into young adulthood at the age of 13 and this felt like part two of that initiation.

As far as I could tell, we were on track. We arranged to travel to Peru in late August, stay there for 10 days and then travel to California for the next stage of Gabrielle's training that we were teaching on. We had to organize a boat plane to pick us up in the forest in order to get to the training on time. Then, with all practical details taken care of, we headed off on our first trip into the Amazon.

We met Hamilton in Iquitos, as well as the other members of our group. We were 12 in total, including our good friends Jake and Eva, whom we had persuaded to travel with us.

We travelled overnight up the Amazon on a 15-hour journey by boat to a village deep in the forest called Jenaro Herrera, on the Ucayali river. We stopped for lunch and had our first contact with the indigenous people. From there, carrying all our luggage and food, including a bunch of live chickens, we travelled by small canoe along the tributaries of the forest. There hadn't been much rain and at times there wasn't enough water to keep the boat afloat, so we were asked to get out and help push. We took off our trousers and boots and, knee-deep in the thick silt of the river, pushed the canoes onwards towards our destination. At times, we were cooled by our first taste of Amazonian rain. We were told not to worry about the piranhas, as they only went into a feeding frenzy if they smelled blood! What a sight we were, muddy and wet and dressed only in our underwear and hats. And what an adventure we were on!

Eventually, close to dusk, we ran out of river next to a small village. The people from the village came down to greet us and, singing and laughing, proceeded to take our luggage and supplies onwards. We were left to follow a young boy, probably nine or ten years old. I walked behind him as he led us, barefoot, through the labyrinth of the forest to our final destination. I was deeply impressed by how in his body he was, how at home and how confident of finding the way as darkness fell.

Eight hours after leaving Jenaro Herrera, we arrived at the camp. Our luggage arrived soon afterwards. We ate and bedded down for the night.

⸙

The next day, we set out early to pick the ingredients to make the medicine for the first of three ceremonies. Hamilton related how he'd come here in quite a state five years before, how he'd found Don Alberto and how he'd taken a full apprenticeship with his *maestro*. He told us how tough his healing journey had been and described the battles he and his *maestro* had had to fight. Don Alberto was well known for standing against those who used the medicine for personal gain and to do harm.

I listened with interest, but felt somewhat removed from the scenes he was describing. I suspected that the *brujos* he'd encountered were just externalizations of his own unfinished business. *Brujo* is a word used in many Spanish-speaking cultures to refer to people who are practitioners of so-called 'dark magic'. In the Amazon of Peru, a *brujo* or *brujeria* usually refers to someone who uses their power to do harm on behalf of those who pay them for their services, rather as we in the West might hire a lawyer to bring an adversary down.

My own experience, up until that point, had been very gentle, kind and powerful, and I felt quietly confident that this would continue. Never have I been so wrong!

We spent all day preparing the medicine as Hamilton continued to talk to us about the minimum 5,000-year-old tradition that we were entering into. He described how each of the ingredients that we put into the big pot over the fire had particular medicine and how during the ceremony he and Don Alberto would be able to call on the power of each plant through the spirit songs, or *icaros*, that the plants themselves had taught them.

He told us that during the ceremony, under the effects of the medicine, we were free to express ourselves as we needed to. He said that we were now in the home of the medicine and for those of us who had drunk before, this was going to be very different experience. He told us that if we needed to shout or cry, we should feel free. He also assured Susannah and me that we could let go and that he would look after Reuben.

I looked around me, wondering who amongst us would be the one to break. I didn't realize it would be me and just what a humbling I was about to receive.

As the sun set and the night began, we gathered in the *maloca,* the ceremonial house, which was beautifully constructed in the traditional way with a leaf roof and, mercifully, fully netted to keep out insects and the tarantulas we could hear moving about beneath us. We all shared our intentions, wished each other well and drank the bitter medicine.

Within minutes, I felt the full effect. I saw a three-dimensional wall of Amazonian energy coming towards me, made up of thousands of different creatures and beings, many of which I'd never seen before. I was frozen like a rabbit in the headlights.

Hamilton and Alberto were playing their *shakapas,* a traditional leaf rattle that the shamans use to clean and direct energy and to accompany their *icaros.*

Hamilton looked at me and told me to stand up and meet what was coming towards me. Amazed that he could see what I was seeing, I struggled to my feet. I felt that I was about to be flattened by that wall of energy, but it stopped right in front of me and a voice emerged from somewhere in its midst.

'Who are you and why are you here? What do you want from us?'

It seemed they had come to interview me.

'My name is Ya'Acov. My ancestors came from eastern Europe. I am here with my family. I am here to learn from you. I was called here in my dreams. My teachers call me a shaman and I wish to deepen my work with your help. Our shamans have been persecuted and we have lost our connection to nature and our own deeper nature. Please help me with this so that I can support others.'

Their only response was: 'Louder!'

I couldn't believe that it was me who was going to be the one shouting. I felt so embarrassed as I repeated, this time more loudly, what I'd already said, to an audience I wasn't even sure was really there.

'Louder!'

At full volume, I shouted out my intention to the spirits. What else could I do?

'So be it,' they replied. 'So be it.'

What followed wasn't pretty. Throughout that ceremony and the two that followed, I was brought to my knees again and again and found myself begging for mercy on several occasions.

'This *is* mercy,' was all I heard in response.

I was in need of help, but the medicine told me that this was between me and her and that neither Hamilton nor Alberto would be allowed to intercede. Hamilton later confirmed that he had heard exactly the same thing from the medicine.

I purged and purged and purged again. I thought that I was dying and at times I wished for any way out of this experience that I'd seemingly asked for of my own free will. By the end of that first ceremony, I was a fully signed-up member of the 'never-again club'. But come the next ceremony, there I was again. Despite there not being human help present in my work, I could hear and feel the Amazonian spirits all around me, caring for me, whispering in my ears and even holding my bucket for me. I could feel their 'hands' on me directing the medicine to where it needed to go.

On top of all this, in the late afternoon of the following day, as I was walking through the small compound of forest huts, all of a sudden, a wind 'hit' me from my left. I felt dizzy and lost my bearings for a couple of minutes. I was shocked. I knew something had happened, but I refused to believe it and so, foolishly, said nothing to Hamilton or Alberto.

That night in ceremony, the cause of the experience made himself known to me. I heard a voice inviting me to ask for whatever I wanted. I was in such a mess that I ignored the warning signs that my body was giving me through a pain in my left ear, and replied, 'I'd like to meet the spirit of the forest.'

'Of course. Look to your left.'

Outside the *maloca*, I had the most intense vision of nature in her full beauty and glory. I felt drawn to go and be with her and ask for her blessing. I was so naive. As soon as my consciousness left that *maloca*, even though my body remained seated on my mattress, I felt as though I'd been grabbed by an icy-cold hand.

I jerked back into my body, gasping, and broke out into a cold sweat.

Hamilton looked at me. 'Don't leave the *maloca*, Ya'Acov. You are safe in here.'

I talked to him at the end of the ceremony and he explained more about the shamanic culture of the forest.

'There are many who have sold their soul for power. When they see you coming into their territory and they see your energy, they see what you have as potential payment for their debts. If you let them, they will take whatever they can.'

I was a mixture of outraged, strangely proud and terrified, all at the same time.

'Did you see the *brujo* who attacked you?'

'Yes.'

'Where is he now?'

I felt a strange tug in my body as if some kind of stretchy, fibrous material was attached to me.

'He's over there,' I pointed to my right, 'about 1,500 feet away.'

'Follow me.'

I felt Hamilton's spirit head into the forest and did my best to follow him with my awareness. We circled the *brujo*, caught him in a net of energy and pulled his spirit into the *maloca*. Although I had no idea how we were doing what we were doing, in the setting and the state I was in, it all seemed perfectly natural.

'He's here now. Talk to him.'

'What am I supposed to say?'

I felt suddenly out of my depth, but Hamilton insisted.

At first I was angry and shouted at the space I felt the *brujo* to be in: 'I'm here to learn, not to take from you! Why did you attack me?'

There was no reply and I felt stupid and tongue-tied.

'Look and speak from your heart,' Hamilton whispered.

As I did, I suddenly saw a small old man, broken by his own design. He looked like someone who had borrowed money from the mafia. He was terrified and seemed more of a child than a powerful *brujo*. I felt a sense of terrible loss.

'I feel for you, grandfather. I pray you find what you need. And I pray you can forgive yourself for whatever it is that got you here.'

I saw him bristle and prepared to defend myself, but then he just faded away.

Hamilton told me that Alberto's *maestro* had trained many people and that more than half of them had chosen the way of the *brujo*. He understood that we all had free will and that in Amazonian shamanism, as in all other walks of life, we had the freedom to make our own choices.

'Who are we,' he asked, 'to judge how someone should choose to live their life?'

I was disturbed by the whole encounter and at the same time fascinated by this new world. This was 'hardcore old school' shamanism.

Alberto joined us smoking a *mapacho*, a jungle-tobacco cigar, which the shamans used for healing. He blew smoke over me and then sat down. He and Hamilton spoke together in Spanish. Then Hamilton turned to me.

'Alberto wants to know who is the raven woman with black hair who won't let you grow?'

'*What*?!'

I was shocked fully awake. Neither Alberto nor Hamilton knew anything about our relationship with Gabrielle and to hear it described in such a way wasn't pleasant. I felt immediately defensive of Susannah and myself, and Gabrielle too.

I asked Susannah to join us. We asked the shamans what they'd seen and they both told us matter-of-factly that they'd been aware of a woman who looked like a raven and had her wings spread in such a way that we couldn't see or receive the light.

It was as if they'd taken a sharp pin and popped a bubble we'd been inside for so long that we'd forgotten it was there.

In Amazonian shamanism, when something is wrong, the cause is usually seen to be a *brujo* who has been hired to cause damage or who has their own reason to do so. In the shamanic and personal awareness culture that we'd grown up in, shit happened between people. We saw the difference, and so neither Susannah nor I had ever taken on the story that Gabrielle had purposefully or consciously done anything to keep us smaller than we were. However, the mirror these two shamans held up to us woke us up to the fact that for some time something had been genuinely out of balance in the space between us.

This unexpected conversation, in the wilds of the Amazon, was the push spirit gave us to face the facts. We both felt the force of the forest supporting us and giving us the courage to take the steps we needed to take. Within less than a year, we would leave our teacher, our practice and our community and begin to teach Movement Medicine.

A *dieta* is a strict regime that apprentices commit to for the period of the *dieta* itself and the 30 days that follow it. No touch, no salt, no fat, no pork, no sex or dreaming about sex, no toothpaste, cosmetics or creams of any kind are allowed. It's a time of deep concentration in which the apprentice comes into personal relationship with the spirits of the lineage. This happens in dreams and in ceremonies, and in the best of cases the spirits teach the apprentice their songs so that they can be called in ceremonies, healings and wherever the need arises. Hamilton told us that it was rather like becoming an apartment block for Amazonian spirits.

∽

By the end of that first visit, all three Darling Khans had been thoroughly cleansed and initiated. Amazingly, I was sad to leave. We took a canoe upriver and the locals came out to wave us off as our boat plane took off over the vast expanse of the forest. Reuben fell asleep in the back of the small plane and as we headed back towards Gabrielle's world, we wondered how our future would unfold.

∽

Chapter 20

FROM *MAESTRO* TO NOVICE – DISMEMBERED, DISILLUSIONED AND REBORN

'The energy which animates the All erupts
through the embodied self and destroys
identification with the sickly contracted ego,
opening the self to merge with new powers.'
ALEX GREY

A few months later, we were with Gabrielle's inner circle in a little house in the woods near Boston. On the agenda was the question of where we were and where we were heading.

We were there for the weekend and we spent the first day trying every conceivable way to fit round pegs into square holes. However hard we all tried, we couldn't craft a shared vision for the future. There wasn't one. There was nowhere to go and it became clear to all of us that it was time for Susannah and me to move on.

It was a relief finally to name this together and at that point there was a deep understanding between us. We all recognized that our 18-year apprenticeship had come to an end and there was all the sadness, honouring and celebration that was appropriate to such a massive moment of change. We left with blessings for the way ahead.

However, the next two years were a painful mess as egos kicked in, fingers were pointed and many people who had been students of ours and Gabrielle's felt the pain of a tear in the fabric of our collective family. At several points, Gabrielle chose to publicly accuse us of stealing her work. With the advice of our elders and mentors, we chose not to answer. Instead, we decided to let our walking be our talking whilst licking our wounds in private and getting down to the work of investigating our part in creating this mess.

Over the years we had seen and been shocked by Gabrielle's capacity to carry out public character assassinations on people who had upset her in some way. Part of our own process was to recognize that although we had privately stood up for those she had attacked, we hadn't done so publicly for fear of being next in line. Once I saw how it felt to be on the other side of the fence, I immediately wrote to previous colleagues and friends and apologized for not being much stronger in my support of them.

This was just the start. It took us years to understand fully how we had played our part in creating such a sad end to such a profound relationship. Despite how painful all this was, I would go as far as to say that the lessons we learned in that time may well be the most important ones I learned in my whole apprenticeship with Gabrielle. I saw how unhealthily entangled I had become with her. Much to my chagrin, I hadn't been strong enough to draw the line on many occasions when I absolutely should have. I'd been attached to my position of power within her organization and had used my rank in unconscious ways, showing off about how close I was to her, how she made Susannah and me miso soup in her home, how we stayed in the same hotels, how she called us up for advice, and so on.

I also saw how unaware of her own shadow and power issues Gabrielle was. Like all of us, she was blind to many aspects of her unconscious, and, as my good friend Jake says, 'When power and unconsciousness go together, there's real trouble.'

People in power need healthy feedback loops. They need people who aren't dependent on them for love, money or anything else and who aren't afraid of telling them the truth.

The first thing we did when we set up our own school was to put that in place. Witnessing our shadows in this way was a humbling experience. Here we were, leaders of a tribal community where consciousness was a central goal, unable to sort out a basic and archetypal conflict between teacher and apprentice.

I'm sad to say that despite our many requests for communication, we only spoke with Gabrielle one more time before she died in 2012. At the same time, my acceptance of my teacher's imperfections helped me to accept my own and, more than that, taught me how important it was to be conscious of power issues, especially as a leader.

Having said all this, once the stable door opened, we bolted for freedom with all the pent-up energy and held-back passion of the last seven years. It was such a creative, challenging and ultimately humbling time for us both.

Since it had first appeared in my dream, we had been working to unlock the meaning of the mysterious symbol of the phoenix, circles and four directions that was to become the central symbol of our new work. Our main method of enquiry was to ask: 'Of all the things we have learned and experienced, which teachings have helped us most and what has helped us to bring these teachings into our day-to-day life?' We asked this in ceremony, in our practice and in hundreds of conversations over three years.

Eventually things fell into place. The synthesis of our collective study and experience came into focus and the School of Movement Medicine was born in January 2007. The vision that we had held since the very early days of our relationship had finally found its form and its place in the world.

∽

Thanks to the Great Choreographer, my apprenticeship in the Amazon happened over this time period. Perhaps unsurprisingly, the focus of this apprenticeship was precisely the same issue as had arisen with Gabrielle. In order to trust my power and learn to use it wisely, I had to look into the purest mirror I could find and get to the roots of my own power stories.

During the time of my apprenticeship, I needed to be super-disciplined about following all the rules of the *dietas*. Not having sex and not even dreaming about sex were the most challenging of the disciplines. I often had so much energy in my body that I would wake up in the middle of the night and have to go for a little run round the woods behind our house! At the same time, it was like a new beginning for Susannah and me, and surprisingly, we found a whole new level of closeness during that time that deepened the intimacy considerably when the taboo was lifted.

The most intense of my visits to the Amazon was a five-week *dieta* in the winter of 2006. Those five weeks were without doubt the most challenging time of my life. Each day of my *dieta* was a study in terror as the light of the day faded and the next ceremony approached. I was alone with my teachers, a few guests and some locals in the middle of the Amazon. There was nowhere for me to turn. There was nowhere for me to hide.

Very early on in my *dieta*, Alberto had shown me in graphic detail the work that was ahead. He and Hamilton both acknowledged that in my work in Europe I was, in their words, a *maestro*. But here in the Amazon, I was a novice.

Alberto told me he admired me for seeing my need to begin again. One afternoon, as he gave me my tree spirit medicine, he told me that

I shouldn't sing in the ceremony, as when I sang, everything that was 'crossed' in me and in need of cleansing came into the space, amplified. He and Hamilton then had to deal with it. As an apprentice, it was my job to watch, listen and learn. They made it clear that they would tell me when it was time for me to take steps within their *mesa*. *Mesa* is the Spanish word for 'table'. In many shamanic traditions, it is used to describe the energy field of a shaman and the lineage to which they are connected. It is the 'safe space' that the shaman holds for the work. Alberto and Hamilton assured me that I would learn and grow and, in time, be working alongside them.

Alberto told me that in our next ceremony, he would sing into my medicine so that I could see exactly what he meant by 'crossed energy'. He was true to his promise. In that ceremony, I was taken down into the basement of my psyche and shown my energy as my *maestros* saw it. I went down and down a long stairway until I came to a corridor with a door at the end. I went through the door into what I can only describe as my nightmare kitchen. There, stacked up to the ridiculously high and greasy ceiling, I found pots and pans and plates and utensils of every description, the result of 17 years of not attending to the washing up. Anyone who knows me will tell you just how fastidious I am around the kitchen. I like things Zen, neat and in their place. This was the perfect image to freak me out. Was this really all *my* washing up? How had it got there? Was it the result of my spiritual niceness? Had I been such a martyr that I'd taken on all the energy the people in my workshops were releasing? Surely there must be a mistake. But no, it was clear. This was *my* energy field. This was *my* mess.

What could I do but clear the sink and get down to the work of finding out what all of this was about?

I had the feeling that I was carrying the results of my own naivety as a group leader and I experienced a mixture of helplessness, humour and a fury that was bubbling around in my belly. I kept coming back to one question and, laced as it was with blame and indignation, it was a clue: 'Why had no one ever taught me how to protect myself?'

For the next week, I made a study of my own lack of boundaries in every area of my life. I saw how naive I had been. For 17 years, I'd been encouraging everyone to let go of any unnecessary weight they'd been holding. I'd never stopped to think about where all that energy ended up.

Now I had two tasks ahead of me. First, to clean the kitchen. And second, to learn to protect myself better.

As I purged, I saw so many situations in which I'd unconsciously cleaned up the energetic fall-out in my work. Like *Groundhog Day*, there I was, again and again, being a self-sacrificing lunatic and clearing up.

And in my dreams and in visions in the ceremonies, the trees taught me about who they were and how they could support me in holding a clearer and cleaner space. They taught me their songs so that I could call them when I needed them.

I couldn't believe that all this help was available to me in non-human form. The generosity of the forest was beyond belief. Of course, I'd worked with my allies for years. But night after night and day after day, I was shown how strangely complacent I'd been not to ask for their help much, much more. I was shown how I'd treated my allies as accessories rather than beings who'd come at my request to help me. It was tough work.

∽

One night, Papa Tua, the head medicine spirit of Alberto and Hamilton's lineage, came to me. He looked like a fusion of Bob Marley and Whoopi Goldberg, all wild hair, firm eyes and natural force. In my vision I was surrounded by 1,000 demons, like Marvel Comic figures, grotesquely ugly and utterly precise. Each was magnificent in its creativity and detail. I felt that I'd arrived in the hell realms to face the shadow world of my unowned selves, but at the same time, they all seemed so real that I felt I was in genuine danger.

Papa Tua was at my side. 'Stand up, man! Look at them, one by one. Look them in the eye. See who they are to you. And tell them you are unafraid.'

'But I *am* afraid. I'm terrified.'

'Do it!'

So I stood up, quite literally shaking in my boots. All of the demons stopped what they were doing, turned around and stared at me. It was like walking into a bar in an inner-city no-go zone. The silence was brutal.

I felt the demons' fury and their menace. 'I'm not afraid of you,' I stammered.

I already had their full attention. Now they looked as though they were preparing to attack.

I honestly felt that I was about to die. I saw Susannah's face, and Reuben's too, and felt devastated to realize that I would never see them again. And from the love I felt for them, my force returned.

I shouted: '*I am not afraid of you!*'

Miraculously, what had started as a fake-it-till-you-make-it charade was now the simple truth. I was no longer afraid of them.

I moved towards them to engage them, not in battle but in conversation. I wanted to know who they were and where they were from.

So, I met my addictions. I met my worst fears. Abandonment and betrayal were there. Pornography too. One by one my dis-eases appeared to me like the fractured shards of a nightmare laid out before me. I talked with them all. I saw their roots – some in my own life, some that went way back in time into my ancestors' lives and the many lives that make up the mystery of each human soul.

And as I engaged with them and saw them as parts of my personality, my repetitions, my stories, they lost their menace and became part of the bigger picture of who I was. I was elated with my work.

Papa Tua returned. He had an anaconda wrapped around his massive shoulders. His jaguar-like teeth shone like ivory in the moonlight when he smiled.

'Nice warm-up. You are ready to begin.'

My terror returned. I thought I'd just faced my fears, but apparently that was just the *hors d'oeuvres*. Now what? My *maestros* were well known for standing up to the sorcerers and *brujos* in the region. People often came to them for healings and I'd already witnessed the kind of battle that healings could entail as curses were undone and energetic darts removed.

One day we'd been lying in hammocks in Alberto's cabin talking. It was very humid and we could hear distant thunder amid the cacophony of the forest. Hamilton and Alberto were both clear with me that their practice and their personal ethics forbade them from using their power to take any form of revenge. They said they felt sorry for any human who had felt obliged to take the road of the *brujo* and they had both had to face temptations in their own training. They made it clear that the same would be true for me.

I didn't believe them. The idea that there might be a *brujo* in me was one step too far. I'd made my choice to work for people's benefit, not for harm. As far as I was concerned, I'd made that choice a long time before. When I told them as much, they just smiled the smile of those who have travelled in regions that most will never visit.

'That choice,' they assured me, 'isn't a one-off choice, but needs to be made again and again, with every step along the road of power you walk. On this path, you must face up to your temptations.'

I shivered involuntarily.

The ceremonies always began as twilight was replaced by night. The *maestros* would prepare themselves in candlelight by spraying protective medicine all around them, smoking *mapacho* to cleanse themselves and then singing into the medicine that we were given one by one. Once everyone had drunk, the candle would be blown out and they would immediately begin to sing their *icaros*, accompanied by the magical sound of the *shakapa*. They would both sing at once.

I had now been given my own *shakapa* and asked to follow the rhythm of the *maestros* and concentrate all my attention on them. Tonight, this wouldn't be possible.

The visionary state came on strong. It was like being strapped into a rollercoaster. There was always that slow ride up the first incline, the gentle approach of that first descent and then whoosh, we were travelling at the speed of light, our normal perception blown out of the water as we entered the world of Amazonian shamanism.

That night, I suddenly knew I was under attack. I'd experienced that before, but this was a whole new story. The *maestros*, too, were dealing with some very heavy energy. Alberto was hunkered down singing defensive *icaros* and Hamilton was alongside him, supporting his teacher. I realized that I was on my own.

As the first wave of energy came at me, I remembered my first night in Iquitos. With the full naivety of someone who doesn't know that they don't know, I'd done a meditation to introduce myself to the local shamans and traditions. It felt like the right thing to do.

Later that night, as Susannah and I slept, there was a loud knock on the door. It was 3 a.m. I got out of bed and went to see who it was. I opened the door and there was Susannah.

'Wait a minute – you're in bed next to me.'

I was very confused. Then it dawned on me that I was dreaming.

'Who are you? Reveal yourself,' I said to the imposter.

The second I did so, Susannah's face melted away and I saw the face behind the mask, cold with evil intent. In the dream, I screamed and slammed the door shut.

Immediately I woke up in bed, sitting bolt upright in a cold sweat.

The next morning, over breakfast, I told Hamilton what had happened. He told me that I might as well be a deer coming out from the forest in the hunting season and announcing to the gathered hunters, 'Hello, I'm a deer.'

'Now they've seen you, they'll come for you,' he said.

It seems they had come. What followed that night and for the four weeks that followed was my Battle of Helms Deep. Night after night, I walked onto that battlefield. I genuinely felt that I was fighting for my life. My *maestros* told me that this was the way I would learn.

A week into the fight, the medicine showed me that if I was intelligent, I would pay very careful attention to how these *brujos* were working.

'They will show you your weakness. Let them lead you to the gaps in your energy field caused by what you do not own. In this way, they can be your teachers and you will defeat them.'

And so each night, holding onto the rhythm of the *shakapa*, staying connected to the medicine songs that my *maestros* were singing and asking the medicine trees to keep me safe and steady, I studied my own fear.

I saw that the only power these beings had to harm me was that fear. But knowing this wasn't enough to stop my fear from taking over. Whenever it did, I was back on the rollercoaster, doing loop-the-loops at great speed, struggling to stay present and hold back the nausea. At times, I felt as if I was being turned inside out.

For years, I'd been told that my lust for power was the problem. I'd believed it and done everything I could to force a little humility into my vocabulary. Trying to impose an idea of humility on top of the fear of power is a recipe for disaster, and it was here in the Amazon that I got to the root of it. The danger for me was *not* owning my power. Trying to squeeze myself into an acceptable self dictated by others' ideas about me had literally put me out of shape. I'd laid down my true power and was therefore open to attack. But worse, in my denial of who I was, I was a far more dangerous human being. Trying to be a nice guy, never drawing a clear line and always smiling a little spiritual smile had built up a pressure in me that was inevitably going to explode somewhere, somehow. I had to own my power. And straightforwardly own my lust for it.

I was here in the middle of the Amazon learning old school shamanism from two of the strongest men I'd ever met. Did I think I didn't want power? Yes! I wanted power! Yes, I was ambitious! And yes, I fully owned my potential to do harm! I knew that only in recognizing and experiencing this, on all levels, would I ever be able to genuinely and wholly make a different choice.

This was the key for me. In seeing this pattern in myself, I understood why so many great teachers seemed to create such chaos around themselves. They would show up, put on their beautiful spiritual face and get other people to do their dirty work and create their boundaries for them. And in this way, they would create an impossible ideal for their followers to live up to. Unowned shadows have a habit of popping up in the organizations and followers of charismatic leaders. And unowned shadows can be very destructive to everyone involved.

It was this process of unmasking that gave me a new touchstone of trust in myself. I realized that if I wasn't prepared to be disliked, to challenge our apprentices and to use my power in the service of life, how could I teach? How could I heal? How could I really be the shaman that my teachers had told me I was?

In those weeks in the Amazon, I felt as if I was being energetically torn to pieces again and again. And again and again, with the help of my *maestros* and the medicine spirits, I returned to that battleground to face my demons.

Brutal as this initiation was, I was utterly grateful to the strength of the forest and its medicines for showing me who I was and showing me that it was both my choice and my responsibility to decide how to use my power.

Each night I would know when we were reaching the end of our work because either Alberto or Hamilton would burst into hysterical laughter at the antics of the other one. Even in my terrors, their laughter never failed to reach me and have me laughing too. God knows what I was laughing at. Perhaps it was the fact this whole journey had come about at my own request! I'd asked to find the trust and the ground to allow my full force to shine through my work. I'd prayed to encounter a power much stronger than me that would challenge me, bring me to my knees and teach me the first steps of what was required to discover that elusive quality that is genuine humility. Now here I was, being humbled and understanding my own power.

❧

Those weeks in the forest were a new beginning. I earned the strength to leave the sticky situation I had enmeshed myself in and break through that glass ceiling so that I could once again see the sky. With my feet now on the ground, my understanding of myself restructured and my beloved at my side, it was time to move into a new chapter of our lives and bring forth the vision that we'd been holding since the day we'd met.

Sometimes, gratitude is the only thing that makes any sense.

❧

Chapter 21

JAGUAR IN THE BODY, BUTTERFLY IN THE HEART

'"How does one become a butterfly?"
Pooh asked pensively.
"You must want to fly so much that you are willing
to give up being a caterpillar," Piglet replied.'
A.A. MILNE

My apprenticeship with Hamilton and Alberto didn't last long. After the *dieta* from hell, I went back twice and completed two more *dietas*. After three years, we all recognized that our work together was done.

Their mastery was a privilege to behold. Their connection to the plants and their spirits and the generosity with which they shared their knowledge with me strengthened me immeasurably for the years ahead.

⌐⁄ ⌐

The end of my apprenticeship with Alberto and Hamilton wasn't the end of my relationship with the Amazon, though. In 2010 Susannah and I would return, this time with the Pachamama Alliance, an extraordinary organization that one of our own long-term students, Bernadette, had introduced us to.

235

The Pachamama Alliance came into existence at the call of the Achuar people of the Ecuadorian Amazon. It began when one of their elder shamans, Don Rafael Taish, had a vision of what contact with the modern world would mean for his people and the forest in which they lived. The Achuar have a belief that is central to their whole way of life: if something scares you, move towards it and investigate. This is the courage of a dream culture, a warrior people who are undefeated and unbroken in their spirit. They even saw off the threat of the Spanish *conquistadores*. Once they became aware of the new threat that was coming towards them in the form of the industrial world's collective thirst for oil, they put out a call in their dreaming. This call was heard by Bill and Lynne Twist and John Perkins, and in 1996 they visited Achuar territory for the first time and the Pachamama Alliance was formed.

The Achuar were very clear about the kind of collaboration and partnership they wanted. First, they asked their new partners to support them in their fight to keep their forest home out of the clutches of the oil companies. They recognized that the ongoing health of their forest was necessary for the ongoing health of the planet as a whole.

Second, they asked their partners to do whatever they could to change what they called 'the dream of the north'. This is the dominant story of the industrialized world in which it makes perfectly logical sense to clear-cut millions of acres of one of the most biodiverse forest regions left on Earth. The Achuar saw our blindness to the long-term effects of such action as a sickness that could only be attributed to the lens or story through which we saw the world and our place in it. And so the Pachamama Alliance got to work on two fronts.

For the past 20 years, in an archetypal David versus Goliath situation, the Alliance has been successful in protecting the forest home of the Achuar and their many neighbours who have joined the Alliance as time has gone on. The work to protect the Amazon against the imminent threat of incursions from oil companies is current and ongoing. It's a microcosm of what we are collectively facing all over the planet. It is a battle between two dreams. The first is the industrial dream that the Earth is a resource that is ours to do with as we please. The second fuses the best of technology with the best of indigenous wisdom to create a sustainable future for life on Earth. This is the key issue for our times. And it is through my contact with the Pachamama Alliance, and particularly the powerfully catalytic symposium they created, Awakening the Dreamer, Changing the Dream, that I have come to a much deeper understanding of my vocation and role as a shaman in these times.

⟨ ⁄ ⟩

Having trained to incorporate the symposium into our work, it made sense to take up the invitation of the Achuar and Sápara peoples and visit them in their homelands.

In the weeks leading up to this first visit, I dreamed about Don Rafael many times. I saw him as a jaguar shaman, powerful and enigmatic, a master of his own domain.

On our third day in the forest, we went to meet him in his village, Wayusentsa. We got up at 3 a.m. to take part in an Achuar ritual that took place every morning. We took an hour's canoe ride downriver from the Kapawi Eco Lodge, where we had been staying, and once we arrived at the village we were invited into the home of the community leader to drink *guayusa* tea from wooden gourds and then to purge in the nearby bushes. This is how the Achuar begin their day in order to cleanse themselves and to share their dreams from a clear place. I know it sounds pretty awful, but in actuality it's a great way to start the day. It's not like being sick – it's more like getting well. Afterwards, guided by their collective dreaming, the Achuar decide on the activities of the day.

We drank, purged and then, as the early dawn light began to filter through the trees, we sat down to share our dreams. Many of them were interpreted as powerful omens connected to the ceremony we'd been invited to attend with Don Rafael that night.

Later in the day, we travelled further downstream to Don Rafael's village, stopping for a time to meditate under the protective expanse of a massive kapok tree, a tree sacred to the Achuar. There we were told about the traditional initiation that young Achuar men and women go through in order to find a guiding vision for their lives. They are given *floripondio* medicine by the shaman and put out under a small shelter at the foot of a kapok tree. The medicine makes them blind to our world for three days but opens the doorway to the spirit world of the forest. Throughout this time, they pray to be visited by Arutam, the divine protector of the forest and all who live there. When Arutam comes, he brings the vision that will guide them during the next chapter of their life.

I asked if anyone from outside the forest had ever done this ritual. Our young Achuar guide, José, thought carefully about this and then replied, 'Not as far as I know. We have grown up in the forest, and for us, this ritual can be very frightening. You would probably die of fear.'

✑

I was invited to be part of a small group to visit Don Rafael and formally accept his invitation to do ceremony. It was around 4 p.m. when we walked into his traditional house, a thatched hut with wooden uprights around the perimeter to provide some privacy. There was a place in the house for visitors to sit and we all sat down on a wooden bench and waited.

For 10 minutes, Don Rafael and his whole family ignored us as if we weren't there. I was told that this was to give the family a chance to get used to having us in their space and for us to get used to being there. Don Rafael was working at something with a knife at a low wooden table with his back turned to us. When he turned round, there he was, the man from my dream.

I said nothing, but witnessed the formal greeting that took place between the Achuar and the way in which they shared their news.

As the formalities took place, we were offered *chicha*, the traditional fermented drink of the region. I had been fasting and the slightly alcoholic liquid brightened my vision considerably.

Then Don Rafael turned his attention to Julian, our Ecuadorian guide. Next he turned to face me. I was about to introduce myself when he spoke instead.

'I know you and I know your wife too. You have been in my dreams these past few weeks. You are shamans from the north. I know your work. I am glad you have come. Tonight I will share my medicine with you, and you will see my power. We offer you this medicine to bring you the healing of the forest, so that you can see the forest as we see it and so that you will stand with us as brothers and sisters to protect this land and my people.'

I was so moved by his powerful, dignified and precise naming of the purpose of our ritual. This wasn't just about our personal healing; we were being invited into the heart and soul of Achuar culture so that we could remove the separation between our personal work and our collective responsibilities and build bridges between inner vision and outer action. This was the everyday shamanism I'd been dreaming of.

'Please tell me how you heal,' Rafael said.

I took a few minutes to explain and he nodded.

'My granddaughter is unwell. I have been unable to heal her myself. Will you work with her tonight?'

I agreed and thanked him for asking. I was moved again by his humility, the obvious clarity of his dreaming and by his trust in asking me to work with a close member of his family.

Night was coming, and with it, another encounter with the primal force of the forest. As Rafael promised, I encountered his undeniable strength. As he sang and delivered his powerful *limpiars* for each member of our group, it felt to me as if the whole forest was listening to him. A *limpiar* is a traditional cleansing or healing using tobacco smoke, the leaf rattle (in Achuar called the *shingu-shingu*), and the power songs of the shaman.

The space Rafael created was nothing short of awesome. I had never felt so safe on my whole shamanic journey.

As the effect of the medicine took hold, Rafael's assistant came to me and asked me if I was ready to do the healing. I said yes, gathered my tools and waited. We were in an open-sided *maloca* in a large clearing. All around us for hundreds of miles in all directions was the wild magnificence of the untouched Amazon. There were no roads. It was nature uninterrupted and, through the eyes that Rafael's medicine opened up for me, as sacred as any temple on the face of this Earth. I felt the force of the jaguar rising in my veins as I thought about what an oil company would do to this place. Sacrilege would be nowhere near a strong enough word.

Rafael's granddaughter came to me, accompanied by her whole family. Parents, grandparents, uncles and aunts, brothers and sisters – a whole entourage had come to witness the healing. People from the outside had been visiting Rafael's compound since the mid-1990s, so to have white people in ceremony there wasn't unusual, but the girl was only nine years old and clearly nervous at being the focus of so much attention.

She sat in front of her grandfather on a stool cut from the trunk of a large tree and I began the healing. The second I invited my spirits to get to work, any nervousness disappeared. A *limpiar* isn't a quiet affair. There are all kinds of noises, from singing to whistling to blowing away what is being extracted and blowing in what is being returned. As I worked, I could hear the suppressed giggles of the children who were watching close by. Soon, they were unable to hold back their laughter at the sounds that were coming from the gringo shaman. They burst into laughter and all I could do was to join them. The tension was broken as the whole family joined in. The connection had been made and I continued my work in an atmosphere of laughter and focused attention.

As I finished, Rafael came to me and shook my hand. He invited me to sit down and immediately returned the favour and gave me one of the most powerful cleansings I have ever had. This ceremony was the beginning of our relationship as partners and allies of the Achuar and Sápara peoples.

Susannah and I returned home with the wildness and force of the Amazon forest pumping through our veins. We understood that our experiences in the Amazon and our allegiance to the people there would find a way both into our work with Movement Medicine and our day-to-day lives.

Our relatively young Movement Medicine work had been going well. We had completed our first apprenticeship programme and led our first professional training course and we were delighted with how quickly Movement Medicine had found its feet in the world. We both felt so much more at home working within our own *mesa*. We had been waiting for the right time to emerge from our cocoon and fly and that time had come.

Movement Medicine is the distillation of all that we have learned. It is the synthesis of all we have received from other cultures, from our teachers and from our journey together as husband and wife. It is a down-to-earth, practical, inspiring form of everyday shamanism that is medicine for the times we live in. It is a recovery of our shamanic roots and a pathway for those who wish to bring their prayers and dreams to Earth on every level.

The essence of Movement Medicine is the Long Dance ceremony, a 72-hour contemporary shamanic ritual. My experience of the Sundance had led me to dream of a contemporary European ritual that was open to people of all denominations and none, that would have all the discipline and power of indigenous ceremony and, more than that, would have a concrete effect beyond those able to participate through raising money for some amazing causes. It took me 18 years and the help of many wonderful people to pull that dream through, and when it landed, I felt fulfilled in a way that I hadn't known was possible.

In the Long Dance, the medicine is movement, repetition, live music, prayer, fasting and the strong intent of a community of dancing warriors. Though plant medicines have supported me to see beyond the known, I've always been taught that we must be able to achieve the same states without the aid of plants in order to integrate what the plants have shown us. And I've experienced no stronger state that that which comes from the total commitment to the prayer that is the Long Dance. When we break through the stranglehold of our learned limitations through our own concentration and efforts, we are taking a very real step in empowerment and in bringing our offering to life.

To be doing what I love doing most – praying, dancing and taking action for all our relations for a prolonged period of time – is my idea of heaven on Earth. I truly believe that this is what we are here for: to discover the evolving landscape of what heaven on Earth is for each of us and to bring that through to express our gratitude for the life we have been given. In my experience, there is simply no better use of a beating human heart.

∞

When we arrived back in the Ecuadorian Amazon in 2011, we were blessed to meet Augustin Tentets, the young Achuar leader of the Sharamentsa community, who has since gone on to be elected president of the Achuar Federation.

Augustin and his people met us in full ceremonial dress, with spears, magnificent black and yellow feathered head-dresses and ceremonial beads. They were an impressive sight as we entered the community house for a formal Achuar welcome.

Augustin soon had us all in tears. It was a difficult time for the Achuar, as the Ecuadorian government had stepped up its efforts to sell the rights to the oil underneath Achuar land to Chinese oil companies, and Augustin talked about the crisis very eloquently. He told us how his great-grandparents had foreseen this time and how they had seen that the forest would remain standing because the Achuar would form alliances with people from all around the world. Just as he and his children could enjoy the beauty of the forest, he promised that his children's children and many generations to follow would do the same. He said that every Achuar man, woman and child was prepared to go to their grave to defend their territory, and we all knew he meant it. He finished his welcome by thanking us for our visit at this difficult time and by asking us to stand alongside the Achuar in their fight to protect what he called 'the lungs of the Earth'.

Through my tear-filled eyes, I watched the group of people we had brought to the forest from all around the world as they felt the impact of Augustin's words. There is no better preparation for ritual than to feel the collective intent to make a difference beyond our own belly buttons. It puts our own personal healing journey into its proper context.

The community shaman, Entsaqwa, the brother of Rafael and a powerful healer in his own right, had been cooking medicine to support us on our journey. During that ceremony, I was shown that there is nothing more disempowering than the idea that this life is a rehearsal for the next one and that if we all behave like good boys and girls according to the 'good book', we will get our reward in heaven. Through that dark spell, I was told, we lose the power, creativity and the holy innocence of our creative-sexual force. We forget how to listen to the wisdom of a body that is connected to the elemental powers and therefore properly resourced. And we forget that we are responsible for taking care of the life we are given so that when our time comes, we can pass it on to future generations in a good way.

I was also invited to acknowledge and be proud of the choices we had made and the direction our lives had taken. I was honoured. The passion we have for standing by our brothers and sisters in the forest comes from our love for the wild magnificence that is the Amazon rainforest and the untamed wildness everywhere, including inside us all. And it comes from our deep admiration for the people who live there. They are far from perfect. Like all of us, they have their own problems and challenges to deal with, but they hold an important piece of the puzzle for our whole species if we are to come through the challenges we have set ourselves.

After the ceremony, Entsaqwa gave me his ceremonial beads and told me that I should always wear them in ceremony so that we would remain connected and the spirits of the forest we wished to protect would protect us in turn.

⁊

The following year, we had the honour of meeting the Sápara people, neighbours of the Achuar. In the past, they had been traditional enemies, but they were now united in a common cause.

The Sápara are a dying people. There are less than 750 of them left and their territory is right on the frontline of the battle between our culture's need for oil at any cost and the new dream that so many people are dedicating their lives to creating. We were painfully aware of the paradox of flying to meet them in a petrol-driven light aircraft.

You might expect that a dying people facing so many troubles would be downtrodden by the weight of their problems. But from the moment we literally skidded to a halt on the short, muddy landing strip, we felt the warmth and generosity of these brave and wise people.

We were greeted by Manari, the leader of the Sápara people, his mother, Mukusawa, Maria, his niece, and many others. Over the past five years, these people have become our family. Little Manari, Maria's son, a young boy who it is clear will grow up to be a shaman for his people, later became our godson.

On our first night in the village of Llanchamacocha, I dreamed about the older Manari's father. Also called Manari, he was known as the peace shaman. Many times, neighbouring tribes had sent out war parties to kill him, because they saw his power as a threat. Somehow, the old shaman had always known they were coming and had gone out into the forest, without weapons, to greet them. He had spoken to them, telling them that he could see the trouble in their hearts, and invited them into his home to drink medicine and be healed of their pain. This had happened many times and those would-be killers had become like family. He had died of natural causes just a few years earlier, but his son dreamed of him every night.

In my own dream, I was called away from the village by the sound of a beautiful forest song. I met the old Manari and he took me into the forest. He brought me to a family of jaguars and told me to lie down between the two eldest, a male and a female. I did as I was asked and felt their warmth and strength. Their deep growls rumbled through my body. Each of them turned to face me and offered me a sharp tooth. I took the teeth and held them together over my heart. As I did so, they melded into one.

When I shared the dream the following morning, Manari seemed very moved. I had told him about my battles with other shamans in the forest and he gave me some great advice: 'They need to know who you are and what your intention is. Introduce yourself to them as you meet them in ceremony and let them know that you are here to support the people and the forest itself.'

I was in such a different place now than when I'd done this on my first night in Iquitos. My introduction then had been more like saying 'Here I am.' What Manari was inviting me to give now was much more of an awareness that I was in their territory and therefore needed to let them know my intent.

Humbled again by my lack of basic courtesy, I thanked him.

There was more. Manari fished out an old stone that had belonged to his father and had been in the family for generations.

'My father was a jaguar shaman,' he said. 'He came to you. He will protect you. This stone is for you to carry with you, so that we can stay connected in our dreaming.'

That night we were offered grandmother medicine cooked by the grandmother of the tribe, Mukusawa. Susannah, David and I were leading the ceremony alongside Manari. This was the first of many times working alongside each other. Twice, Manari has travelled to the UK and joined us in holding the Long Dance ceremony, and what a joy it has been to sit side by side in each other's land and pray.

As the medicine became strong, I felt totally overwhelmed by the responsibility of holding the intensity of the space. We were in ceremony with our group and we'd been joined by several young people from the tribe. They asked me to blow into their medicine before they drank, a sign of deep trust. Though a part of me wanted to run, scream, purge and lose myself in the forest night, I called on all the years of my training to steady myself. I also called on the spirit of Manari's father, asking him to stand behind me. As I did so, a large moth landed on the back of my head. His wings moved fast as he walked over the naked skin of my scalp. I felt this was the help that I'd asked for. Manari's spirit calmed me and we got down to work.

After the ceremony, the Sápara gave me a beautiful beaded headband with feathers and asked me to wear it in ceremony so that I could carry them with me. With each gift I received from the forest and its peoples, my commitment to stand with them grew stronger and stronger.

In the morning, as Susannah and I washed in the Conambo river, several butterflies swarmed around me. Several of them landed on my head, my chest and on my back behind my heart. They stayed on my body for a long time, fluttering their bright orange wings. I felt a deep sense of peace and connection and knew I'd been blessed by the spirits of the forest.

Over the past five years of visits to the Achuar and Sápara peoples, our connection has grown deeper and deeper. We have worked with Rafael,

Entsaqwa, Jimpickit and Sumpa, a quartet of elder shamans who, even after 50 to 60 years of training and work, still have their own elders from whom they learn.

When we first met Sumpa, whose strong open heart led us to name him 'the flower shaman', news of our work in the forest had preceded our arrival. Susannah, David and I were travelling alone on that occasion so that we could do our own work in the forest without holding a group. We'd already visited Rafael. He'd asked what we needed and I'd told him that I wished to experience the power of the jaguar so that I could carry its strength back home and be more effective in our work for the forest. That night I had an extraordinary experience of becoming a jaguar and running and hunting in the forest. I had never felt such force.

When we got to Sumpa's compound, after all the formal introductions, I offered to do whatever work might be helpful during our stay. The next morning, Sumpa came to the small hut where we were staying as guests of the family and invited David and me to follow him into the forest.

We walked for 20 minutes until we heard the sound of a group of people laughing and talking. We arrived in a clearing where there were hundreds of bundles of the kinds of leaf material the Sápara use for thatching their roofs. They were piled high on top of one another. Sumpa was building a new house, one that befitted his status as an elder in his community, and the whole community was helping. Though at that moment they were taking a rest and drinking *chicha*. It was very hot.

We drank *chicha* with them and soon it was time to get back to work. The Achuar men and women walked up to the bundles, swung them up over their backs and started walking. Our bundles were pointed out to us by a young man who had a cheeky smile. I soon found out why. As I swung my bundle onto my back, I nearly crumpled under its weight. I couldn't imagine how I was going to manage it. I heard David grunting loudly behind me and the humour of the situation got to me. We'd offered our help and I'd meant as healers, but I was being taught a good lesson by Sumpa. Work is work. The house of an elder is a sacred space. The shaman's role is no more or less important than anyone else's in the village and when help is needed, everyone joins in. This was everyday shamanism.

I took a deep breath and started to struggle along the path. Half an hour later, soaked in sweat, I walked over a small bridge, made of an upside-down canoe, and back into the compound. The Achuar had arrived 10 minutes before. There were smiles and pats on the back as David and I dropped off our loads. We had passed the test of friendship.

∽

Our hosts had also asked if I could do some healing work during the ceremony that was due to take place that night. As is the protocol, I asked the elder if this was okay and he gave his permission.

The ceremony was strong. I began with a question that had been a central dilemma for me for many years. I wanted to know how to blend the raw power of the jaguar with the parts of me that were quieter and more sensitive. In order to see clearly, you have to be super-sensitive. And I'd learned time and time again that in order to be super-sensitive in our world and stay safe, I needed to be super-strong. How could I allow my full power through and still be receptive to others?

It was another life-changing night and one that I will remember for the rest of my days.

I did the healing that had been requested of me and then, as I finished, the husband of the woman I'd worked on came to me and asked if I might do some work on him. I agreed. When I completed that work, I was ready to go back to my banana leaf, lie down and enjoy the beautiful clear night sky. But as I stood up to go, I saw a group of 10–15 people sitting down. I wondered what they were doing there.

Sumpa's son looked at me with a kind smile. 'They have come for healings. Are you ready for the next one?'

For the next four hours, I worked without a break. Women, men and children lined up and I did what I could for each one of them. The trust these people placed in me was my strongest ally.

When I eventually came to the end, I sank to the ground, exhausted. As I lay there, I felt as though I'd just run the shamanic equivalent of a marathon. At the same time, I felt so grateful to have the opportunity to give something directly back to these people from whom I'd received so much. And more than that, in trusting in my work as a shaman, they'd given me something that I hadn't even realized I needed.

As I settled in next to Susannah on a banana leaf, I felt the echoes of the last 30 years of initiation rippling through me. I sang a song of gratitude, and as I did so, I was given the answer to my dilemma. I heard the spirits of the forest whispering into my ear and even more deeply into my heart: 'Jaguar in the body, butterfly in the heart, Ya'Acov. Jaguar in the body, butterfly in the heart.'

Epilogue

AN EVERYDAY SHAMAN

Excellence is an art won by training and habituation.
We do not act rightly because we have virtue or
excellence, but we rather have those because we
have acted rightly. We are what we repeatedly
do. Excellence, then, is not an act but a habit.

Aristotle

Throughout this whole journey, Bikko Máhte had been quietly alongside me. With so very few words, he had taught me so much.

A few years ago, he made me a drum. It was beautifully crafted. When I went to his house to receive it, he insisted that we play together. As we fell into the hypnotic rhythms of the overtones and undertones, he suddenly stopped.

'What is this drum made from?'

'Silver birch, silver, reindeer antler and the skin of a reindeer,' I replied.

'What does it mean to you that an animal died for you to have this drum?'

I was a little shocked by the sudden question. 'I don't really know,' I said.

'I thought not, by the way you play. If you wish to learn to play this drum, you must learn what it is to hunt and kill. How can you own and play a drum like this if you don't know what it means to do so?'

I knew immediately that he was right. I promised him I would find a way.

A few months later, I spent some days with a friend of a friend called Will. He looked after the wild deer that roamed across three organic farms in Wiltshire. Deer are without natural predators in the UK. Humans have destroyed them. Without natural predators, the deer herds can grow too large and this can lead to sickness in the herd and in the land. Will had grown up as a landsman. Hunting had always been part of his life. He'd agreed to take me hunting too.

He began by teaching me to shoot. He made it plain that unless he could be assured that I was a good enough shot, there would no hunting. He then taught me the rudiments of stalking.

We had risen very early on my second morning with him. At 9 a.m. we returned to his home to rest and I went back to bed. I dreamed I was hunting a three-year-old healthy buck that I would kill later in the day. In the dream, I spoke to him and he told me that he would be my prey.

I woke up feeling a mixture of excited and sad. I'd told Will about my reason for hunting and he understood that taking life was a big deal.

Late in the afternoon, we went out to hunt. We had no luck at first and as the light faded, Will seemed to think that we'd missed our chance for the day.

I was certain the deer would show up. 'Can we wait a little longer?' I asked him.

We were perched on a high-seat hunting tower where a field met some woods. As I spoke, he hushed me.

'Over there.'

At first I saw nothing, but then I realized that not more than 130 feet away from us, a young buck had come into the field and was standing in the one place in the field where I could safely shoot him.

I slowly raised my rifle, breathing slowly as Will had taught me. I had no idea whether or not I would go through with it.

As I saw the deer in the sights of my rifle, I felt a deep connection with him. He stayed where he was and I had the uncanny feeling that he was aware of me and of his own death. My finger was on the trigger. I said a quiet prayer and fired.

Immediately I saw the spray of blood that signifies a hit in the heart and the deer took off.

I was shaking and even though I very rarely smoke, I was glad of the tobacco.

Soon we were on the red trail and we found the body of the deer about 300 feet from where I'd shot him.

'I'll leave you with him for a while,' Will said kindly.

I sat with the body of the deer and my tears flowed. I had killed him. Of my own free will.

I had such mixed emotions. On the one hand, I felt devastated and my tears were appropriate. On the other hand, something as old as the hills had been awakened in me. I looked at my trigger finger and saw that death was in my hands.

Being the bringer of death changed my relationship to dying. At that moment I was able to take another step towards accepting death as part of life and, in so doing, accept my own mortality.

I sat with the deer and offered tobacco for his spirit. As I did so, I heard the name Ré ir Ré and a song came to me with which I could honour the life I had taken. It was a fierce moment as I sat there singing, my throat sore and yet my voice strong.

Will waited patiently and when I let him know that I was done, he taught me how to take care of the carcass. We hung the body overnight and the next day I skinned and butchered the deer. My family and I ate the meat over the following months and a good friend, Dorrie, made a drum for me from the skin.

As Bikko Máhte had thought, my relationship with my drums deepened immeasurably after that. Now when I pick up a drum to play, I feel what has been given and I do my best to receive the gift again and to honour the one who gave it.

In 2015 Bikko Máhte decided to give me his own drum, a drum he'd been playing for many, many years. He spoke to me about our work together and told me that the reason we'd been close was that I'd never tried to take anything from him or from the Sami culture. He told me that the work that Susannah and I were doing was pure medicine. And he gave me permission to tell you his story and the story of our relationship.

Receiving his drum was the closest I will ever get to receiving a PhD. When he honoured me with the gift, he told me, 'If you ever feel you have finished with this drum, please either bring it back to the Sami museum in Kautokeino or pass it on to your son.'

☙

A shaman is called into being by their own predilection for matters of the spirit, a journey interspersed with healing crises through the shadowlands of their own psyche and, finally, by their community and elders. It has taken me half a century to recognize and accept my own nature.

When I look back over my life so far, I see clearly that the healing journey I've taken has been focused on changing the stories that have imprisoned me. 'Being who you have been told to be is more important than being who you actually are' and 'You are not enough as you are' were the messages I found again and again at the roots of my unhelpful behaviour. I was more than a little hypnotized by these stories. I found it hard to come out from behind the masks I'd learned to wear. For years, all my shamanic experiences fed those hungry ghosts inside me. But the ghosts just chewed them up and demanded more. And I didn't feel that I was good enough, magical enough, shamanic enough. My focus was firmly on how others saw me, just as it had been trained to be. At the same time, my visions opened my eyes to the majesty and the joy of life. They reminded me of what I'd known as a child. But deep down, I continued to sing the painful song that is doing so much to destroy the fabric of life on Earth: 'I am not enough. I don't have enough. I need more.' I believe that shifting our identity from this debilitating mantra is the healing task of our times.

Round and round I went, until I eventually found a ground of being inside myself, rooted in my body and in a sense of self that wasn't dependent on the approval of others.

I couldn't have landed in that simple everyday acceptance of my own nature without the help and validation of the indigenous shamans, indigenous people and many others along the way who gave me their trust over the years. Trust is a validation far more real and valuable than approval.

When we were last in the Achuar village of T'inkias, I was asked to give a healing to an old shaman who was visiting from another village. He had terrible pain in his legs. I went to work with him in the late afternoon. His relatives were close by and I did my work to the best of my ability.

On the other side of the house we were working in, a tiny old woman was watching us carefully. She was the shaman's wife. Once we'd finished, I was asked to work with her as well. Through translation, it was explained to me that she was having some problems with her breathing. She was the archetypal Amazonian grandmother. The lines on her face told many stories of life in the forest. She was beautiful.

I sat down on the packed earth floor in front of her and started to drum in order to get myself into that hollow-bone state. When I opened my eyes to begin my work, she had calmly removed her top and was sitting half naked in front of me. I will never forget how humbled I felt at that moment. I was in the home of this woman's family. The smoke from the fire was drifting through the open-sided house and there were sounds of children playing and village life all around us. And here in front of me, open to whatever I could offer her, sat this dignified woman, made stronger than I could ever hope to be by her total vulnerability. She smiled and I wondered if she knew the gift her trust was giving me.

⸱ ⟋ ⸱

Ever since I discovered there was such a thing as shamanism, I've wanted to find a form of it that is appropriate for the place and time we live in. Susannah has been my constant companion on that journey and Movement Medicine is the result of our search.

We have been blessed by meeting and working with many shamans from different cultures, and there is the temptation to imitate those we admire, but I've always been told that the point is to rediscover the medicine in myself, my culture and my lands.

So, yes, I have feathers and drums. Yes, I use a *shakapa*. Yes, I have beautifully coloured wristbands and seedpod shaman's belts. I carry many gifts from those I have met. I wear them and use them for three reasons. First, because I have been asked to do so for my protection, and I have recovered from my naivety and recognized the need for protection. Second, I wish to honour the people who gave them to me and, in the case of our Amazonian family, the unbroken lineages they have come from. When I put my shaman's gear on to work, I remember them and what they stand for and I say a prayer for them. And I remember what it is like to have an unbroken shamanic lineage that goes back thousands of years and I am strengthened by it. And the third reason is that I have learned that accepting help and guidance from trustworthy sources is a necessity.

But I was brought up in the modern world and one of the reasons why it took me so long to accept my nature as a shaman was because despite the fact that I was having all these experiences, part of me didn't believe they were real. I often experienced a clash of cultures or stories inside myself. In the rational world, these things didn't happen. And yet they were my experience.

Modern science is, however, beginning to show us what shamans have always known: all things are connected. And I've found that the more I've paid attention to how things are connected, the more connections have made themselves apparent to me. When I've allowed my cynicism to take over, it has taken over. And the world has been all the greyer for it. When I've allowed my curiosity to open my mind and my senses, on the other hand, some of what is hidden in plain sight has become visible to me. For me, the most basic practice of everyday shamanism is the simple act of noticing.

In June 2013 Susannah and I moved into a new home. It was the first time we'd ever taken on the guardianship and ownership of a significant piece of land. Learning to look after that land has turned out to be the missing cornerstone that has finally given my life a balance I'd previously only dreamed of. Working on the land has made me pay so much more attention to the value of simple things.

As the years go by, life feels more and more precious to me. Not just when I'm in a ritual space but in the everyday rituals of how I relate, work, shop, learn to look after the land I live on, eat, laugh, pray and make love. My journey has woken me up to the magic that is present in the most ordinary of circumstances and it has shown me that it is in being who I am and giving what I've got that my fulfilment as a human being lies.

Nine months after we moved into our new home, I was doing a birthday ritual on our new land. I was sitting under an oak by the stream that runs through the land, drumming with the drum Bikko Máhte had recently given me. I sang for several hours, giving thanks to the waters, the trees, the rocks and all the many blessings of my life. I was in a whimsical mood and a question popped out of me before I could censor it: 'Great Spirit, I know you're busy and I've never asked before, but would you mind sending me a little sign to show me that my prayers have been heard?'

I wasn't really expecting an answer, but immediately after I'd finished speaking, I spotted a kingfisher flying towards me from my right. The kingfisher is the closest we have in Britain to the hummingbird. This one flew right up to me and circled my head three times. As usual, I burst into that sweet blend of laughter and tears as the spirit of life revealed a little of its mystery.

When I went back to the house, I told Susannah the story and she smiled a strange smile. Later she gave me my birthday gift and card. When I opened the card, I found it showed a beautiful kingfisher, all blues and silver light as it dived for fish.

This time we both fell into the delight of our laughter and tears. Susannah told me she'd bought the card for me three months before.

So, what have I learned on the journey so far? Over the years, I've had a real battle with the fear of being who I was and the bitter lack of self-acceptance that underlay it. I struggled to balance the parts of me that wanted to fit in and be acceptable with my existential need to stay in touch with the magical wild of the imaginal world of pure spirit.

This is still ongoing. The part of me that feels bewitched by the spell of the times can easily be overwhelmed by fear of what is happening in the world. In that fear, I see those parts of myself that cling to certainty and flee from the unknown. And what a temptation certainty is! But the more I rest in the knowledge of who I am and what I am committed to, the more I am free.

In my freedom, I choose to do my best to take small, consistent, everyday steps (and occasional quantum leaps) in the direction my heart calls me. On this road, there is dignity. There is the remembrance that my perception of myself and what is or isn't possible is radically affected by the story I tell. And there is the remembrance that though I don't decide what happens in life, I'm free to choose how to dance with it to the best of my ability.

I've come to accept that good and evil exist in this world. And, equally importantly, these forces exist inside me and I have the free will to choose the road I walk on. And the responsibility for that decision.

Shamanism isn't nice. It's as much about the darkness as it is about the light. It's as much about the jaguar as it is about the butterfly. For those of us brought up in the modern world, it has to embrace the body and the heart every bit as much as it embraces the mind. *Jaguar in the Body* invokes the raw, embodied power of our true and wild natures and of nature itself. The jaguar is a fierce protector of what it loves. *Butterfly in the Heart* invokes the shining and fleeting beauty that we catch glimpses of in one another when we feel safe enough to see and be seen. The butterfly is the miracle of transformation that touches us with its soft and silent wings.

As in the micro, so in the macro. Shamanism has a role to play in reminding us that we all have a lot of jaguar power inside us and we are often blind to the effect its unconscious use has on ourselves, on others and on the environment. And shamanism consistently reminds us how important it is to protect those parts of the complex web of life that are fragile and butterfly-like, and that our modern way of life is deeply damaging to them.

By recognizing this dance in myself and owning all aspects of it, I am bound to do my best to stand up for what I believe in. The shamanism I practise demands more than sitting still in pretty visions singing about the light. Movement Medicine invites us to stand up and do all that we can to bring our visions and dreams to Earth as an act of gratitude for the great mystery that gives us life. I have learned that we weren't given this Earth to do with as we pleased, but we came out of it and we are part of it.

Movement has been and remains my central medicine. In our Movement Medicine rituals, when the door to spirit opens, I know it is through my own effort and concentration that the connection has been made. And, perhaps paradoxically, my work with plants has helped me to know this more and more.

In the dance, I've found a way to acknowledge the paradoxes of life. In each ritual, I know and commit more and more to what matters to me. And yet at the same time, I'm bowing at the feet of the great mystery called living and dying, and acknowledging how very little I know.

I'm sitting in front of a small lake with a lively stream behind me. I'm surrounded by the old oaks who have lived here an awful lot longer than I have. They stand majestic in the landscape, singing and dancing in the wind. I am one of the guardians of this land. I have been learning how to look after it and what it needs from me. I have received such strength in return from the land I now call home. The sun is up and I've been here all night praying. Again.

Last night was New Year's Eve. Susannah and Reuben and I spent some time in our ritual drumming giving thanks for the life we live and praying for the year ahead. Reuben is about to head off to continue his training in shamanism, yoga and outdoor survival skills. Susannah has a new album out. And I have this book coming into the world in June.

As we drummed, I entered the realms of the chaos we are living through as a species. I witnessed the turmoil of clashing ideologies and the horrible suffering of innocent peoples, animals and landscapes. Our voices and the rhythms of the drums made a path for me to follow. I saw shamans all around the world doing the same thing. And people, spiritual and practical and political and musical and young and old, and black and white and red and yellow, all in their own ways, their own traditions, carving pathways through the chaos, dreaming and weaving, being and doing what was needed to find a way through.

Warmed by the heat of the winter fire and with the musical sound of the stream rushing past, I felt the power of these elemental forces inside me and all around us. In the sauna, sweating, I felt the blessing of the fire. Afterwards, we washed in the stream.

The rituals of everyday shamanism help me to remember the bigger picture of my life and to connect to the bigger powers that shape it.

This book is dedicated to the medicine generation and to all those who wish to bring heaven to Earth and aren't afraid to do the work of facing themselves in order to find themselves. The harvest of that work is being who we are and giving what we've got. There is only one difference, I've discovered, between those who keep their dreams in the sky and those who attempt to bring them to Earth. And, as old school as it may sound, that difference is *work*.

Not long after I finished writing the first draft of this book, I felt a strong need to drum for my dear friend and guide Bikko Máhte Penta, White Eagle. The next day I received the sad news that he had died. He had been out gathering wood for the winter when his heart had stopped.

As Susannah and I were driving to work a few days later through the lanes of Devon on a bright autumn day, I was astonished to see a blue morpho butterfly in front of the car. I stopped on the narrow lane to watch it and it flew back to us and fluttered around the windows for a while, coming as close as it could without actually entering the car.

We were both open-mouthed. Magic was in the air. Blue morphos live in the Amazon rainforest. For our friends there, their appearance often signifies the blessing of an ancestor or a last visit from someone who has just died.

There was a butterfly farm close to where we were driving and I assumed the blue morpho had escaped from there, but the timing of its appearance and the wonder we felt in its presence led me to believe that Bikko Máhte had come to say a final goodbye.

In the days after he died, I drummed for him every night. One evening, as I was drumming in our kitchen, I saw him – playful, free and with a big smile on his face. His antics made me laugh as I travelled on the overtones of the drum he had given me. And then he turned to face me and looked me in the eyes.

For the fourth time in my life, I felt the touch of lightning. For the fourth time, I felt hammered into the ground. My body shook violently as I struggled to maintain balance and consciousness.

At that moment, between the worlds, White Eagle gave me his last gift. I can't tell you what it was. I don't yet know. I can only tell you that all the ancient strength of our meeting, all the humility he had displayed, the trust he had placed in me and the faith he had had in the work Susannah and I had carried out landed in me in a new way.

I will be forever grateful for the love, guidance and support I and my family received from this gentle yet powerful man. He courageously held the essence of his people's shamanic traditions in his shaman's heart. He was consistently at my back throughout my journey and I will miss his physical presence on this Earth more than words can say. But more than that, I send a prayer every day that his spirit continues to fly on the wings of the white eagle and finds its way home.

Ya'Acov Darling Khan
January 2017

ACKNOWLEDGEMENTS

I have been supported in sharing this story by many exceptional people who have given their testimonials for this book. I promised them that I would make it clear that their testimonials are for the book, not necessarily for the teachers I write about. None of my teachers have been perfect. Like me, and probably like you too, they are all very human and all have their shadows and their blind spots. I have learned that to expect anything different is part of the problem. Therefore, I never recommend teachers. I only recommend that people follow their instincts wherever they lead, just as I have done. I haven't seen many of my former teachers for many years. I am grateful that this book has given me the chance to honour them for what I received from them and to thank them for what they have shared with me along the way.

There are many people who have made huge contributions to my journey who I wish to acknowledge. Most of all, Roland Wilkinson, our work partner for more than two decades. Your dedication to bringing what Susannah and I dream into this world is a fundamental support without which our lives and the lives of the people that our work reaches would be much the poorer. Thank you for all your work that is truly love made visible.

Bee Quick, you were the first to support us. Susanne Perks, you picked up the bare threads of what we were dreaming and wove a beautiful community from them. Fly with the dragons.

Richard and Elizabeth Darlington(RIP), two very fine parents-in-law. Your generosity, patience and love for us as a couple and for Reuben were a bedrock of our lives.

David Rose, from the moment we met on the lawn at CAER, we lovingly struggled our way through many years of crazy adventures. You were there when I needed you and you have been a fine playmate for more than three decades.

Neil Caplan, you purposely found and mercilessly pushed my buttons and you put me on the road to being real. You were the first man that met me where I was and encouraged me to go further. You were a friend who saw the shaman in me and challenged me to find him for myself.

Matthew Barley, the only person I've ever met who is more stubborn than I am. I have loved our friendship and watching our families grow up and our marriages deepen. You saw me and I saw you.

David Tucker, you questioned me fully and then leapt in with both feet. It's through you that the Amazon Forest and its people opened their doors to me. Your generosity and dedication are genuinely awesome.

Sue Kuhn, your loyal, loving friendship and seeing has given me and so many others so much over the years.

Jo Hardy, you were part of our original apprenticeship team and your wisdom and experience gave and continue to give us and our apprentices such support and love.

Dorrie Joy, your capacity to see what I see and then bring it into form has brought me such sweet medicine. You are a true artist.

Michelle Pilley (and all the team) at Hay House. Thank you for suggesting I throw away my first draft and start again and for encouraging me to allow the story to tell itself. Your support over the years has been and continues to be so important.

Lizzie Henry, a finer editor I could not wish for. Your sharp, bright humour and your unfussy clarity make the editing process a genuine pleasure. Valeria Huerta, my agent, for teaching me, with a smile, that I don't have to do it all myself.

I wish to thank and honour: all our local organisers who do so much to bring our work to their communities, our faculty and staff at the School of Movement Medicine, all our apprentices, past, present and future, and all who follow the desire to remember the wild wisdom inside them and come to work with us. Lawrence Abelson who never pulled out of a tackle and always encouraged me to follow my dreams, Helen Poynor and Maura Sills for mentoring and supervising us so brilliantly (Helen for more than 25 years!), Heather Campbell and Sue Jamieson who opened the door at the beginning, Malcolm Barradell and Derek Finch who held the fort for Reuben and became such an important part of our family, Johnathan Mathys for pouring such Phoenix medicine into the land we now call home, and David Cole for being the best neighbour and for offering such steadfast and warm support.

And to the indigenous peoples of the world who continue to maintain and strengthen the bridge between what we dream and how we live and to show us what 'civilized' actually means. I dedicate myself to return to you tenfold the healing I have received from the ways in which you have accepted me as I am and welcomed me into your world.

RESOURCES

If this book has inspired you to begin or further your own shamanic journey, you will find a whole bunch of useful resources on this page. If you are particularly interested in my work, you can find me on Facebook: www.facebook.com/yaacovandsusannahdk/

For full information about Movement Medicine embodied shamanic practice including online courses, apprenticeship and professional training, check out: www.schoolofmovementmedicine.com

You can also find out about Movement Medicine being offered worldwide: www.movementmedicineassociation.org

We are currently designing a whole new set of online courses for those who wish to join our online community and study everyday shamanism from home.

These are challenging times and times of great opportunity for us all to make a difference in this beautiful world. We have found help and support from a wonderful variety of places and organizations. In this resource section, you will find the names of books and organizations that I have found to be particularly helpful. I hope you will too.

Books

- *Movement Medicine* by Susannah and Ya'Acov Darling Khan
- *Choosing Happier: How to be happy despite your circumstances, history or genes* by Jem Friar
- *Dreams of Awakening* by Charlie Morley

- *Coming Back to Life* by Joanna Macey and Molly Brown
- *Buddha's Brain* by Rick Hanson Phd, with Richard Mendius MD
- *Animals in Translation* by Temple Grandin
- *Mind Wide Open* by Steven Johnson
- *The Brain That Changes Itself* by Norman Doidge
- *The Age of Empathy* by Frans de Waal
- *The Tears of the Ancestors* by Daan van Kampenhout
- *The Wisdom of No Escape* by Pema Chödrön
- *Grace and Grit* by Ken Wilber
- *Stealing Fire* by Steven Kotler and Jamie Wheal

Organizations

- The Pachamama Alliance – protecting the Amazon and changing the dream of the modern world: www.pachamama.org
- Freedom from Torture – working to bring an end to torture and to support victims of torture: www.freedomfromtorture.org
- Survival International –working for indigenous peoples worldwide: www.survivalinternational.org
- Trees for Life – a wonderful reforestation project: www.treesforlife.org.uk
- For information about the work of Victor Sanchez, go to: www.elartedeviviraproposito.org
- Ecosia – an eco-friendly search engine: www.ecosia.org
- Flight-free travel throughout Europe: www.seat61.com
- A site with the intent of ending hunger worldwide: www.thehungersite.com

ABOUT THE AUTHOR

Jim Wileman

Ya'Acov Darling Khan was, from a young age, drawn to the down-to-earth connection with the spirit world that shamanism invites. He has pursued this yearning throughout his adult life, studying and practicing with many gifted teachers from the Amazon to the Arctic Circle. He has been recognized as a practicing shaman by Elder Shamans from the Sami (European tradition), and Achuar and Sápara peoples of the Amazon.

Ya'Acov is the Co-creator of Movement Medicine, a contemporary, embodied, shamanic practice and runs the School of Movement Medicine with his wife, Susannah. The school offers a full programme worldwide and online, as well as an apprenticeship programme and professional training.

Since 1989, he has been travelling the world encouraging thousands of people to move beyond their held patterns and self-limiting expectations, and discover themselves and their gifts through embodied shamanism. His journey has taken him to meet and work with some extraordinary people. His Movement Medicine workshops are inspiring, empowering, contemporary and practical, and are attended by people from all walks of life.

Ya'Acov's creations include co-authoring *Movement Medicine: How to Awaken, Dance and Live your Dreams* (Hay House) and the CD, *Movement Medicine CD 1* (with Susannah). You can hear him on the Long Dance CDs, *21 Gratitudes* and *Another 21 Gratitudes. Jaguar in the Body, Butterfly in the Heart* is his second book.

www.schoolofmovementmedicine.com

HAY HOUSE

Look within

Join the conversation about latest products,
events, exclusive offers and more.

 Hay House UK

 @HayHouseUK

 @hayhouseuk

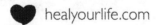 healyourlife.com

We'd love to hear from you!

Printed in the United States
By Bookmasters